OXFORD HISTORICAL SOCIETY
General Editor: Alan Crossley

THE BUILDING ACCOUNTS OF
CORPUS CHRISTI COLLEGE, OXFORD
1517–1518

Oxford Historical Society
NEW SERIES, VOL. XLVIII

THE BUILDING ACCOUNTS OF CORPUS CHRISTI COLLEGE, OXFORD 1517–1518

Edited by

BARRY COLLETT, ANGELA SMITH, AND JULIAN REID

THE BOYDELL PRESS

OXFORD HISTORICAL SOCIETY

MMXIX

© The Oxford Historical Society 2019

All rights reserved. Except as permitted under current legislation no part of this work may be photocopied, stored in a retrieval system, published, performed in public, adapted, broadcast, transmitted, recorded or reproduced in any form or by any means, without the prior permission of the copyright owner

First published 2019

An Oxford Historical Society publication
Published by Boydell & Brewer Ltd
PO Box 9, Woodbridge, Suffolk IP12 3DF, UK
and Boydell & Brewer Inc.
668 Mt Hope Avenue, Rochester, NY 14620-2731, USA
website: www.boydellandbrewer.com

ISBN 978-0-904107-28-9

A CIP catalogue record for this book is available
from the British Library

The publisher has no responsibility for the continued existence or accuracy of URLs for external or third-party internet websites referred to in this book, and does not guarantee that any content on such websites is, or will remain, accurate or appropriate

This publication is printed on acid-free paper

Typeset in Monotype Bembo Book by Word and Page, Chester, UK

Printed and bound in Great Britain by
TJ International Ltd, Padstow, Cornwall

CONTENTS

List of Plates	vi
Preface	ix
Abbreviations	xii

INTRODUCTION
Richard Fox, *by Barry Collett*	xiii
The Building Accounts, *by Angela Smith*	xliii
The Manuscript, *by Jane Eagan*	lvii

EDITORIAL NOTE, *by Julian Reid*	lxi
EDITION OF THE MANUSCRIPT, *by Julian Reid*	1

APPENDICES
1. Chronology of the development of Bishop Fox's plans, *by Barry Collett and Angela Smith* — 91
2. A set of missing building accounts, *by Angela Smith* — 99
3. Purchase of land from master mason, John Lebons, *by Angela Smith* — 103
4. Indenture of 1513 between Bishop Fox and the Prior and Convent of St. Swithun's Priory, Winchester, *by Angela Smith* — 107
5. John and Jane Huddleston and the Manor of Temple Guiting, *by Angela Smith* — 127
6. Carved details in the hall at Corpus Christi, *by Angela Smith* — 131
7. Bishop Fox's Berkshire endowment of the College, *by Barry Collett* — 139
8. Educational opportunities for craftsmen's sons, *by Angela Smith* — 143
9. Building industry legislation, 1514, *by Barry Collett* — 145
10. Craftsmen, suppliers, and carriers listed in the building accounts, *by Angela Smith* — 153

BIBLIOGRAPHY	161
INDEX	167

PLATES

Frontispiece. Portrait of Bishop Richard Fox at Sudeley Castle

1. Fox's chantry chapel in Winchester Cathedral
2. The hall at Corpus Christi College
3. David Loggan's view of Corpus, 1675
4. Oriel window above Corpus gate
5. Detail of the fan vault over the main entrance to Corpus
6. Detail of woodwork in the library at Corpus
7. Fol. 2r, the account for 2–16 March 1517
8. Fol. 18v, payments of daily wages, 9–24 May 1517
9. Fol. 44v, showing marginal entries in a distinctive hand
10. Fol. 52r, purchases from a blacksmith
11. Agreement of 1512 between Bishop Fox and John Lebons
12. The carved date 1516 on a shield in Corpus hall
13. The carved motto of Bishop Fox on a corbel in Corpus hall
14. Heraldic and other details on a corbel in Corpus hall
15. Fox's pelican device in the nineteenth-century glass in Corpus hall
16. Details of the frieze in Corpus hall, including Bishop Fox's device of a pelican vulning
17. Further details of the hall frieze, with monograms referencing the Virgin Mary

The Oxford Historical Society records its gratitude to the President and Fellows of Corpus Christi College for a generous grant towards the publication of this volume.

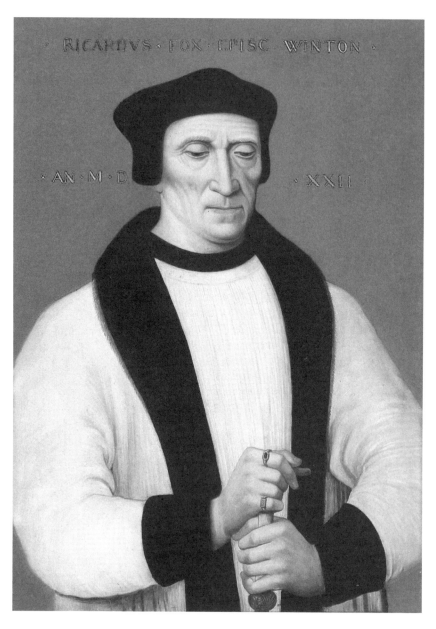

Portrait of Bishop Richard Fox, 1522, at Sudeley Castle. (photo. by Nicholas Read)

PREFACE

Bishop Richard Fox of Winchester founded Corpus Christi College, Oxford, specifically to teach *studia humanitatis*, Renaissance classical studies. He purchased or leased various properties on the site, acquiring them one by one, had the site progressively cleared, began construction in 1513 and continued in this manner for the next few years until the hall, part of the chapel, the gate-tower and sections of rooms were completed during 1516. In January 1517, while clearing and building was still in progress, Fox purchased the last land and building on the site, a small hall used by the nuns of Godstow. Corpus Fellows came into residence in March 1517 while work was in progress, and the first students arrived perhaps then or in July 1517.

In 1519, Erasmus praised this 'biblioteca trilinguis' (trilingual library: Latin, Greek and Hebrew), which he declared was 'inter praecipua decora Britanniae' ('among the greatest glories of Britain'). Corpus Christi College however was more than England's Renaissance jewel. The story of Fox's building comprises much of his *curriculam vitae*, a long and complicated story – beginning in Lincolnshire with childhood episodes that influenced both his piety and, later, his foreign policy, his education in law at Oxford, his career in royal service, his reaction to the usurpation of Richard III, his exile in France with Henry Tudor as chief councillor, and after the battle of Bosworth in August 1485, his rapid rise as Henry VII's, Secretary and Keeper of the Privy Seal (virtually 'Prime Minister'). As Henry VII's principal diplomat, Fox steadily developed England's involvement in Europe, well before the better known diplomacy of his protégé, Thomas Wolsey. He was widely recognized as a shrewd political analyst and councillor, 'a wise man and one that could see though the present to the future'. Despite his immense importance in English and European history, little direct evidence about his thinking survives. When he died in 1528, apart from Corpus Christi College and his splendid chantry chapel in Winchester Cathedral, he slipped from historical sight like a shadowy Fox with which his contemporaries compared him.

The College Quincentenary in 2017 has stimulated new interest in Fox's College. Rodney Thomson recently published an edition of the medieval Greek and Latin holdings of Corpus, Nigel Wilson an edition of the College's Greek manuscripts, and Peter Pormann a catalogue of the Hebrew manuscripts.[1] Thomas Charles-Edwards and Julian Reid have completed a history of the College from 1517 until the present. The three authors of this edition of the building accounts, CCCO H/1/4/1 have combined their different historical skills. Angela Smith is an art historian who has studied Bishop Fox's architectural projects, Julian Reid is the College Archivist and Barry Collett is separately writing Fox's biography.

Richard Fox's foundation of Corpus Christi was entwined with his own personality and political complications, as was the contemporary trilingual college [between 1500 and 1528] at the University of Alcalá with the personality and political life of its Founder Cardinal Ximines [Ximenes de Cisnero]. The Spanish and English colleges are striking examples of European intellectual reform based on classical languages and literature, and intended to reform and reinvigorate Church, universities, government and nation, both driven by one man's personality and circumstances. For that reason, this critical edition of the building-site accounts of Corpus includes a lengthy introduction to its Founder.

The building accounts of 1517–18, CCCO H/1/4/1, contain useful historical evidence. They reveal the human thinking, planning and the daily physical labour needed to build this Renaissance 'beehive' of *studia humanitatis*. They show a well-organized and efficient site, showing its various stages of construction, the senior craftsmen's consultations with Fox, materials used, items of equipment, names of workers, days worked, both morning and afternoon shifts, wages, holy days and missed days, group and individual tasks, contracts and specialist subcontracts for walls, paving, decorating, making tables, beds and library desks, costs of materials and cartage, fortnightly *summae* of costs, and several human asides. Item by item, they slowly bring to life people on that building site in 1517–18. It is most disappointing, therefore, that account books for 1514, which were discovered in the 1920s, had disappeared again within twenty years. An account of this loss is given in the second appendix.

ACKNOWLEDGEMENTS

A large number of people helped us in the preparation of this volume. First, the President and Scholars of the College of Corpus Christi in the University of Oxford, who have been helpful, hospitable and patient in the face of delays, while also taking an active interest at every stage. They have

---

[1] R. M. Thomson, *Descriptive Catalogue of the Medieval Manuscripts of Corpus Christi College Oxford* (Cambridge, 2011); N. G. Wilson, *Descriptive Catalogue of the Greek Manuscripts of Corpus Christi College Oxford* (Cambridge, 2011); P. E. Pormann, *Descriptive Catalogue of the Hebrew Manuscripts of Corpus Christi College, Oxford* (Cambridge, 2015).

given permission to use illustrations of Corpus Christi College, including images of CCCO H/1/4/1. They generously made a substantial grant towards publication of this volume. A timely and generous Small Grant from the British Academy enabled digital photography of CCCO H/1/4/1, transcriptions and editing. We are also grateful for the generosity of Lady Ashcombe of Sudeley Castle, who gave permission to use the 1522 portrait of Bishop Richard Fox, and Sudeley's Archivist Mr Derek Maddock, who arranged the photographic work of Mr Nicholas Read of Oxford. The authors would also like to thank Jane Eagan, Head Conservator of the Oxford Conservation Consortium and the staff at Durham Castle Buildings Archive, Hampshire Record Office and Lincolnshire Archive, the British Library, the Bodleian Library and the Library staff of Corpus Christi College – whose daily work is in the original library of the Founder.

Innumerable colleagues have helpfully asked searching questions and offered ideas. Eliza Hartrich and Jane Borgeaud were assiduous Research Assistants. My fellow authors, Angela Smith and Julian Reid (the College Archivist), invariably transformed sober discussions of puzzling material into cheerfully perceptive analyses, and my wife Paula characteristically offered firm comments from a discreet distance. The Oxford Historical Society was most encouraging in accepting this volume, and Alan Crossley, its General Editor, and its past Chairman, the late Jeremy Catto, gave guidance and skilled advice distilled from their wide historical knowledge.

Barry Collett
Feast of Corpus Christi, 2018

ABBREVIATIONS

Allen	P. S. and H. M. Allen, eds., *Letters of Richard Fox, 1486–1527* (Oxford, 1929)
BL	British Library
CCCO	Corpus Christi College, Oxford
Emden, *BRUO*	A. B. Emden, *Biographical Register of the University of Oxford to A.D. 1500*, 3 vols. (Oxford, 1957–9)
Fowler	T. Fowler, *The History of Corpus Christi College with Lists of its Members*, OHS 25 (Oxford, 1893)
Harvey	J. H. Harvey, *English Medieval Architects: A Biographical Dictionary down to 1550* (2nd edn., Gloucester, 1984)
HLRO	House of Lords Record Office
HMSO	Her Majesty's Stationery Office
HRO	Hampshire Record Office
McConica	J. K. McConica, ed., *History of the University of Oxford, III: The Collegiate University* (Oxford, 1986)
ODNB	*Oxford Dictionary of National Biography*
OED	*Oxford English Dictionary*
OHS	Oxford Historical Society
PROB	Records of the Prerogative Court of Canterbury
RCHM	Royal Commission on Historical Monuments, *An Inventory of the Historical Monuments in the City of Oxford* (London, 1939)
Salzman	L. F. Salzman, *Building in England down to 1540: A Documentary History* (reprint, Oxford, 1967)
Smith, 1988	Angela Smith, 'The Life and Building Activity of Richard Fox, c.1446–1528' (unpublished Ph.D. thesis, Warburg Institute, University of London, 1988)
VCH	*Victoria County History*
WAM	Westminster Abbey Muniments
Ward	G. R. M. Ward, *Foundation Statutes of Bishop Fox for Corpus Christi College, All Souls College and Magdalen College, Oxford* (London, 1843)
WCL	Winchester Cathedral Library

INTRODUCTION

RICHARD FOX

Despite his importance in English and European history, Bishop Richard Fox (1448–1528) has been little studied, partly because he deliberately kept in the shadows, working mainly behind closed doors, otherwise keeping his mouth shut and his quill under control, leaving little paperwork or other evidence that might reveal his analyses of contemporary political and ecclesiastical problems, or his contributions to discussions, or his influence upon decisions. No sermons have survived, although there are several surviving letters with expressions of his piety. Some letters are tinged with dry humour but others quite secretive. He used trusted servants to carry documents and letters on important matters, sometimes simply asking the recipient to speak with the courier, 'geve unto hym therin asmoche feith and credence as if I spake personally with you my selve', and like Wolsey he sometimes conducted highly secret conversations on horseback in an open space, such as a garden.[1] Some of Fox's political and administrative ideas, however, may be deduced from his letters and actions, or the Statutes he wrote for Corpus Christi College, or even his translation of the Benedictine Rule for nuns and (both 1517). Recently, there has been more interest in him, yet, like his contemporaries, historians are often obliged to speculate about this elusive man, a Fox seen as if in a mirror, glimpsed over the viewer's shoulder, a dark shadow swiftly and silently slipping away. Young Henry VIII told an aristocratic Spanish ambassador, 'In England, we think he really *is* a fox'.[2]

When Corpus Christi College, Oxford, opened in 1517, Richard Fox was about seventy years old and Bishop of Winchester. He had planned the College, developing his ideas for several years (Appendix 1). In July and

---

[1] Allen, 12, letter to John Gunthorpe, 5 September 1489; see W. P. Baildon, ed., *Calendar of the Manuscripts of the Dean and Chapter of Wells*, vol. 2 (London, 1914), 116.

[2] There were several small chronicles about Fox and his works. About a hundred years ago, Edmund Chisholm Batten and Margery Howden wrote small but reliable biographies to accompany their editions of Fox's episcopal registers and Bath and Wells and Durham respectively. Within the last thirty years there have been a number of works: in 1987, Richard Carless completed a biographical thesis and Angela Smith a lengthy doctoral thesis in 1988, and Cliff Davies's entry in ODNB (2004) is an accurate and perceptive work. In addition to this present volume on the building-site records, Clayton Drees published a full-length biography in November 2014 and another full-length biography by Barry Collett is forthcoming.

August 1513 he took the first steps by sending personally chosen craftsmen to develop the site of Urban Hall, a dilapidated student residence, and construct a new kitchen to feed building workers. This first step was followed by further work, though not rapidly because Fox was fully occupied in foreign and domestic politics and, in any case, still did not hold the title to any of the several properties on the site – merely their owners' agreements to lease or sell. The earlier stages of building from 1513 until March 1517 are barely documented because the building accounts are lost, though the accounts of 1514 were found in the late 1920s but were misplaced again, and their present whereabouts are not known (Appendix 2).[3] The sole surviving building accounts (CCCO H/1/4/1) cover work from 5 March until autumn 1517 and include a few final tasks in 1518.

❖

Fox founded Corpus Christi College to teach the Renaissance *studia humanitatis*, studies of classical languages and literature in their original purity, in order to educate minds in understanding humanity, society, especially its politics, and Christianity. Erasmus greeted the College as a new dawn in the intellectual life of Renaissance Europe, praising it as 'biblioteca trilinguis' (trilingual library: Latin, Greek and Hebrew), and 'inter praecipua decora Britanniae' ('among the greatest glories of Britain'). Bishop Fox was a sophisticated and devout man, and his foundation and endowment of Corpus Christi College could easily be seen as a politician trying to achieve national and international fame, or as an aged prelate, trying in a late-medieval manner to merit heavenly salvation – or both.

Fox's intentions, however, were far more than hopes for fame and salvation through conventional acts of late-medieval piety. The roots of his intentions for Corpus stretched back into his childhood. Fox was a typical case of late-medieval social mobility. He was born in the village of Ropsley near Grantham in Lincolnshire in 1447 or 1448, three or four generations after the Black Death, the second of three children of relatively prosperous yeoman landowners, Thomas and Helena Fox. He was probably first taught by his mother and the parish priest, and later attended elementary classes conducted in Grantham by the parish clergy and chantry priests in St. Wulfram's Church, or perhaps at the 'Grange', the priory of the Greyfriars who led Grantham's annual Corpus Christi procession and were responsible for practical civic works, having built the town's water supply system and

---

[3] It is probable that the building accounts were hurriedly used, as were other documents, to pack and hide College plate in 1643, during the Civil War, using water to soften the paper. This would explain why the sole retrieved set of accounts has strong water stains; J. G. Milne, 'The Muniments of Corpus Christi College', *Oxoniensia*, 2 (1937), 129.

supervised the leper hospital. The schoolboy Fox probably stayed with his Rous relatives in Grantham for the week, riding home for Sundays and holy days.[4] His family was close-knit (and remained so when several members later migrated to London) and an exemplar when he later tried to build up a sense of close-knit *familia* in all organizations, especially his College.

Like other country boys, Richard Fox and his older brother John probably helped with farm work and were taught by older men how to maintain ditches, dykes and fishponds – important in Lincolnshire, where flat areas were prone to flooding – and to use quarries for buildings and other stonework. Fox's lifelong interest in water management, stonework, building maintenance and other practical skills were used in adult life when he devised effective water defences at Calais and Norham Castle. Practical skills also served him well later, in maintaining church buildings in his care and designing new buildings.

Bright boys usually went from elementary school to a grammar school to study Latin language and literature. There are no local records for young Richard's time, but grammar teaching may have been available, since Grantham had a long history of schooling, beginning with Walter Pigot, clerk, appointed schoolmaster at Grantham from the feast of Michaelmas 1329 for one year, and renewed until 1335. When Fox was a boy several local clergy were graduates (mostly of Oxford), and local worthies were keen on education, and in 1478, when Fox was thirty, the father of an old school friend died and bequeathed land to pay for two priests to pray for his soul and to instruct local boys 'in good manners and the art of grammar in a certain fine house built near the church'.[5] The quality of his childhood education in Ropsley and Grantham had laid the basis of Fox's Oxford studies and his social advancement out of the yeoman class, and stimulated his lifelong encouragement of merit amongst working-class children. Shortly before his own death in 1528, when Fox handled the will of his old school friend, Richard Curteys, he re-endowed the school at Grantham as a grammar school (today known as the King's School), using that 'certain fine house'. The school became a feeder for Corpus Christi, as did another school Fox

[4] Smith, 1988, 59–61. It was common for children of both sexes to be sent to board and be educated in wealthy households. Later, when Bishop of Winchester, Fox himself had children boarding and educated in his household.

[5] Anthony Wood, *Colleges and Halls in the University of Oxford* (Oxford, 1786), 382–3; Fowler, 2; also see CCCO 280(c), ff. 169r–v; 188r–203v (lives of Fox). A. F. Leach in *VCH Lincolnshire*, ii, 421–92. The will was of Henry Curteys (Curteis), a wealthy merchant and alderman of Grantham. The Guild of the Blessed Mary was probably an earlier school attached to a religious house, and in 1492 Fox joined the Boston Guild of Corpus Christi (BL Harleian MS 4795), but the guild did not have a school. In 1329, the dean and canons of Lincoln Cathedral interviewed and appointed six teachers to grammar schools in the county of Lincoln. A. F. Leach, *The Schools of Medieval England* (London, 1915), 192.

founded in Taunton, and Corpus itself became a major means of social mobility for commoner children.

In 1460, when Fox was twelve or thirteen years old, the Wars of the Roses brought violent conflict and brutal retributions along the Great North Road through Grantham, and the village of Ropsley was close enough perhaps to experience the violence. Shortly after, his mother died, and his father remarried. When he was a young man at Oxford, his region was again the epicentre of ferocious fighting followed by executions in Grantham close to his former school. We can only conjecture the effect upon Fox of nearby military violence, his mother's death, folk memories of the Black Death and religious devotions on Christ's Passion, but they probably confirmed in this intelligent and sensitive boy the biblical and Augustinian refrain that life is flimsy and transitory, yet human suffering is embraced by Christ's suffering – symbolized by the *Arma Christi* (symbols associated with the Passion) above the altar in Fox's chantry chapel and carved on the roof bosses over the quire in Winchester Cathedral. During his later political career, Fox single-mindedly pursued peace, carefully using his skill with words to avoid ambiguity and strengthen agreements in foreign policy, diplomacy and treaties. Although his peace policies were always based upon political calculation, they were also a product of character and temperament formed in childhood.

About 1465, Fox travelled south to study law, very probably at the recently founded Magdalen College, Oxford. After graduation, he worked as a crown lawyer and was connected with the diocese of Salisbury, where several influential men appreciated his potential. John Davyson, Dean of Salisbury, had been a prebend (a salaried cathedral post) at Grantham, and he may have spotted Fox's schoolboy talent. In his will Davyson named Fox, who later set up a chantry at Cambridge to pray for Davyson's soul. In 1477, Fox was ordained as an acolyte in Salisbury Cathedral, placing him on the classic route of social elevation: a commoner, an intelligent boy from a self-sufficient but not wealthy family, passing from grammar-schooling to university studies in law, ordained a churchman, and steadily promoted by those who saw his talent. Nevertheless, he did not forget his own background.

In 1478 Fox was given work in Edward IV's royal council, probably at the instigation of another patron, James Goldwell, who was present at the meeting. Goldwell was Bishop of Norwich and a diplomat, and in 1499 left a bequest of his best robes and a ring to Fox who was the only person mentioned by name in his will, apart from a godson and relatives. The following year, Fox joined a delegation in Flanders and received an honorary matriculation at the University of Louvain. He was now marked for a high career in royal service, and soon after, the new Bishop of Salisbury, Lionel Woodville, brother to Queen Elizabeth, the wife of Edward IV, gave him a wealthy prebend. He continued working with other royal servants connected with the family of Elizabeth Woodville.

Fox was close enough to the centre of government to see that high-level conflicts weaken good governing at all levels, as expressed in his later correspondence and woven into his translation for nuns and the Statutes of Corpus. When Edward IV unexpectedly died in 1483, the ensuing changes altered Fox's life. Conflicts within the royal family between the surviving brothers and sisters of Edward IV and the family of his wife, Elizabeth Woodville, became open violence, with Edward's brother, Richard, Duke of Gloucester, arbitrarily murdering some of the Woodville family. Edward IV's young son was crowned as Edward V, but Gloucester usurped the throne as Richard III. Fox had been working close to the Woodville faction, and may have been personally hostile to Richard III, but he could have kept his head down and quietly served the new regime. However, when young Edward V and his brother disappeared in the Tower of London, people supposed that they were murdered and publicly expressed repugnance at the presumed crime. This reaction was countered by Richard III's emphasis upon his own personal morality, but presumably Fox saw this as hypocrisy in pursuit of power – a usurper who secured the crown by the 'unnatural murder' of his nephews, but claimed to be a righteous king.

In October 1483, Henry Tudor, Earl of Richmond, and Henry Stafford, Duke of Buckingham, organized a rebellion, but it failed, and Richard III's bloody retributions drove a stream of both Lancastrians and Woodville Yorkists to flee across the Channel to join Henry Tudor in Brittany. Fox, too left England and went to Paris, perhaps as a theological student, perhaps sent by the Woodville faction to be both a student and a 'sleeping agent' until needed. Henry Tudor himself feared extradition from Brittany, and in 1484, fled into France. When Henry arrived Fox left his studies in Paris and joined him. By a remarkable stroke of luck, the two men struck up a strong rapport and Henry immediately gave Fox high responsibility in organizing the invasion of England. Apparently any doubts Fox felt about war were outweighed by the necessity for military rebellion against Richard III. The main problems were the complicated uncertainties of French politics and bureaucracy and the need to move fast before autumn's unpredictable weather, but he completed the task efficiently. In this matter he learned another lesson – how important it was for a working team to remain close-knit, determined and swift.

Richmond's small fleet sailed in the late summer of 1485 and landed in Wales. His army marched inland and, despite unfavourable odds, defeated Richard III at the battle of Bosworth on 22 August 1485, and he became Henry VII by military conquest. Immediately after the battle, his secretary and adviser Richard Fox showed how close he was to the king by his countersigning one of the first royal orders with his surname, in bold capitals – FOX. The victorious army marched to London, and was welcomed by the City. Henry VII faced huge long-term tasks in securing his new government, but in the short term he established his legitimacy by being crowned at Westminster Abbey, calling a parliament to ratify his reign, married Elizabeth of York to fulfil the promise to unite Yorkists and Lancastrians, obtained papal approval of both his reign and the marriage and suppressed uprisings, notably at the crucial battle of Stoke.

Fox remained Henry VII's intimate counsellor – informally behind the scenes and formally as royal Secretary, and through his presence at nearly all meetings of the royal Council – and in 1487 was appointed Keeper of the Privy Seal. In addition to exercising multiple and overlapping roles in Henry VII's government he was the king's foreign minister and leading diplomat at a time when England was increasingly involved in European politics. Fox was also Bishop of Exeter (1487–91), Bath and Wells (1491–4), Durham (1494–1501, when Scottish military threats were high) and Winchester (1501–28), the wealthiest diocese in England. He was a dominant force in government, religion and learning between 1485 and his resignation from royal service in 1516, and he exercised considerable sway in political decisions, both domestic and foreign, during years when England was on the edge of enormous changes. Contemporary diplomats – usually, though not invariably, shrewd observers – more than once called him *alter rex* (the other king).

The victorious Henry VII needed to subdue further resistance, and persuade English people, including resentful Yorkist opponents, to accept his victory. In broad terms, his policies were to avoid reprisals, be tolerant and restore efficient and stable government, which had been eroded by two decades of conflict – ambitions at the core of Fox's character. Thus, Henry VII's closest adviser possessed personal qualities aligned with policies that could make the new Tudor regime acceptable. In that sense, Fox was the man for the occasion, even in 1485. Henry VII was fortunate, indeed lucky, in having Fox close beside him, but Fox was not his only capable councillor. Good government, however, requires more than solid morale. It needed competent and highly co-ordinated administration. This would be crucial to Henry's survival and he was highly fortunate in having few men of high status whom he was obliged to appoint, and he could therefore select the men he wanted as royal councillors. Moreover, he was a shrewd judge of personality, and chose on merit 'vigilant men and secret', 'the ablest men that then were to be found', as Francis Bacon put it.[6] Despite their polit-

---

[6] Francis Bacon, *The History of the Reigne of King Henry the Seventh* (London, 1628), 40, 242. Also W. C. Richardson, *Tudor Chamber Administration 1485–1547* (Baton Rouge, Louisiana, 1952), 98.

ical inexperience, Henry's royal councillors in 1485 were all capable, 'sad' (serious) men who learned quickly, and whose competence and steadiness during crises he already knew. More importantly, they were personally close to him in another way: although he chose them, in another sense most had first chosen him by the act of joining him in exile and battle. They were his subjects, but no mere subordinates. They were his former comrades, whose shared experience of uncertainty, exile, danger and battle inevitably engendered bonds of comradeship that strengthened common purpose and inhibited factions. This meant that the royal council had at its core the strength and solidarity of veterans shared by all ranks – soldierly bonds that included the king and lasted long after Bosworth.

Henry VII needed to secure peace with other nations. Fox took responsibility and proved to be a natural diplomat: pacific, rational in agreeing terms, amiable and highly intelligent (as Thomas More said, 'vir minime stupidus'). He swiftly negotiated an end to Richard III's war with France, and in the conflict between France and Brittany successfully juggled Henry VII's difficult position as a grateful friend to both countries, keeping England out of involvement. He arranged a temporary truce with Scotland that, in fact, lasted for ten years. Fox also worked hard with Spain, reasoning that an Anglo-Spanish marriage alliance would protect England, provide long-term security and stimulate trade. For this, English diplomacy had to be strengthened by reforms in education.

A competent and acceptable Tudor administration and expanded English engagement in Europe both needed good education, and Fox looked to universities for scholars who were potential priests, lawyers, teachers, doctors and royal servants. He knew that England's expanding diplomatic engagement in Europe (and even beyond) required a large cohort of well-educated men from whom to recruit. So did the English Church and English prosperity in general. He also looked to grammar schools to feed the universities. From 1485 to 1517, the problems of Tudor survival – good government and expanding diplomatic engagement abroad – pushed him towards later ideas of integrated government, Church and universities.

During the first major royal progress in 1486, Fox left the royal party to visit Ropsley to see his family and the parish priest, Thomas Dalton MA (Oxon.), and arranged to have a porch built as a thanksgiving gift for St. Peter's church where he had been baptized.[7] After some days with his

---

[7] Thomas Dalton, rector of Cottesmore, Rutland, from 19 April 1481, vacated the parish before February 1493. Cottesmore is ten miles south of Ropsley, where a priest, also named Thomas Dalton, was incumbent from 1477–88. It is reasonable to suppose that it was the same man serving both parishes in 1486. Emden, *BRUO*, 538. N. Pevsner, J. Harris and N. Antram, *The Buildings of England: Lincolnshire*, rev. edn. (New Haven and London, 2002), 613–14. The porch, still standing, has pinnacles and a parapet with shields in pointed quatrefoils, the date 1486 carved

family, around 20 March he rode twenty-five miles northwards to Lincoln to deal with another personal matter. Although committed to the king's service, Fox now had a parallel vocation – to move beyond the minor clerical orders towards the priesthood. At Lincoln, he spent some days in solitary retreat; on 25 March 1486, the feast of the Annunciation, the first day of the Christian year, Bishop John Russell ordained him sub-deacon, the first of the major orders.[8] As the royal progress returned from the north towards London, Fox again left the royal party to visit Oxford, and at Magdalen College met the young John Claymond a student of Greek. He appointed Claymond master of a grammar school in Durham diocese in 1500, and Master of St. Cross near Winchester in 1508, a post he held until 1517, when he was appointed first President of Corpus.[9]

Fox's definition of education was widening. As a student at Oxford during the 1460s, he would have received a sound, partly scholastic-style education in Latin literature and law. He would also have encountered Italian humanist influences coming to England, such as Tito Livio Frulovisi during the 1440s: by the mid-1480s royal service had recruited Italian humanist scholars such as Giovanni Gigli, Bernard André, Pietro Carmeliano (who lived in Oxford for several years and lectured at New College) and Cornelio Vitelli.[10] There were also Englishmen who had been classically educated in Italy, including Peter Courtenay, Bishop of Winchester, who had studied law at Oxford, Cologne and Padua; John Gunthorpe, formerly an ambassador for Edward IV and Privy Seal for Richard III, had pursued *studia humanitatis* at the University of Ferrara under Guarino da Verona in 1460 and later in Rome.[11]

Fox's appreciation of classical studies as preparation for political and diplomatic work was reinforced in October 1489 by a small incident when Fox and other English ambassadors travelled from Calais to London in the

---

inside and an inscription *Hac non vade via, Nisi dicas Ave Maria*, 'Do not enter here without saying an Ave Maria'– the prayer of the Annunciation whose feast day was imminent, and the occasion of Fox's ordination at Lincoln.

[8] Emden, *BRUO*.
[9] CCCO 280, ff. 204r–210v. Also, MS 303, ff. 66r–75v (both catalogued in William Fulman, *Collectanea*, ix), ff. 67r–v (lines 107–12): Shepreve's 'Lament for Claymond' has been edited and translated by Professor Stephen Harrison; Fowler, 110; *VCH Durham*, ii, ed. William Page (London, 1907), 129; J. G. Milne, *The Early History of Corpus Christi College, Oxford* (Oxford, 1946). The school is uncertain but probably Staindrop College.
[10] J. Gairdner, ed., *Memorials of King Henry the Seventh, Historia Regis Henrici Septimi*, vol. II (London, 1858), 54–7; H. L. Edwards, 'Robert Gaguin, and the English Poets, 1489–90', *Modern Language Review*, 32 (1937), 430–4; E. G. Duff, *Fifteenth-Century English Books* (Oxford, 1917), 56–8. Trapp, *ODNB*.
[11] Barry Collett, 'British Students at the University of Ferrara, 1480–1540', in *Filosofia, scienze e cultura alla corte degli Estensi: lo Studio di Ferrara nei secoli XV e XVI. Proceedings of the Commemoration of the 600th Anniversary of the University of Ferrara in March 1992*, ed. M. Bertozzi (Ferrara, 1994), 125–46.

company of classically educated French and some Italian diplomats who worked for England. The scholar-diplomats argued at length in Latin, especially Giovanni Gigli was notable for his fast-thinking, sophisticated and audacious ripostes. Fox saw in action the additional hard edge given by a disciplined study of the humanities through classical languages, literature and history – a vocabulary strengthened by Greek and Latin, an ability to analyse complicated problems and make connections, define concepts precisely, back them with historical examples and deliver elegant, powerful arguments.[12] That encounter strengthened Fox to give education for royal service a new emphasis provided by *studia humanitatis*. By the time he became Bishop of Durham in 1494 Fox was encouraging classical studies in England not only to prepare diplomats, but also to develop wider political potential.

When the Scots invaded England in 1497, Fox faced another, sudden, but indirect need for education, born out of war. Defending the north against the Scots was expensive for Henry's government and the whole country was heavily taxed, but the West Country vehemently protested against taxation to protect the remote northern country. A rebellious Cornish army marched on London but was defeated at Blackheath. The Scots were stopped in the north by the English army and by fortifications at Norham Castle (supervised by Fox), but it had been a close call. The need for national unity was now urgent, but it would take time, and not be easy, and in the meantime required a better-educated royal service.

In 1501 Fox became Bishop of Winchester and he began moves for Church reform, which were part of his ideas for good government. Some priests and a few monks misbehaved by spending too much time hunting or in taverns, and other forms of laxity. But at a deeper level than these abuses, the Church had too few educated priests, and too little spiritual understanding of the kind that could be nourished by education. Much clerical education seemed based on the scholastic syllabus, which trained minds in logic but gave inadequate understanding or insight into the human condition. Humanists wanted more of *studia humanitatis*, which sowed seeds of virtue and knowledge and human understanding through study of the classical and biblical languages of Latin, Greek and Hebrew and their literature and history. *Studia humanitatis* were to be followed by vocational subjects for clergy, lawyers, administrators, physicians – those whose enriched professional skills would improve the human condition and the world. In Italian city-states the classical humanities had been doing this for

---

[12] Gairdner, *Memorials*, 54–7; Edwards, 'Robert Gaguin', 430–4; Duff, 56–8. Trapp, *ODNB*. A characteristic application to diplomacy is Lucretius, *De Rerum Natura*, 1, 402 'these small traces are enough for the sharp mind, through which you may come to know everything' ('Verum animo satis haec vestigia parva sagaci sunt, per quae possis cognoscere cetera tute'). The classically educated Arthur Conan Doyle used Sherlock Holmes to illustrate this.

the professions for a hundred years. In Fox's reforming intentions, religion, education and the professions began to intermingle with the new ways in which the two English universities and the grammar schools were already moving steadily towards humane studies.

During the first years of the century, the king's mother, Lady Margaret Beaufort, co-operated closely with Fox. She obtained a new charter for Christ's College, Cambridge, in 1505 and then endowed and expanded it, with *studia humanitatis* in mind. Her considerable influence in the university helped her spiritual adviser, Bishop Fisher, become President of Queens' College, Cambridge, in April 1505. She was also posthumous foundress of St. John's College, Cambridge, in 1511, having earlier bought considerable property to endow the colleges. These three Cambridge reformers intended to produce high-quality university graduates for service in both Church and the secular world.

At the same time, Fox encountered severe political troubles. Henry VII's eldest son, Arthur, who was married to Katherine of Aragon as part of Fox's Anglo-Spanish alliance, died in 1502, and Henry's wife, Elizabeth of York, died in childbirth in February 1503. With what were possibly the first signs of tuberculosis, the king went into a long personal decline, and his personality became less stable and obsessively avaricious. Henry VII and his Council had imposed a system of bonds and recognizances soon after Bosworth as a means of keeping wealthier subjects under control and enforcing peaceful behaviour, and now these bonds and recognizances were expanded into money-making practices by a group of counsellors, principally Empson and Dudley, who employed a small army of informers, lawyers and enforcers. The consequence was the development of excessive and dangerous revenue-raising through officious minor officials making major financial impositions. By exaggerating small legal lapses or making false accusations of improper or criminal behaviour, officials forced many nobles, gentry and others towards bankruptcy, often taking the opportunity to demand bribes or buy their victims' land cheaply. There was enormous resentment at the law being manipulated to enrich the king and crown administrators to the detriment of justice and the property of subjects. Worse, King Henry VII was compliant with the extortionate and corrupt behaviour of Empson, Dudley and their managers. Several councillors, including Fox, had been involved in earlier bonds and recognizances as instruments of keeping the peace, and although not implicated in these recent abuses, they were uneasy. The Tudor monarchy became the focus of widespread unpopularity and outrage, with talk of tyranny, the abuse of Magna Carta and seething political discontent so hostile that Fox, the king's mother, Lady Margaret Beaufort, and other members of the Council feared that popular acceptance of young Prince

Henry was at risk. For a second time Fox was caught up in a crisis of monarchy. Lady Margaret and other members of the Council secretly plotted to make Empson and Dudley and their agents scapegoats and use their punishment to increase the popularity and acceptance of the Tudor monarchy. In 1508, their first step was to arrange for a young humanist-educated clergyman, Alexander Barclay, to translate Sebastian Brandt's hugely successful allegorical satire *Das Narrenschiff*, published in 1494. Barclay's English translation, known as *The Ship of Fools*, had been modified to address high-level corruption in England, including, for example, word-plays on angels (gold coins), 'Angels Work Wonders in Westminster Hall'. Satire on lawyers as pigs in a trough was blended with praise for the new king in waiting, who would rule much more wisely.

Henry VII died in April 1509. The plotters kept his death secret for forty hours while they moved troops into position, arrested Empson and Dudley and imprisoned them in the Tower. The royal Council decided not to charge them with corruption because a trial would reveal how deeply the king himself had been involved in their conduct. Instead, a charge of treason was devised, on the grounds that their personal bodyguards were brought to London to take over the Council and the new king. The accusation was flimsy, but it reduced public discrediting of the late king, and allowed the royal Council to maintain the standing of the monarchy and promote the popularity of young King Henry VIII. Fox, however, had dirtied his hands and compromised his integrity. He was upset by what he had done, although his Florentine contemporary Niccolò Machiavelli would have understood. The plot succeeded: the anger was directed away from the dead king and directed towards the two scapegoats, Empson and Dudley. There was widespread acclaim of the young king and the popular expectations of his new rule.

Having quietly saved the monarchy in 1509, Fox now became the organizer behind the revival of the Spanish marriage alliance, through the marriage of Prince Henry with Katherine of Aragon, the widow of Henry's older brother Arthur. Actually, Katherine's status as a widow was uncertain, because she claimed that her earlier marriage had not been consummated and she was therefore not Arthur's widow – an uncertainty that later had immense consequences. In 1509, Fox wanted the marriage to provide heirs to the throne and avoid England slipping back into the kind of civil conflict that marked the Wars of the Roses. The marriage was part of Fox's plan to secure long-term peace in Europe by union with Spain and by diplomatically securing neutrality with France, Scotland and the Holy Roman Empire. Moreover, a spectacular wedding to the glamorous young Spanish princess, amid a public display of English technical expertise in pomp, ceremonies and stage-managed political theatre, bolstered the popularity of the handsome young Henry VIII.

Fox's plans for peace, however, soon began to go awry because Henry VIII was bent on war with France to recapture former English territories there and bolster his personal honour. The tension between the young king and the elderly and experienced Keeper of the Privy Seal since 1487 continued for three or four years, between 1509 and 1513, as Henry, helped by Fox's former protégé, Thomas Wolsey, gradually loosened Fox's domination of the royal Council and foreign policy. Fox was aware of other damage that royal authority could inflict on otherwise good government, as Henry VII's did in his later years, but war was his greatest worry. He supported the various prelates who proposed peace, including John Colet, the Dean of St. Paul's, who told Henry bluntly and publicly that war was almost always immoral. The king took the clergy's criticisms of his war policy seriously, but he did not change, and Fox was left with the long-term implications of Henry VIII's personality.

If the Church were a moral guide for government, monks and nuns should be amongst those to guide and inspire rulers, but after more than twenty years of being a bishop, and handling problems with lesser monks and nuns, he knew that the monastic life in its present condition was inadequate to inspire the nation. He still hoped that if monks were educated in *studia humanitatis*, the Renaissance study of the humanities, they would stimulate reforms within the English Church. Fox was familiar with several notable humanists, including Erasmus, Vitelli, Ammonio and Colet, who had demonstrated the powerful educational potential of the humanities, and he knew well and held in high regard many monastics, including the Scottish friars at Greenwich, his friend Prior Castell and the monks at Durham Priory, and the Carthusians at Sheen.

In November 1511, Fox had evidently chosen a site for his monastic foundation, to the west of Merton College on the edge of Oxford's red-light area, at the south end of Gropecunt Lane. He hoped that the monks of his college would help transform the Church and spread spiritual regeneration into government and secular society. Fox now began discussions with the Fellows of Merton College in the hope of acquiring part of their property for his site. Merton gave tentative assent, and preliminary work began and on 21 December 1511 the governing body of Oxford University wrote to Fox acknowledging his plan to establish a college.[13] On 8 February 1512 a contract was drawn up between Fox and the mason John Lebons (Appendix 3) concerning the sale of property in Hampshire, to be part of the endowment for the bishop's foundation.

[13] Milne, *Early History*, 2; Fowler, 65; Allen, 55–6; McConica, 18.

In June 1512, Fox was still waiting for a decision from Merton College, but was evidently confident of the outcome because he sent four senior craftsmen to survey the site on 4 July 1512, William Vertue, master mason, and William East (Est), mason and master of works, who answered to Vertue, Humphrey Coke, master carpenter, and Robert Carow, a well-known Oxford builder.[14] Coke had designed and supervised the refurbishment of the episcopal lodgings in Durham Castle in the 1490s during Fox's episcopate. Coke and Vertue had also worked for Fox more recently at Winchester, when Fox showed marked respect and generosity towards them and other skilled craftsmen. They hired workmen, and began clearing the site of Urban Hall, which was owned by Merton College but was now in a dilapidated state. In his history of Corpus, Thomas Fowler suggested that the college kitchen had been the refectory of Urban Hall, but this theory was disputed by J. G. Milne, who thought that Fox's masons merely reused some footings of Urban Hall.[15]

In August 1512, a group from the building site of Brasenose College, encouraged by two Fellows of Brasenose, came on the site and violently assaulted Vertue, East and Coke, though not Carow the Oxford man, or the local labourers. On 23 August, the leader, a scholar named Hastings, appeared before the chancellor's court, where Fox had arranged to have an agent present, probably his Oxford attorney. Violence on a building site was shortly to be forbidden under 'An Acte Concernyng Artificers and Labourers' of 1514; 'if any artificer or laborer reteyned in s[er]vice with any p[er]son for bilding or Rep[ar]acon do assaute or make or cause to be made any assemble to assaute herme or hurte any p[er]son assigned to countroll and ov[er]see theym in thair working', which appears to punish violence on a worker's own site, though not on another site. This court had powers of investigation and in the end sent Hastings to prison. However, the Brasenose authorities, possibly pleading the ambiguity, interceded for him and the Principal and bursar stood bail for the very large sum of £40 so that Hastings could be released on probation.[16]

The attackers were probably members of an Oxford academic gang, calling themselves 'Trojans' because they strongly opposed Greek studies of *studia humanitatis* and supported the traditional scholastic curriculum. The 'Trojans' were so well represented in Brasenose, and active in the University as a whole, that a few years later the government, through Thomas More, intervened to suppress them. Also, the dispute may have been partly industrial, with local craftsmen objecting to 'foreigners' from London

---

[14] *RCHM*, 48
[15] Fowler, 68.
[16] Ibid., 64–5.

being in charge at the new site, and fearing that Fox's men would bring in outside skilled workers. This accords with the fact that the only senior man untouched was the local man, Robert Carow, who became a master carpenter on the Corpus building site.[17] Or perhaps it was an intriguing combination of the two motives, an unusual alliance of town workers and gowned scholars.

Fox now offered the Fellows of Merton College a large preliminary payment of £120 in cash. The understanding was that in return for the money they would convey the freehold but reserve an annual rent-charge (then permissible at law) in consideration of loss of the rents of Corner Hall and Neville's Inn, at the market value of what their properties were now earning, and for losing the use of the Bachelors' Garden. In January 1513, Merton agreed and Fox went ahead with his side of the arrangement. He gave the £120 in cash to John Claymond, who delegated its distribution to Walter Morwent, who on 16 January began disbursing it at regular intervals, receiving carefully worded receipts for each payment.[18]

When Henry VIII's military campaign to invade France got under way in 1513 Fox joined it, but feared that he might be killed or taken prisoner in France and so be unable to complete the college and his chantry chapel in Winchester Cathedral (Plate 1). He drew up an indenture with Prior Thomas Silkstede of St. Swithun's Priory, Winchester (Appendix 4), which he signed shortly before sailing. It included a list of his belongings, which he had assigned to the monks, so that if he did not return from France, the goods could be valued and sold, and the money used to purchase properties from Merton College, St. Frideswide's and Godstow Abbeys, complete the work already done on the hall and the College and then finish his chantry chapel. Fox designated four men to appraise the value of his possessions in the event of his non-return to England: Abbots Kidderminster at Winchcombe, Bere at Glastonbury (a highly capable monk whose abbatial election Fox had manipulated), the Abbot of Reading and the Prior of Lewes – all four humanist scholars. Fox knew them well and held them in high regard – they were clerics who shared his enthusiasm for the New Learning. The 1513 indenture also reveals that Fox had already prepared the foundations for his chantry chapel and he intended to have it completed in tandem with

---

[17] E. A. Gee, 'Oxford Carpenters, 1370–1530', *Oxoniensia*, 17/18 (1952/3), 134. Carow, the local man, prepared the library's timber work to a design of Humphrey Coke, contracted with Roger Morwent to make a long bench for the Master's parlour, panel between the windows, make two doorways, one in the parlour and one in the room above, two cupboards one above the other, 5 feet high and 20 inches broad, seal the parlour roof, and make a door at the bottom of the stairs. The college supplied materials and he was paid £5 for his work.

[18] The paperwork in the College archive is carefully worded, but not entirely clear. Julian Reid, the College archivist, clarified the legal process, and suggested the term 'rent-charge' instead of 'quit rent' Also, Fowler, 65–6.

the completion of his college at Oxford. Indeed, Fox's chantry chapel was designed by Humphrey Coke and William Vertue, who were responsible for designing and overseeing work on Fox's college at Oxford. The indenture even mentioned that Fox wanted two chantry priests to celebrate daily Masses for his soul. Any monies left over were to be used for the construction of new vaults over Winchester Cathedral's retrochoir, the presbytery aisles and transepts.

The invasion of France was inconclusive, but the king was still resolved on war, and towards the end of 1513 he and Thomas Wolsey further pushed Fox aside, as Wolsey steadily became more prominent in the Council and in shaping royal policy. Fox was now about sixty-five years old, and his political influence had become weaker. He had come to the conclusion that the problem of maintaining good royal government was now too urgent to be remedied by the uncertain and slow influence of learned monks, and considered the possibility that Corpus Christi College could teach secular as well as monastic students. A few may be monks, but most students would become secular priests, or remain laymen as lawyers, doctors, teachers or royal servants, thus creating in the priesthood, professions and royal service a group of classically educated men who would influence king and court more effectively than pious monks could. Corpus thus built more than an English contribution to Renaissance pedagogic glory. More important was Fox's intention to improve the morality and competence of secular clergy (as distinct from monastics), and to improve the morality and competence of secular professions, including diplomacy, at a time when England was rapidly becoming more involved in European politics and conflicts, and mercantile trade in the Orient and New World.

The construction of the new college was presumably more active in 1514, though that year's building accounts kept by the clerk of works are now lost.[19] They may have held information about yet another assault in August 1514 on the senior Corpus workmen by the academic thugs of Brasenose. The presence of two academics who encouraged the violence, John Formby, the former Principal of Brasenose, and John Leigh, both scholastic 'Trojans' in opposition to Greek studies, suggest strongly that some attackers opposed *studia humanitatis*, but the attack probably also involved local hostility against outside workmen in a year when town conflict with the university was particularly high and the belligerents may well have been an alliance of town workers and gowned scholastics. It is further possible that the attack was connected with John Huddleston the younger, who was intensely hostile to Fox. Although the widow of Sir John Huddleston wanted to sell Temple Guiting, her stepson believed that Fox and the new college were depriving

---

[19] A more detailed account of this curious matter may be found in Appendix 2.

him of his family legacy, and he remained implacable. Whether or not her stepson John was involved in the attack on the building site, there was blood spilt, and the grievous assault on East (now Master of Works at Corpus) nearly became a murder charge.

Fox now tried to smooth the purchase by contracting to hold a mass, daily prayers and an annual obit in perpetuity for John and Jane Huddleston at an altar in Corpus that would be dedicated to St. Cuthbert. A contract was drawn up between Fox and Christopher Urswick, an early Tudor humanist who had known Fox since their time in exile in France with Henry, Earl of Richmond, and was now archdeacon of Oxford and acting on behalf of Jane Huddleston. On 6 December 1514, Urswick drew up an indenture with Fox, with plans for the consecration, dedication and use of the college chapel for the Huddlestons. In the meantime, Fellows from All Souls College, an institution whose *raison d'être* was to pray for the dead, would be paid for a monk to recite daily prayers for the Huddlestons (Appendix 5).[20] In the indenture, Urswick referred to Fox's college as being built 'in honour of Corpus Christi', but named 'Winchester College' in the same way that another Benedictine college, built in honour of St. Cuthbert, was named Durham College.[21] At the end of 1514, Fox still intended his college to include monks.

In September and October 1515, Henry VIII's policy and outrage began to overtake Fox's intentions. As the gateway, chapel, refectory and library of Corpus were being built, Henry VIII, deeply pious in his own way, was nevertheless increasingly antagonistic to the Church's rights. Friar Standish, one of his 'Spiritual Council', continued to give public lectures and sermons arguing that it was not against the law of God for secular judges to summon clergy for criminal causes. In October 1515, the Convocation of Clergy summoned Standish to explain why he publicly 'read, taught, affirmed and published divers matters which were thought not to stand with the laws of God and the determination of Holy Church'. As tensions between Church and state grew during 1515, Fox still remained indecisive. Despite having guided monarchical dominance over the Church since 1485, and having helped Henry VIII transfer cases from Rome to England during the quarrel with William Warham, Archbishop of Canterbury, his actions show that by now Fox was wary of further royal supremacy over the Church. Moreover, the dispute between the king and Convocation of Clergy had showed the Church's weakness in having too few learned men, either clergy or laity, to

---

[20] CCCO F1/Cap.1/Fasc.1/Ev.25.
[21] I thank Julian Reid for the deft observation. The focus of the sculptural decoration on the college gatehouse, which was completed in the first phase of building, is the eucharistic cup supported by angels that denote a dedication to Corpus Christi.

defend its liberties and jurisdiction. In fact, some of most effective disputants on both sides were laymen, demonstrating the power of well-educated laymen in religious and moral matters and showing the astuteness of Fox in using Corpus to educate not only secular clerics, but also pious professional laymen well trained in theology.

Henry VIII ordered royal judges, councillors both spiritual and temporal, and certain Members of Parliament to meet at Blackfriars, where Convocation's bill of heresy against Standish was read. Standish then aggravated the debate by drawing a sharp distinction between spiritual and secular authority and arguing that bishops had no place in Parliament merely on the grounds that they were 'spiritual' people. After robust discussion, the judges asserted that by summoning (and accusing) Friar Standish, members of Convocation were vulnerable to charges of *praemunire* (appealing to an alien jurisdiction, the papacy).[22] The bishops protested again, claiming that the Convocation of Clergy had the same right as Parliament to 'treat of things concerning both lay men and also the laws of the land'. They asserted that they had 'ever been loyal subjects', and had never said, done or intended to do 'anything contrary to the King's prerogative or prejudicial to the Crown', and asked Henry to support the Church according to his coronation oath.[23]

Fox still did not reveal his own thoughts, but was certainly aware of what that clash between spiritual and secular authority would imply for him as a bishop and obedient royal servant. Fox was already very reluctant about Henry VIII's war with France, and now, during these two intense weeks in the autumn of 1515, he was undoubtedly worried about Henry VIII's attitude to the Church. Presumably he now made up his mind about Corpus and put pressure on Warden Rawlins and the Fellows of Merton College to act upon their earlier agreement of 21 November 1512 to sell him the land. Rawlins and the Fellows reacted swiftly, and on 20 October 1515 conveyed Corner Hall, Neville's Inn and the Bachelors' Garden to Fox in consideration of the £120 already distributed and a perpetual rent-charge of £4 6s 8d, 'upon the which ground where the said meases now stand and gardens the said Bishop intendeth and purposeth by the grace of God to build and edify a college that shall be called Corpus Christi College'.[24] There was no mention of monks. Merton's draft conveyance with St. Swithun's Priory was now put aside and never engrossed. The wording of this agreement of 20

---

[22] Anthony Pollard, *North Eastern England during the Wars of the Roses* (Oxford, 1990), 46. Robert Keilway, *Relationes quorundam Casuum selectorum ex libris Roberti Keilway, Armiger* (London, 1602), 180.
[23] *Letters and Papers, Foreign and Domestic, Henry VIII*, II.ii, ed. J. S. Brewer (London, 1864), 350–61. Seven pages were written by Brian Tuke, the King's Secretary.
[24] Fowler, 67; a 'mease' is a dwelling house with outbuildings. A plan of these properties is reproduced in Fowler, 69.

October 1515 narrows down Fox's change of mind to October 1515, when the Church–state crisis became intense before the second Blackfriars conference, in November. Corpus was to be predominantly a secular college.

Once Merton College took action to convey the land, Fox's plans for Corpus were more secure and he could more easily show his own views. Henry VIII was now in hot anger against the Church, as became apparent at the third assembly convened at the royal palace of Baynard's Castle on 21 December 1515 with judges, King's Council, and some of the Commons. At that conference, Henry VIII again declared that he would no longer countenance the separate and superior authority of the Church and was determined to assert his royal supremacy. Cardinal Wolsey knew that the Church was in a weak position, and in a dramatic gesture interposed himself between the clergy and the king. He knelt before Henry VIII, asking him to forgive the clergy for supposed *praemunire*, and both as a cardinal and the Archbishop of York begged for royal forgiveness. His intention was to divert royal hostility away from the English Church, towards Rome and the papacy, and he told the king that when they appealed to the papacy, the English clergy had not intended to derogate Henry VIII's jurisdiction.

The irony of a priest, indeed a cardinal, kneeling before the secular power to confess and seek forgiveness was not unnoticed, but Wolsey was, in fact, playing a double game; a vigorous reformer, he was using antipathy to Rome in order to divert the king's assertion of royal power against Rome, rather than the English Church. Wolsey cautiously asked the king if the pope and his council at Rome might sort out the preliminary tangled matter of 'whether the summoning of clerks [clergy] before temporal judges for criminal causes was against the law of God'. But Henry would not put into Rome's hands even this uncertain aspect of royal authority over the Church, nor was he going to prolong the discussion. He abruptly told Wolsey, 'We think Dr Standish has sufficiently replied to you in all points'. There was to be no debate. The king had spoken and he was implacable.

At that point, unexpectedly, and uncharacteristically, Fox burst out, saying sharply to the king in English 'Sir, I warrant you Dr Standish will not abide by his opinion, at his peril'. The remark implied that Standish, and by implication the king, had gone too far. At this awkward moment, several people all spoke at the same time, in confusion. Archbishop Warham, at this moment Fox's ally, spoke up, saying that many holy fathers had resisted the law on this point, and some suffered martyrdom. Lord Chief Justice Fineux, although himself wary of royal power, cautiously agreed with Standish, noting that many clerics had been arraigned by holy kings and fathers of the Church had agreed to it. In response, Henry VIII had the last word, asserting that he was

King of England, and the Kings of England in times past never had any superior but God; know, therefore, that we will maintain the rights of the crown in this matter like our progenitors ... as for me, I will never consent to your desire, any more than my progenitors have done.[25]

The Archbishop of Canterbury then made his last throw. He asked, as Wolsey had done, that the matter be referred to the court of Rome, but the king did not reply. Henry VIII's pointed silence was a heavy rebuke for the archbishop. The next day, Saturday 22 December 1515, at one o'clock in the afternoon, Warham resigned as Lord Chancellor and was replaced by Thomas Wolsey.[26] With a few aggressive words, and a cold silence, the young king had opened up the deep conflict inherent in Church–state relations. The case for Fox keeping his foundation a partly monastic college was further weakened. He now needed his college to fulfil a more urgent long-term function than educating a few monks.

Some time after the Baynard Castle episode and Henry VIII's harsh treatment of Archbishop Warham, Fox altered the building plans to accommodate its new purpose and its larger number of scholars. At his manor at Esher, Fox conferred during Christmas 1515 with Vertue and Coke, England's most distinguished (and highly paid) master mason and master carpenter, both in royal employ – and his acquaintances for more than eighteen years.[27] Coke was the skilled project manager whom Fox had recommended to Lord Darcy some years earlier.[28] The craftsmen used the old plans ('double plattes' of two-storeyed modules, each of four rooms, two upstairs, two downstairs, and a central staircase) and adapted them to increase accommodation. Instead of a prior, eight monks and a few servants, the college would now have one President, 20 Fellows, 20 students or *discipuli* (perhaps including some monks), three lecturers and the chapel staff. To do this, instead of two modules comprising eight rooms to house eight monks

---

[25] Keilway, *Relationes*, 180. A detailed account of the debate on liberties of the Church is on 180v–185v. Fox's outburst is on 184v–185r. Keilway does not give his sources. He compiled the report soon after the events but it was not published until 1602. T. Rymer, *Foedera, conventiones, literæ, et cujuscunque generis acta publica, inter reges Angliæ*, 13 (London, 1727), 52–4. Pollard, *North Eastern England*, 46, 53–4.

[26] *Letters & Papers*, II, ii, no. 1313; Rymer, *Foedera*, 529–30. P. Gwyn, *The King's Cardinal: The Rise and Fall of Thomas Wolsey* (Pimlico, 1992), 49.

[27] The costume and the historical circumstance point to William Vertue being almost certainly the standing figure of a master mason in the stained glass northernmost light at the bottom of the great west window of St. George's Windsor; H. M. Colvin, ed., *The History of the King's Works*, 3, 1485–1660 (London, 1975) 313; also, see J. H. Harvey, *Report of the Society of Friends of St. George*, iv, no 3 (1962), 92.

[28] 'ryghte cunnynge and diligente in his werkes; and whan so euer ye shall have any werkes ... if ye take his advise therein, he shall advauntage ye large monee in the buldynge thereof, as well in the devisinge as in the wirkenge of yt'; Allen, 19; Gairdner, *Memorials*, 84. Colvin, *King's Works*, 30.

(one to a room), Fox, Vertue and Coke decided on five modules, along the north and west sides of the Front Quad, providing twenty rooms. Moreover, each Fellow would share his chamber with his pupil, doubling occupancy to forty. Fox's new plans required a much larger chapel on the site abutting the library. To feed the building workers, and later the College, the kitchen was enlarged, perhaps by extending the earlier kitchen, the 'small house' of 1512, which was originally intended to feed the monks. The new replanned College kitchen recalls Fox's insistence upon ample good food, and Coke's earlier designs for the great kitchen at Durham Castle, built during Fox's tenure of the see in the late 1490s.[29]

The royal assault on the Church and Fox's sharp rejoinder to Friar Standish coincided with changes in foreign relations as Henry VIII and Wolsey dismantled Fox's policy for peace in Europe, instead allying England with the Holy Roman Empire and planning another invasion of France. With his political influence diminishing, Fox faced a dilemma. If he stayed within the government he would be partly responsible for what was happening, but might still be able to modify or change policies. On the other hand, if he left government he would no longer be in the royal council, his resignation would be a strong protest and he would retain his own integrity. Meanwhile, although Henry VIII and Wolsey largely excluded Fox from policy-making, they still needed his administrative and diplomatic expertise. When the king asked him directly for assistance Fox usually obeyed, as a loyal and obedient subject should, but when Wolsey asked him, he often prevaricated or refused. His predicament was extremely awkward, for although his departure seemed inevitable, he still hoped to influence policy. His acquaintance, Thomas More, added a portrayal of Fox's dilemma in his famous 'A dialogue of Counsel' to Book I of *Utopia*, which was finished in the spring of 1516, precisely as Fox's crisis came to a head.

In May 1516, Fox's anger reached breaking point: Cardinal Schiner, a Swiss dealer-financier in arms and mercenaries, arrived in London, and at court first spoke privately with the king and Wolsey and was then ushered in to meet the Council. In a polite but cold rage Fox stalked out of the royal Council Chamber together with Archbishop Warham, a personal adversary in ecclesiastical politics, but now an ally. Fox resigned the Privy Seal, left government and returned to Winchester, apprehensive about the government of Henry VIII and Wolsey, but now firm about revising his original plans – so that Corpus Christi College might educate a few monks, but it would mainly produce well-educated pious graduates for royal service, the Church and the professions.

[29] A college kitchen was often called 'a house'.

INTRODUCTION   xxxiii

 Hugh Oldham, Bishop of Exeter, was Fox's dearest friend ('carissimus') and a major donor of funds to Corpus. Oldham was not a scholarly bishop but a good administrator and advocate of educational reform, and had just purchased the site upon which he was soon to found Manchester Grammar School in 1516. Oldham bluntly told Fox not to waste money on 'bussing monks' (monks). 'Bussing' may mean kissing, gossiping or boozing, but Clayton Drees, Fox's recent biographer, points out that the word may have been mispelled, and was 'buzzing', meaning talkative or noisy. Also, according to Ralph Holinshed, the date of Oldham's utterance was 1518, which seems three years too late, but perhaps that date is correct, and Oldham's comment came after, not before, Fox's change of mind. Both men had a sense of humour and Oldham may have used a slight change of pronunciation to make a pun, joking that the College was now, in 1518, safely filled, not with 'bussing' monks but with 'buzzing' bee-like students who busily made honey.[30]

 Whatever the date and meaning of Oldham's utterance, he very probably agreed with Fox's worries about Henry VIII's foreign policy and attitude to the Church, and the need for a 'reformacion', both spiritual and secular, a 'reformation' which could not be brought about by monks alone, but needed both the secular clergy and the professions to acquire skills and moral energy through a study of classical languages and literature. Winchester diocesan tradition from Bishop William of Wykeham (d. 1404) onwards held that godly education strengthened secular society, although Fox's experiences with several religious including with Prior Salyng of Merton Priory, whose lax discipline was well known, showed that it did not always strengthen monasticism. The Bishop of Lincoln, William Smyth, took a similar secular attitude with the newly refounded Brasenose College. Fox also knew that St. Swithun's Priory had few scholarly monks, and, as the visitation of 1521 later revealed, there was considerable laxity in Prior Silkstede's financial administration. Most of all, Fox's painful departure from government, full of ominous political portents, suggested the urgent need to build up an educated cadre at court rather than educate monks for a cloistered life at Winchester.

 Construction of his foundation had begun well before Fox legally acquired all the properties on the site. Presumably, Warden Rawlins had firmly assured him that Merton College would finalize the sale of its properties, and there were similar promises from the Prior of St. Frideswide

---

[30] C. J. Drees, *Bishop Richard Fox of Winchester: Architect of the Tudor Age* (Jefferson, 2014), 127–8, has an excellent discussion on Oldham's advice that was first mentioned in Ralph Holinshed, *The firste volume of the chronicles of England, Scotlande and Irelande* (London, 1577). See vol. 3, 617 of the 1807–8 reprint.

and the Abbess of Godstow. These assurances were sufficient for Fox to proceed. From the start he intended that Corpus should be built with little elaboration but with high-quality workmanship, and for that reason had employed Coke, Vertue, East and Carow. In 1516 Carow and his workshop completed the new dining hall with its magnificent hammerbeam roof (Plate 2). The carved detail on the frieze beneath the roof includes the date 1516, and imagery showing that the college was originally designed for the education of monks (Appendix 6). Similarly, some of the corbels in the hall were (and still are), decorated with the heraldic arms of St. Swithun's Cathedral in Winchester and the initials PTS for Prior Thomas Silkstede. The other corbels were decorated with Fox's own motto, *Est Deo Gracia*.[31]

Fox was now buying properties, including farms, to give to the College as endowments to provide income. Most purchases were in the south of England, and in the counties or dioceses from which he wished to draw students. Oxford colleges already took students from other parts of the kingdom, mostly the north. Fox now partly addressed this imbalance as bright young men were drawn from all over the nation, as he, Lady Margaret and her confessor, Bishop John Fisher, had similarly done some years before when establishing colleges at Cambridge. One property at Arborfield, near Reading in Berkshire, some thirty miles from Oxford, was purchased during 1516–17, illustrating Fox's policy of preferring to purchase properties for the endowment of his college in the south of England, and the counties or dioceses and social class from which he wished to draw students. This purchase also shows his methods of buying land. Fox sought the advice of a local farmer, Thomas Barker, about the quality and value of his proposed purchases. Barker replied, evaluating the land, and thanking Fox for encouraging his son Anthony, 'my poor lad', to study at Corpus – which the young man later did, and then became a priest. This attitude, often reflected in the Corpus statutes, reveals that Fox deliberately pursued a policy of meritocracy and social mobility, in both urban and rural areas (Appendices 7 and 8).

In the autumn of 1516, as Corpus hall was finished, the heads of the four nunneries in Winchester diocese asked Fox to translate the Latin Benedictine Rule for women, and he agreed. Fox's reply to the nuns implied that he saw more potential for improvement amongst the nuns of his diocese than the monks. That autumn and winter he translated the sparse Latin sentences into equally sparse English and added his own commentaries, which reveal much about his thoughts on responsibility, personality, management and the exercise of authority. Fox's thinking was in the Stoic philosophical

---

[31] *Est Deo Gracia* means 'Thanks be to God' and is an expression of gratitude. It can also mean that grace comes from God, and indeed, entirely from God, so that, for example, salvation is totally a gift of grace.

tradition and he showed few reservations about women exercising authority: the essential thing was that authority was exercised properly, and he made plain the full authority of abbesses by calling them 'my diocesans'. Richard Pynson published Fox's translation in January 1517 under the title of *Here begynneth the Rule of St Benet*.[32]

After Christmas, the building of Fox's college recommenced, possibly on 5 January 1517, much earlier than Fox usually preferred, but his plans were now under pressure, or perhaps on 2 March, the date from which the site accounts begin recording. The accounts reveal carefully planned project management. The kitchen and dining hall already provided secure storage, cooking and eating facilities for the workers. Scaffolding was erected with safety walls made of rush-matting and loads of stone were carted mainly from Headington Quarry and timber from Nettlebed near Henley, while building supplies were brought up-river by barge from London or purchased locally, and other equipment and material bought or borrowed from other colleges as necessary – with all quantities and times planned. Sub-contracts were given for internal specialized carpentry, especially in the library, and separate contracts for the exterior walls and a tiled yard with a security fence for timber and building materials.

The workers had long hours, but under industrial legislation of 1514 they were given a break for meals and in hot months additional rest-time to sleep after lunch (Appendix 9). The accounts also show that workers had some say in work arrangements, for example a team which dug foundations for buildings chose not to work for wages but as sub-contractors. One lime supplier, Elys Larden, who made regular deliveries to the building site, could be erratic in delivery, but was guaranteed by his friend, Lewis, a stone mason who constructed the boundary walls of the college. Lewis would see that Larden delivered the lime on the right day for the plasterers to complete their work in time for the fresh plaster to dry out over the Easter break.[33] Such active participation of workers reflects Fox's and his senior craftsmen's way of thinking about the exercise of authority at all levels and how to achieve high-quality work through planning, teamwork and speed. After the publication of *Here begynneth*, Fox wrote the Foundation Charter for Corpus Christi College, dictating passages to secretaries, and on 1 March 1517 signed the completed document. Four days later, on 5 March 1517, Fox officially handed over responsibility to his old friend, John Claymond, as the first President of Corpus.

---

[32] Richard Fox, *Here begynneth the rule of Seynt Benet* (London, 1517). Also, B. Collett, *Female Monastic Life in Early Tudor England: with an Edition of Richard Fox's Translation of the Benedictine Rule for Women, 1517* (Aldershot, 2002).
[33] CCCO H/1/4/1, f. 4r.

By March 1517, the college hall was complete, the chapel and gatehouse with its carved detail (Plate 4) were structurally finished, the kitchen was in full operation and some Fellows (no more than eleven out of the full complement of twenty) and the President were in residence.[34] During the rest of 1517, more Fellows and scholars came into residence, perhaps first housed in other colleges and moved into Corpus as each room in the front quadrangle was completed and ready for occupancy. At the same time the library was completed, occupying the entire south side of the Front Quad, directly opposite the gateway, in full view of everyone who entered Corpus by the main gate. This arrangement is evident in the earliest detailed illustration of Corpus, published by David Loggan in 1675 (Plate 3). The library reflected the importance that Fox gave to learning. It was furnished with book presses and glass windows on either side of a central aisle, and its east end abutted the west end of the chapel, a structural reminder to all library readers of the intimate connection between learning and religion. The library and the chapel were together the heart of Fox's Renaissance academy of knowledge and virtue, a beehive of classical scholarship to sweeten good government with the honey of learning.

Fox's next task was to draft the statutes of Corpus. He began with the familiar reflection 'We have no abiding life on earth', for life is uncertain and there is no sure stability.[35] This was not a pious commonplace, but the starting point for Fox's serious business of government, Church and universities, remedied by the acquisition of both virtue (character) and knowledge, which together enable people to ascend to the heavenly City of God as if by a ladder. For Fox, virtue was not an abstract quality, but consisted of good works done with awareness. Hard work is necessary to acquire both virtue and knowledge skill, and competence. It was a social programme, but Fox expressed it poetically: as bees work hard to gather wax and honey, so do scholars work 'like ingenious bees ... by day and night to make wax to the

[34] Allen, 89; Fowler, 57. The Bishop was then resident in his episcopal residence of Wolvesey Palace, Winchester. Fowler states that John Claymond and seven (possibly eight) Fellows were admitted 5 March 1517 (NS); Robert Morwent as *compar sociis* on 22 June; and the first five discipuli on 4 July.

[35] CCCO A4/1/6. This is Claymond's copy, with annotations in his own hand, such as, for example, who should administer disciplinary action in the absence of more senior officials f. 9r–v (at the end of chapter 7 of MS), withdrawal and expenditure of expenses, f. 9v, ch. 8 of MS; ch. 9 of MS, ff. 10r–v, on the birthplaces and abilities of Fellows and passages on seniority depending upon length of membership and not position; deputing responsibilities and punishments. The solemn ideas were balanced by a bawdy drawing: the large initial 'N' is inscribed with a sketch of a monk's face, his mouth slightly open with his tongue or teeth slightly visible and his nose shaped like a large flaccid penis. The volume was ceremonially presented to President Claymond, perhaps before the sketch was inserted, but the copy given to Morwent lacks the insertion. Fox's Winchester registers contain numerous doodles of caricature-like faces drawn around the capital letters.

honour of god, and honey dropping sweetness to the profit of themselves and all Christians'.[36] Even in the midst of poetry Fox touched upon practical meritocracy – to the 'profit of themselves'.

Corpus Christi was to be a college for the new learning, the *studia humanitatis*, based on classical Latin and Greek and eventually to include Hebrew, all to be studied in association with scriptural theology. Fox was making a clear statement about the value of humanist classical studies in general and Greek in particular. Claymond was a scholar of Greek, and the study of Greek was to dominate Corpus and, in passing, encourage the university to provide its own Greek teaching. There were to be daily lectures in Greek language and literature, and precise instructions were given for the contents, time and the place of Greek lectures and their subject matter, and how students were to continue their study of Homer, Plato and Greek Patristic writers during summer. The College's chained library was given books from Fox's own library and he donated more books, buying them in London and sending them packed in barrels or crates up-river to Oxford on barges.

Having defined College studies, Fox designed the rest of the Statutes to keep the College administratively functional and smooth-running, using the statutes of Merton, Balliol and Magdalen (where, as Visitor, he conducted a visitation in 1506–7, when Magdalen was very dysfunctional), and statutes of the Cambridge colleges, Pembroke and more recently St. John's – Fox was executor to its foundress, Lady Margaret Beaufort, who had died soon after her son in 1509. The principle behind all college statutes was the Benedictine monastic Rule, with its quasi-paradoxical concept that the abbot or abbess held absolute authority but could exercise it only after full consultation with all the monks, or the nuns. Fox wanted Corpus to become a small *familia* of scholars living and working together amicably and efficiently, a small and tightly knit community based on strong authority, but exercised with counsel, giving rise to efficiently organized college life, free from factions and conflict as were seen at Magdalen College.[37]

Magdalen College's faults of 1507 thus guided Fox's idealistic Statutes of Corpus in 1517 as a *familia*. It could not be a coincidence that he deliberately intended its members to live and work together as a family, like each community in More's *Utopia*. Fox knew that the greatest dangers to his beehive were internal conflicts, personality clashes, malice, grudges and vendettas amongst the bees, as seen at Magdalen only ten years earlier, and

---

[36] An interesting discussion of Fox's bee analogy can be found in J. Woolfson, 'Bishop Fox's Bees and the Early English Renaissance', *Reformation and Renaissance Review*, 5.1 (2003), 7–26.

[37] Fox's ideas about morality in politics and exercising authority with virtue were matched by contemporary thinkers including the Venetian Gasparo Contarini, the Florentine bureaucrat Niccolò Machiavelli and the troubled Augustinian Friar Martin Luther, who pinned his ninety-five theses to the castle door at Wittenberg a few weeks before Corpus opened.

his detailed regulations and procedures were designed to avoid, or control, such conflicts. The Statutes were also designed to engender working equality between all persons and promote teamwork and efficiency. Authority within the College was to be self-contained. He prescribed internal oaths to bind them together, but was practical enough to have oaths of loyalty to the college backed up by 'one hundred pounds of good and lawful money of England'. He also forbade interference by, or appeals over the College to, 'the Pope or the court of Rome or any other person or place', so that both the loyalty and internal authority of the College were entirely self-contained.

The statutes provided for twenty Fellows, according to provenances by birth, which were specified in detail. Most were chosen for obvious personal reasons, but there was also an underlying political purpose. First, he provided for his dioceses, and the county of his birth and that of Oldham, Lancashire, where Hugh Oldham, 'a principal benefactor of this college, was born'. He required (in chapter nine) that fifteen Fellows were to have been born in southern counties, five in the diocese of Winchester, two in the diocese of Bath and Wells, two in the diocese of Exeter, two in the county of Gloucester, one in Wiltshire, two in Kent and one from either Oxfordshire or Berkshire.[38] Three Fellows were to be from the Midlands: two from Lincolnshire and one from Bedfordshire. Finally, two Fellows were to come from the north, one of whom was to have been born in the diocese of Durham. Fox also gave scholarships and fellowships to fill or augment gaps left at Magdalen by Waynflete, who himself had developed a deliberate geographical policy, making provision for counties not already well represented at other colleges in Oxford or Cambridge. Some Oxford colleges, such as Queen's, University, Balliol (the last two with very small fellowships) had a northern catchment but others, like Exeter and New College, were distinctly southern. Merton and Magdalen had mixed catchment areas, Lincoln and Brasenose took from the Midlands, while Oriel was unique in having no clear regional bias. Fox provided only one scholarship and fellowship each for Lancashire and the diocese of Durham, but that may be because they were not supported from a local endowment but from funds derived from estates outside the catchment area. The predominance of southerners (75 per cent) in Fox's pattern of intake reflected the location of Fox's dioceses, but also made a more even distribution across the nation.

During June 1517, the building of Corpus was almost completed. The accounts showed the pace of building work slowing and more Fellows and scholars coming into residence.[39] On 7 June 1517, the President, Fellows and

---

[38] Chapter 9 of Fox's Statutes is chapter 10 in Ward's translation.
[39] This was not unusual as colleges often opened to students before the buildings were fully

other members of the College were officially discharged from canonical obligation to the see of Lincoln, and jurisdiction over the College was transferred to the Bishop of Winchester.[40] Fox completed the Statutes while staying at the Hospital of St. Cross near Winchester, which was his favourite residence. A scribe produced the Statutes as a formal presentation manuscript of fifty-four folios (108 pages), bound in one volume. On 20 June, Fox read them aloud in the chapel at St. Cross, and, exercising his new jurisdiction, signed a licence permitting divine offices to be performed in the chapel at Corpus.[41] There were, however, some consequences. When Fox had changed his mind in 1515, the monks of St. Swithun's Priory effectively lost the bishop's foundation at Oxford. Prior Silkstede seems to have taken the loss badly, for neither he nor his monks attended the ceremony at St. Cross, or the formal presentation of the Statutes at Winchester.

By July 1517, at least five *discipuli*, nine Fellows and the President were resident in Corpus, though there were probably more. That month an outbreak of a deadly sweating sickness that killed within a few hours of the first signs struck Oxford and nearly four hundred students died, including several at Corpus, one of them Fox's kinsman. On 17 July, Fox wrote to President Claymond, urging him to be patient with 'the great tempest that has lately been amongst your company' and expressing the hope that his kinsman had been in a state of grace when he died. An immediate corporate problem for Corpus was therefore whether the College had the right to bury their own dead on land recently purchased from Merton College. Fox himself, as bishop, ruled in favour of Corpus, thus removing the possibility of jurisdictional conflict before it arose. The outbreak of sweating sickness also made several benefices vacant by death, which Fox was able to give to Claymond and others as a form of income. Fox's college was now virtually completed and functioning well. The building site accounts for 1517 and most of 1518 recorded a total expenditure of nearly £700, to which was added the bill of a smith called John Banks, dated June 1518, for c. £463, making the total about £1,163. Apart from unrecorded expenses, met

---

finished or furnished. Wykeham's students, for example, had been farmed out to other halls whilst New College was being completed: E. F. Jacob, 'The Building of All Souls College', in *Historical Essays in Honour of James Tait*, ed. J. G. Edwards, V. H. Galbraith and E. F. Jacob (Manchester, 1933), 121. Similarly, St. John's College, Cambridge, opened in 1516 when still unfinished: R. Willis, *The Architectural History of the University of Cambridge*, 2 (Cambridge, 1886), 242.

[40] Fowler, 67.
[41] It is possible that the wooden fittings in the chapel at St. Cross which are carved with Fox's pelican device and heraldic arms were made specifically for the occasion; see Angela Smith and N. Riall, 'Early Tudor Canopy Work at the Hospital of St. Cross, Winchester', *Antiquaries Journal*, 82 (2002), 125–56. This theory would accord well with the inclusion of humanist-inspired details notably the mix of traditional Christian imagery such as figures of Prophets, with Renaissance sibyls. An alternative and slightly earlier dating has recently been made for the stalls by N. Riall, *The Renaissance Stalls at the Hospital of St. Cross* (Winchester, 2014), 12. Also, see Fowler, 67.

directly from his purse or covered by donations, Fox had spent about £1000 in this period of only eighteen months, and by extrapolation (difficult to guess), perhaps four thousand on the whole project, and more on purchasing properties to endow Corpus.

The College had begun to fulfil its purpose of extending the work that Fox, Lady Margaret Beaufort and John Fisher had begun at Cambridge. During the ten years since then, by 1517 and 1518 the political situation and Fox's doubts about Henry VIII and Wolsey had presumably worsened. Thomas More was now writing his *Richard III, a Plain Tract on Tyranny*, ostensibly a description of the Yorkist king's government, but also providing a comparison with Henry VIII's approach to rule. The work explains tyranny as the result of personality, as had mirrors-for-princes literature. In More's *Utopia*, a satirical work published in 1516, wayward personalities were curbed and good government safeguarded and sustained by old customs, practices and institutions, but in real life, problems caused by personalities cannot be easily resolved the same way. Nevertheless, in 1518 More took Fox's dilemma upon himself by joining Henry VIII's government. More's *Utopia* and his entry into government were therefore alternative ways to deal with the problem of unwise government. There, one of his first acts was to intensify educational change by ordering the University of Oxford to suppress the anti-humanist Trojan faction.

More's great friend, Desiderius Erasmus, who was one of the leading early-sixteenth-century humanists, admired Fox's new College and its contribution to the European renaissance of classical learning. Prior Silkstede, on the other hand, remained distant. The Statutes still allowed the Priory some formal functions and to send students, but none of the monks from St. Swithun's Priory in Winchester went to Corpus. In December 1518, Fox drew the Prior and Convent closer by allowing the considerable lands and treasure of June 1513 to remain with them as an endowment, enabling them to take responsibility for his chantry chapel and its accoutrements – and with two of its monks appointed as chantry priests. The funds would also finance further building and operation of Corpus Christi College. The College and Fox's chantry chapel would be thus two sides of the same coin: both were in effect chantries, with the bishop of Winchester as Visitor of the College, while the President and Fellows of Corpus were Visitors of the chantry chapel, whose annual task it was to annually check that all was in order and functioning properly.[42] The arrangement was maintained, but Prior Silkstede and Fox seem to have communicated little, and relations were not

---

[42] One of the chantry priests, Basyng, changed his name at the Dissolution, to Kingsmill, and became the first dean of the reorganized chapter. Kingsmill removed some items from Fox's chantry as they were listed in an inventory of his personal possessions at his death in the 1540s.

improved by an official episcopal visitation of St. Swithun's Priory on 26 August 1521 and the Visitors' report of February 1522. The report found that administration was inefficient and, significantly, that Prior Silkstede and the Convent had not sent scholars to university in accordance with Benedictine constitutions. The report, which was partly a rebuke to an inefficient and ill-humoured prior, gave six months to make improvements.[43]

Soon after he had become Bishop of Winchester, Fox had begun to rebuild the east end of Winchester Cathedral. Over the quire he placed an array of roof bosses, some of which are carved with heraldic armorials relating to Saxon kings. Iconographic evidence reveals that the bosses were carved and put in place in 1508, and were part of a grand scheme presenting the Tudors as the legitimate royal heirs to the English throne, being the latest in a long line of monarchs. The bosses were part of Fox's much more elaborate plan to save the dynasty as Henry VII lay dying in 1508 and the kingdom was in uproar at the corrupt and repressive behaviour of tax officials. The bosses showed Fox's interest in 1508 in bolstering the Tudor dynasty and their claim to the throne.

The structural work at the east end of the cathedral, which involved reconstruction and glazing of the east gable and clerestory, the re-vaulting of the presbytery aisles and construction of Fox's chantry chapel, was probably completed as work on the College was coming to an end. This was of course well after the political crisis of 1509. It is warrantable to conjecture that the bones of the Saxon kings were not yet elevated in the wooden chests that are seen at Winchester today, but were arranged as relics and displayed, to impress the Holy Roman Emperor Charles V when he visited Winchester in 1522, and perhaps for pilgrimage profit by the monks. (Fox himself was apparently not interested in relics except in using them to support the Tudors). The monks continued in charge of the bones until 1522 when there was an important reason for change. With the emperor's visit, strenuous efforts were made to emphasize the historical line of Tudor authority and its presumed links with royal Saxon forebears, such as by painting the portrait of Henry VIII on the supposed table of King Arthur. The wooden chests were evidently commissioned and displayed to impress the emperor.[44] It was perhaps soon after the visit that Fox and his

---

[43] Fox, *Register*, IV, ff. 67r–v (the visitation).

[44] It is possible that the portrait of Bishop Fox at Sudeley Castle illustrated in the frontispiece above and dated 1522 was painted by a Flemish artist travelling in the Emperor's entourage (see Smith, 1988, 428, 436, n.19). The small portrait (42.5 × 29cm) is painted in oil on panel and depicts the bishop in half length. The panel is inscribed RICARDUS FOX/EPISC.WINTON./ AN.M.D.XXII. It may have been made to commemorate the visit, or as a memento of Fox who had recently suffered a stroke, and it probably served as a model for the Bishop's portrait that was made for Corpus posthumously. The provenance of the Sudeley portrait is unknown. It is first recorded in the collection of Mrs Dent-Brocklehurst in the late nineteenth century (Smith,

steward, William Frost, co-commissioned the screens that now surround the presbytery; the screens were finished in 1525. The chests containing the bones of Saxon kings were placed on top of the screens, a visual reminder of Fox's belief in the legitimacy of the Tudors but at a height where they could not be displayed to yield a profit to the monks.[45]

In summary, Corpus Christi College was born partly out of Fox's reaction to weaknesses and corruption in England's monarchical governments. His first monarchical crisis was with Richard III and took him into dangerous exile as a traitor. The second came when Henry VII, to whom he was close, connived at authoritarian, corrupt and greedy practices, and an angry public reaction simmered for five years and endangered the monarchy by 1509, when Henry died, and Fox took unusually devious steps to protect the monarchy, though in order to do this he allowed two men to die unjustly.

The accession of Henry VIII, however, was attended by extravagant rhetoric (partly organized by Fox and others for political reasons) about a new Renaissance dawn arising and how the young, learned, virtuous king would ensure good government. Fox was aware of weaknesses in the character of the young king, and he faced his third monarchical crisis when Henry VIII took England into war with France in 1513, and showed his determination to override the Church's separate spiritual jurisdiction. It was unlikely that Fox had shared the euphoria of Henry VIII's accession, but for those who had, the dream of 1509 was now turning sour. This time, Fox could not plot a solution to the problem, but he hoped that humane studies, and clerical reform, would encourage, indeed accelerate, rational policies of peace, as set out in Erasmus's book on war and peace, the *Complaint of Peace* (*Querela Pacis*) of 1516. Fox's initial hope, that Corpus Christi College would produce learned and virtuous monks who would reform the Church, and thereby the whole of society, was improbable. By 1513, it was clear that even with classical education, the piety of learned monks would be too little and too slow in improving Church and state.

Instead, if his college could train other first-class minds, whether monks, secular priests, lawyers, civil servants, doctors or teachers, Corpus graduates, and those of other colleges, would have a rapid impact upon society. In particular, those who became civil servants at court, could, as far as possible, advise and guide the court, and in modern parlance 'ring-fence' vagaries of the monarch and over-ambitious courtiers. The foundation of Corpus Christi College in 1517 was Fox's last throw, an attempt to assist good government during what would be the long reign of a young king about

---

1988, 428).

[45] J. M. Luxford, *Art and Architecture of the English Benedictine Monasteries: 1300–1540*, Studies in the History of Medieval Religion (Woodbridge, 2008), 80.

whom he had doubts. During the last ten years of Fox's life, however, events worked out in different directions, more so after his death in October 1528. Even he could not have linked the sharp lesson he had learned from the king at Baynard's Castle in 1515 to his experience with minor heretics in his diocese. Nor could Fox have foreseen how a few years later Henry VIII's political style and relations with the Church would become entangled with theological changes from Germany.

THE BUILDING ACCOUNTS (CCCO H/1/4/1)[46]

On 1 March 1517 (New Style), Bishop Fox signed the foundation charter for Corpus Christi College Oxford.[47] Four days later, he handed over administrative responsibility for Corpus to his old friend, John Claymond. The hall at Corpus was complete, the chapel, kitchen and gatehouse with its oriel window structurally finished and work was under way on the living quarters for the Fellows, students and President. Much remained to be done: a cloister and boundary walls around the college were yet to be built and the internal quadrangles needed paving. Although the works would not be finished for another eighteen months, this did not prevent the first Fellows from arriving in March 1517 or the first scholars a few months later.[48] All documentary record of the first phase of construction at Oxford is lost but for a brief reference in an agreement drawn up in June 1513 between Bishop Fox and Prior Silkstede of St. Swithun's, Winchester, which states that work on the college had begun.[49] All that survives today is a solitary book of building accounts in the college archive, covering the second phase of work at Corpus, from 2 March 1517 until 21 November 1518.[50]

The Corpus building accounts comprise a series of short *bokes* or books of payments and wages, each one generally of a fortnight's duration. They were written in English in a neat secretarial hand by a clerk of works who remains unidentified. The accounts offer details on the provenance of materials used

---

[46] Much of this section is based on chapter 8 of my doctoral thesis: Smith, 1988.
[47] Fowler, 57. The Bishop was then resident in Wolvesey Palace, Winchester.
[48] See above, p. xxxviii, n. 39.
[49] See Appendix 4.
[50] Building accounts are a rarity, for few pre-Reformation building accounts made in connection with Oxford colleges have survived. An exception are the recently published accounts for All Souls College, Oxford; see S. Walker, ed., *Building Accounts of All Souls College, Oxford, 1438–1443*, OHS new series 42 (Oxford, 2010). Fragments of accounts for Wolsey's foundation of Cardinal College, Oxford, were discovered in the 1930s in the archive of Corpus; see J. G. Milne and J. H. Harvey, 'The Building of Cardinal College, Oxford', *Oxoniensia*, 8/9 (1943–4), 137–53. A few fragments pertaining to the construction of Magdalen College, Oxford, exist; see J. Newman, 'The Physical Setting: New Building and Adaptation', in McConica, 604. For Brasenose, see E. W. Allfrey, 'The Architectural History of the College', in *Brasenose Quatercentenary Monographs*, I, OHS 52 (Oxford, 1909), 5. For other fragments, see Harvey, 90, 94, 298.

in completing Corpus, the costs involved and details about the day-to-day organization of building. They also record the payments made to the many tradesmen employed on the works, including masons and carpenters, and the names of the master craftsmen who designed the college for Bishop Fox and whose presence on site was still occasionally required. Lists of specific craftsmen, their days worked and wages are interspersed among the accounts (Appendix 10). The accounts include details of workplace practices and relations and fortnightly *summae* of all costs. They also include copies of contracts with several craftsmen. An antiquary, Thomas Hearne, was shown the Corpus accounts in the early eighteenth century and was the first to publish extracts from them; further details were published in the 1870s for the Historical Manuscripts Commission.[51] The economic historian, L. F. Salzman, referred to the accounts in his documentary history of medieval building published in 1952, and two years later, the architectural historian John H. Harvey included details in his biographical dictionary of English architects.[52] In recent times, John Newman discussed aspects of the second phase of building Corpus using information drawn from the accounts.[53]

Most of the entries in the Corpus accounts concern the purchase and purveyance of materials required for completing the college buildings, in particular stone and wood. Where possible, materials were sourced locally though almost one half of the entries in the Corpus accounts relate to payments for the transport of stone and timber to Oxford. Several types of stone were used for building Corpus, mostly acquired locally from the well-established quarries at Headington, a few miles to the east of Oxford.[54] One of the chief suppliers of stone was John Franklin, who belonged to a family of quarrymen operating at Headington in the late fifteenth and early sixteenth centuries. Franklin and many others named in the accounts carted several grades of stone to Corpus, including chunks of freestone and the much smaller and irregular-sized pieces known as ragstone. The clerk of works who recorded the accounts for Corpus provided the names of the various suppliers and carters of stone and the costs of carriage by cartload. Freestone usually cost about a shilling a load and ragstone sixpence. The Corpus accounts reveal that freemasons squared off the freestone on site in Oxford, and the stone was then laid in courses by setters or layers to form

---

[51] Thomas Hearne, *The History and Antiquities of Glastonbury* (Oxford, 1722), 285–9; *Second Report of the Royal Commission on Historical Manuscripts* (London, 1874), 126.
[52] Salzman, 15, 121, 217.
[53] Newman, 'The Physical Setting', in McConica, 609.
[54] The Headington quarries were first worked in the late fourteenth century, when stone was quarried for the building of the bell-tower of New College in Oxford. For the quarries, see M. D. Lobel, ed., *VCH Oxon*. v (Oxford, 1957), 163–4. No mention is made in the surviving Corpus accounts of the quarries at Hinksey, Sherborne and Sunningwell that had provided stone for the building of All Souls College in the 1440s; see Walker, *Building Accounts*, xix.

the lower courses of walls. Freestone was also used for making steps in the college buildings. Ragstone set into a mortar was used for the upper parts of walls and it was also laid and covered with sand to form a solid base upon which paving could be set.[55]

The Corpus accounts show that lesser quantities of a better-quality stone were procured from quarries further afield, including Taynton in Oxfordshire, some twenty-two miles from the college, and also Little Barrington in Gloucestershire, which was a few miles further west.[56] The stone from these quarries was a hard oolitic limestone, prized for its appearance and much in demand for use in building Oxford colleges. At Corpus the limestone was used for masonry that required careful shaping, such as window openings. The Taynton limestone was carried to Oxford, where it could be carved on site, though sometimes specialist work was undertaken off site. One entry, for example, records that Taynton stone was delivered to a mason called John Ward, of Little Barrington, who was paid for making the traceried windows for the cloisters at the college.[57]

Many entries in the Corpus accounts record purchases of lime that was put to use at Corpus as a constituent in the mortar made for use with the stonework. It was also used in the process of roughcasting or plastering the roughly textured external walls, and it formed the basis of the whitewash used for internal surfaces.[58] According to the accounts, most of the lime was brought from the quarries at Headington and was measured by the quarter load and bushel.[59] In March 1517 lime was *borrowed* from Balliol College. The accounts indicate that the purveyors of the materials for building Corpus frequently *borrowed* (or acquired) surplus stocks from neighbouring sites in Oxford. The practice known as borrowing was widespread in the later Middle Ages and not only helped to lessen the costs of sourcing materials but also alleviated the problems (and costs) associated with carriage over long distances.[60]

Large quantities of wood were also required for completing Corpus Christi College, for flooring rooms, for the *seallyng* or panelling of walls and also for making furniture. Most of the wood used to build Corpus was

---

[55] CCCO H/1/4/1, f. 2v. Franklin was a member of an established dynasty of quarrymen operating in Headington; see *VCH Oxon. v.* 146. In the mid-1500s, Corpus began to lease a quarry in Headington.
[56] CCCO H/1/4/1, f. 6v.
[57] CCCO H/1/4/1, f. 35r.
[58] Most of the external walls at Corpus were faced with stone in the nineteenth century; see Newman, 'The Physical Setting', in McConica.
[59] CCCO H/1/4/1, f. 4r.
[60] It is possible that the Master and Fellows of Balliol were keen to offer Fox assistance in the building of Corpus since Fox had drawn up new statutes for the college which had been promulgated in 1507.

oak, though the college accounts include entries concerning the purchase of ash and elm. The accounts record that the ash was purchased to make items for the kitchen including, a kneading trough and pastry boards, whereas the purpose for which the elm was bought is not recorded. The accounts suggest that much of the timber was acquired from the Oxfordshire area, in particular from the woodlands at Nettlebed, eighteen miles south-east of Oxford and near Henley. Evidently hewers stripped and squared the cut wood before delivering it to Oxford by the cartload, where the timber would be used in making frames or supports and for flooring. The accounts record that timber from Nettlebed cost 2 shillings a load. Pre-cut planks of wood were sometimes sourced from suppliers; Henry Thycart and Robert Gely, for example, both provided elm boards for Corpus.[61] Some timber was also acquired from other Oxford colleges, where it was presumably left over after recent works.[62] In March 1517, a thousand laths, for example, were *borrowed* from Queen's College.[63] Laths were used in roofing or as supports in walls prior to plastering. The Corpus accounts do not specify the purpose for which the laths were acquired but since the entry is followed with another recording the purchase of lime (presumably bought for plaster), we may deduce that they were purchased for use in making the walls. Wainscot, the term applied to a good-quality oak that was used for panelling interior walls and making doors, is mentioned in several entries in the Corpus accounts.[64] This was sometimes sourced from local suppliers, including Robert Devyn and John Coterell. A number of payments recorded in the accounts were made for the carriage of wainscot by cart from Henley-on-Thames to Oxford, which suggests that the wood was purchased in London and then brought upriver to a suitable staging post. The wainscot acquired from London was probably the fine-quality split oak that was imported from the Baltic region in the fifteenth and sixteenth centuries.[65]

Of particular interest in the Corpus accounts in connection with the acquisition of wood is an item concerning the comparatively large payment of £4 for one hundred wainscot panels that were acquired in July 1518 from

---

[61] CCCO H/1/4/1, ff. 7v, 10v.
[62] For example Magdalen and New Colleges; see CCCO H1/4/1, ff. 6r,11v. Fox was *ex officio* visitor of both Magdalen and New Colleges and it may have been through his influence that the goods were made available.
[63] CCCO H/1/4/1, f. 4v.
[64] CCCO H/1/4/1, ff 3v, 4v, 7v, 9r.
[65] For wainscot, which was also known as *Estrichbord*, see Salzman, 245–6. Wainscot was purchased for use in panelling rooms of All Souls College, Oxford (see Walker, *Building Accounts*, 6); in 1510 a carpenter was paid for travelling from Cambridge to London to buy wainscot for the ceiling in the chapel at Christ's College; see R. Willis, *The Architectural History of the University of Cambridge and of the Colleges of Cambridge and Eton* (Cambridge, 1886), 198, n.2.

the Master of the Savoy.⁶⁶ The Savoy Hospital was an establishment in London that had been founded by Henry VII in 1505 and its construction was a project with which Bishop Fox was closely involved in his capacity as executor to the late king. It was Fox who drew up the statutes for the Savoy and he was in regular contact with William Holgill, a priest who supervised the building of the hospital. Indeed, Holgill often acted as an agent for Fox in land transactions in connection with the endowment the bishop planned for his Oxford college, and it was probably Fox who ensured Holgill's appointment as the first Master of the Savoy Hospital.⁶⁷ It has long been thought that Holgill was appointed to the mastership in 1517, but it has remained unclear when construction of the Savoy Hospital was finished.⁶⁸ The reference in the Corpus accounts is therefore significant, for not only does it imply that building work on the Savoy had finished by mid-1518, but it also confirms the timing of Holgill's appointment as Master. The Corpus accounts reveal that sundry other items were taken from the Savoy Hospital for use in the completion of Corpus. These items included, for example, a door that cost 8 shillings.⁶⁹ Holgill may have advised Fox of the availability of surplus supplies at the Savoy. Alternatively, details of the excess supplies available could have been passed to Fox by Humphrey Coke, who was Master Carpenter of the hospital. Like Holgill, Coke was also well known to Fox and had been employed by the prelate several times down the years. Moreover, it was Coke who had been appointed with the royal mason, William Vertue, to design and oversee construction of Corpus.⁷⁰

The key role that Coke and Vertue played at Corpus is revealed, not in the surviving building accounts, but in an agreement made in 1513 between Bishop Fox and the Prior and Convent of St. Swithun's.⁷¹ The agreement names both craftsmen as the designers of Fox's college, a foundation that was constructed in tandem with the bishop's chantry chapel at Winchester Cathedral and which the two men also designed.⁷² A year earlier, as Fox's

⁶⁶ CCCO H/1/4/1, f. 45r.
⁶⁷ For Holgill, see R. Somerville, *The Savoy: Manor, Hospital, Chapel* (London, 1960), 256–7. Fox and Holgill had known each other for many years and early in his episcopate, Fox presented the cleric to several livings in the Winchester diocese including Chilcombe and Boldre. Holgill was evidently trusted by Fox for he was involved in the purchase of many properties for Corpus as his signature on numerous deeds in the archive at Corpus reveals. See also Allen, 128.
⁶⁸ See H. M. Colvin, ed., *History of the Kings Works*, 1485–1660, 3 (London, 1975), 14.
⁶⁹ CCCO H/1/4/1, f. 45r.
⁷⁰ Coke worked for Fox at Durham in the 1490s where he oversaw the refurbishment of the episcopal quarters in the castle. Both were involved in royal projects with which Fox was also involved and it is likely that they offered advice to Fox regarding the extensive works he instigated at Winchester Cathedral in the early 1500s, which included the rebuilding of the east gable.
⁷¹ CCCO A1/Cap.1/Fasc.1/Ev.1, transcribed above, see Appendix 4.
⁷² Angela Smith, 'The Chantry Chapel of Bishop Fox', *Winchester Cathedral Record*, 57 (1988), 27–32.

plans were coming to fruition, Vertue and Coke had visited Oxford in order to discuss the bishop's plans and consider the site chosen for his proposed foundation.[73] Since the early building accounts for Corpus have been lost, the extent of the craftsmen's precise role as construction began is unclear. As a mason, Vertue may have taken greater responsibility for the structure of the college buildings. It is generally assumed that he was responsible for the design of the college gatehouse with its fan vault (Plate 5). Though a carpenter by training, Coke was evidently experienced when it came to structural design and probably collaborated with Vertue in this respect. It is Coke who is credited with the design of the great hammerbeam roof over the hall, which, according to dates carved onto corbels and the wall plate beneath the roof, was finished in 1516.

Coke and Vertue were probably frequent visitors to Oxford in the early stages of the construction of Corpus. In the final year of work, the men were required less often and as such are named just a handful of times in the surviving building accounts. Several entries show that Coke was paid for visiting Oxford, presumably to offer advice on site. In the spring of 1517, for example, Coke received 1s 8d a day for his services on site, a higher rate of pay than he had received as an employee in royal employment and a more generous allowance than the daily rate of 12d, that was usually given for such services.[74] The Corpus accounts reveal that Vertue and Coke were sometimes present on site in Oxford together; on 22 June 1517, for example, the two men were each paid for eight days on site.[75] The nature of their work on that occasion is not recorded but it may be assumed that they visited in order to assess and advise on the works in progress. Both men were on site again the following October.[76] Sometimes their expertise was required off site. One entry in the accounts records, for example, a visit that Vertue made to the quarry at Taynton.[77] The purpose of that visit is not recorded but it may be safely assumed that the master mason visited the quarry to select stone for a specific project at Corpus. Coke is named in the accounts more often than Vertue.[78] As a skilled and experienced carpenter, his advice was vital in connection with the flooring and panelling of rooms at Corpus and the making of furniture. Both men continued to be actively engaged

---

[73] On that occasion, Vertue and Coke were joined by William East or Est and it was during that visit that all three were assaulted by or at the instigation of individuals associated with Brasenose College.

[74] CCCO H/1/4/1, f. 6v. Craftsmen generally received higher remuneration when employed privately than for work undertaken in royal pay; see D. Knoop and G. P. Jones, *The Mediaeval Mason* (Manchester, 1933), 109–10.

[75] For example, CCCO H/1/4/1, f. 9v.

[76] CCCO H/1/4/1, ff. 9v, 29v.

[77] CCCO H/1/4/1, f. 29v.

[78] CCCO H/1/4/1, ff. 3r, 6v, 9v, 29v, 31v, 39v, 55r.

in overseeing Fox's foundation as construction continued, despite the fact that both had commitments elsewhere in the royal works.[79] Since Vertue and Coke were rarely on site, responsibility for overseeing the completion of the structure and fittings of Corpus fell to an executant mason and carpenter who could supervise as well as carry out specific tasks. It is possible that the mason who held this position at Corpus between 1517 and 1518 was William East or Est who had visited Oxford with Coke and Vertue and was badly injured in the attack the three sustained. East recovered sufficiently to continue working on a contractual basis for various clients, amongst them Bishop Fox, and he is recorded in the surviving Corpus accounts for 1517–18 seven times. The accounts do not always make clear precisely what works he undertook as work on the college buildings progressed, though on two occasions he was paid for making *cresse table*, which was probably a variant of the squared-off stone *gresys* or *grasse table* used for steps and the lower levels of walls.[80]

The local Oxford carpenter Robert Carow seems to have been the craftsman charged by Coke to oversee the timberwork at Corpus. Carow was the most active master carpenter resident in Oxford in the early sixteenth century.[81] It is generally thought that the great hammerbeam roof for the hall at Corpus, designed by Coke, was made in Carow's workshop. Though there is no documentary evidence to confirm the supposition, the enormous payment of £73 13s 4d recorded in the Corpus accounts and made to Carow in the spring of 1517, might be payment for the roof.[82] The Corpus accounts show that Carow was involved in making the roof and floor of the cloister chambers after Coke's designs.[83] He also supplied wood for finishing the library and he was contracted to make beds, probably 'high beds', at 2 shillings apiece.[84] Carow was one of several local craftsmen who were later employed on the construction of Cardinal College for Wolsey, which included a larger and more elaborate version of the hammerbeam roof that he had made for Corpus.[85] One of the team who later worked with Carow

---

[79] Both men were involved in supervising the building work at Eton College in Windsor. Intriguingly, work on Lupton's gateway at Eton, which was designed by Vertue and is very similar in design to the Corpus gateway, began on 2 March, 1517, the day that the surviving building accounts for Corpus begin.
[80] CCCO H/1/4/1, ff. 9v, 48v. For *grasse table*, cf Salzman, 89; for *greses*, ibid, 488.
[81] Newman, 'The Physical Setting', in McConica, 611. Carow had been master carpenter for the bell tower at Magdalen College; see E. A. Gee, 'Oxford Carpenters, 1370–1530', *Oxoniensia*, 17/18 (1952–3), 112–84, in particular, 129–33. He also worked at Queen's, All Souls and Oriel Colleges. For biographical details see Harvey, 48–9.
[82] CCCO H/1/4/1, f. 6v.
[83] CCCO H/1/4/1, ff. 30v, 35v, 53r. The cloisters were rebuilt in the early eighteenth century.
[84] CCCO H/1/4/1, f. 9r; also Newman, 'The Physical Setting', in McConica, 611.
[85] The design of the hall roof at Corpus was also copied with slight adaptations for the roof

at Cardinal College was James Lynche, who is very likely to have been the carpenter called James Lenche who is named in the Corpus accounts.[86]

Many individuals were required to complete the building work at Corpus and the names of those men are recorded in the building accounts (Appendix 10). Some of the men were probably involved in the first phase of construction between 1513 and the end of 1516. Most of the suppliers and a substantial number of the craftsmen would have been local to Oxford and a good number were employed on the building of other colleges. A carpenter called Roger Wryght, for example, worked at Magdalen College, and Richard Pytfeld, who supplied timber for Corpus, worked as a sawyer for Lincoln College. Some of the men who helped to complete Corpus and whose names are recorded in the building accounts went on to work on Cardinal College in Oxford in the 1520s; amongst them were the labourers Wylliam Brytton and William Hobbys, who worked together. Similarly the carpenters William Collyns and Nicholas More are recorded in the Corpus accounts and are known to have worked together at Cardinal College. Collyns's involvement at Corpus and Cardinal Colleges, and possibly More's too, can be attributed to the fact that he had learned his craft as an apprentice to Humphrey Coke, who supervised the carpenters at Wolsey's foundation.

Another local man whose name features in the Corpus accounts was the carpenter-joiner Cornell Clerk. The accounts include a copy of a contract whereby Clerk was commissioned for a set of sixteen desks for the college library. These desks were of the lectern type, twelve whole or full-length desks and four half-desks or table-top lecterns. The desks would have been arranged as the presses that replaced them in 1604 are today, tenoned into the groundsill.[87] It is not clear whether the current benches are original or if they are part of the refurbishment of the library that was undertaken in the early seventeenth century, when Fox's desks were replaced. The wording of the contract reveals Fox's specific wishes concerning the smallest of details. Whilst he wanted Clerk to base his design for the Corpus desks on those in Magdalen College, he stipulated that they were to include plain poppy heads rather than the carved ones that ornamented the library furniture at Magdalen (Plate 6).[88] Fox evidently believed that such detail might prove a

---

of the hall of the Austin Canons in Oxford which is now over the chapel at Brasenose College; see Gee, 'Oxford Carpenters', 131–3; J. Blair, 'Frewin Hall, Oxford: A Norman Mansion and a Monastic College', *Oxoniensia*, 43 (1978), 82.

[86] For brief biographical details, see Gee, 'Oxford Carpenters', 136.

[87] CCCO H/1/4/1, f. 5v; Hearne, *History and Antiquities of Glastonbury*, 286. For Clerk, see Harvey, 54. The scars of the nails fixing the desks to the brackets, can still be seen, though they probably relate to the replacement of the desks in 1604.

[88] The entry is important in providing some idea of the original library furniture at Magdalen; see Burnett Hillman Streeter, *The Chained Library. A Survey of the Evolution of the English Library* (London, 1931), 149. A careful historian with an eye for detail, some of Streeter's

distraction to students trying to study, though the rounded finial in place of fleur-de-lys may also be seen as a departure from traditional forms.[89] The accounts record that Clerk received 10 shillings for making each desk.

Entries in the Corpus accounts recording wages paid to the workers reveal that they received typical rates of pay for their skills. Masons and carpenters generally received a daily rate of 6d, with less-skilled men receiving a penny less. Plasterers, on the other hand, took home a slightly higher wage. Carriers were needed to oversee the carriage of materials to Corpus, and on site, a mix of skilled craftsmen and unskilled labourers was required to finish the buildings. Many worked a regular six-day week, with rest taken on Sunday. The accounts show that no payments were made to workers on site on Wednesday 25 March 1517, for this was the Feast of the Annunciation that marked the beginning of the Church year.[90] Work on site at Corpus also stopped for several days in the middle of April for Easter, and analysis of payments made to workers shows the thought and planning given to holy days by those who organized work on site. They acquired equipment necessary for making plaster, including a large tub or cowl, and Elys Larden was contracted to deliver four loads of lime before Palm Sunday (2 April). The delivery was crucial for the building schedule and the entry in the accounts ends bluntly, 'and this bargen to be done. Richard Leowse is suertye'.[91] The lime was delivered on time and the plasterers finished before the end of work on Maundy Thursday (9 April) and the plaster could dry over Easter.

Other joiners named in the Corpus accounts include Roger Gryffyth, Roger Morwent and Robert More, who panelled the library, chapel and President's lodgings with wainscot.[92] Morwent's work also included the making of a long bench, doors and cupboards. These men were all working inside the college buildings and as such their activity was curtailed from time to time by poor light. It is no surprise therefore that the Corpus accounts record payments in November 1517 when *candellys* were purchased specifically for the use of the carpenters. Generally, building works would tail off in the late autumn each year and resume the following spring; however, the admission of Fellows and scholars to Corpus in 1517 necessitated that the college be completed swiftly and so work con-

---

conclusions about the library furniture at Corpus were mistaken. Fox may have attended Magdalen as a young man but in any case, he was *ex officio* visitor of Magdalen. Clerk had been engaged on various projects at Magdalen in the first decade of the sixteenth century; see Harvey, 54. The early-sixteenth-century bookcases at Corpus were heightened in 1604 (*RCHM*, 52) and the finials of the library desks were changed.

[89] Streeter, *The Chained Library*, 149.
[90] CCCO H/1/4/1, f. 14v.
[91] CCCO H/1/4/1. f. 4r. The entry suggests that Larden could be unreliable.
[92] CCCO H/1/4/1, f. 19v.

tinued throughout the winter months. It was not a practice that Bishop Fox usually endorsed.[93]

It is clear from the Corpus accounts that certain tasks required to complete the college were sub-contracted to craftsmen many miles distant from Oxford. In 1517, for example, an entry records that a part-payment (*in preste*) was made to Thomas Roossell of Westminster, who is described as the carver of the *knottes* for the chapel. The knottes were the set of wooden bosses commissioned from Roossell for the college chapel at Corpus, and the accounts state that the carver was to make ninety-eight large or 'hole knottes' and fourteen small or 'halff' bosses.[94] Roossell was a member of a dynasty of carpenters and presumably a specialist carver. The initial payment to Roossell was made by Humphrey Coke, who probably also delivered the wainscot required for the bosses that is recorded in the next entry and cost 16 shillings. Coke may have appointed Roossell himself, for he knew the carver's work through their earlier involvement together in the building of the Savoy Hospital.[95] Moreover, the craftsmen were related through marriage, since Coke's daughter, Christine, was married to John Russell, who was a member of the dynasty of carpenters to which Thomas Roossell belonged.[96] Roossell received a payment of 16d for each boss that he made, a sum of £7 9s 4d for making the complete set.[97] The Corpus accounts also reveal that Coke received a considerably higher sum of almost £20 for gilding the bosses. Coke was paid the extraordinarily large sum of £19 5s in total for gilding each of the ninety-eight large bosses at 3s a piece and 22d for each of the fourteen smaller bosses.[98] The bosses made by Roossell and gilded by Coke can still be seen in the chapel at Corpus and include a variety of religious imagery in addition to royal badges associated with the Tudor dynasty as well as the pelican device used by Bishop Fox.[99]

Many general labourers were required to complete the building of Corpus. The accounts sometimes record simply a Christian name or a surname: a labourer called Johan, for example, is named in connection with paving various parts of the college, including 'the wood yard to the kechyn', an area adjacent to the kitchen. More often than not, full names are recorded

---

[93] CCCO H/1/4/1, ff. 30r, 31v, 32v, 34v. In the college statutes, Fox specified that repairs or new building works on properties belonging to the college should not be undertaken between 28 October and 1 March following; see Ward, 179

[94] CCCO H1/4/1, f. 29v. Salzman wrongly gives the number of half bosses as 43 and is followed by Harvey.

[95] Russell made shutters for the windows at the Savoy Hospital; see WAM MS 63509, no pagination.

[96] Gee, 'Oxford Carpenters', 134.

[97] CCCO H/1/4/1, f. 29v.

[98] CCCO H/1/4/1, f. 39v.

[99] See J. Reid, 'The Bosses of Corpus Christi Chapel', *The Pelican Record*, 49 (2013), 15–24.

in the accounts: thus Richard Lewowse or Lewis was paid for constructing the boundary walls round the college and Nicholas Herne and William Brytton were paid for digging the foundations of the cloisters. The traceried windows for the cloisters were made off site, as noted above, by John Ward. The accounts record that one Robert Glasyer provided fifty-seven feet of glass at 5 shillings a foot for these windows.[100] The glass was probably plain, though it is clear from surviving fragments from other windows at Corpus that some rooms were glazed with armorials and Fox's pelican device. The accounts reveal that the window surrounds of the cloister were made by Richard Parker, who, like so many of those employed on site at Corpus, could apply his skills to various tasks; the accounts reveal that Parker was also paid to construct five freestone chimneys in the chambers above the cloister.[101]

There is no evidence in the surviving accounts that Bishop Fox visited Oxford during work in 1517–18, though he is likely to have visited in the first phase of building between 1513 and 1516.[102] Despite his absence, Fox was regularly informed about the progress of the work; he corresponded with those who were supervising construction through letters, plans and instructions. It was usual practice for those supervising building work to visit the client from time to time.[103] After his resignation as Keeper of the Privy Seal in May 1516, Fox was generally resident in Winchester or at one of his other episcopal properties.[104] There is no record that William Vertue visited Fox during the later stages of work on Corpus. Humphrey Coke, on the other hand, travelled to see the bishop in Winchester on at least one occasion, present for example at the episcopal palace of Wolvesey for the institution of the President and Fellows of Corpus in March 1517. On his return to Oxford, Coke carried with him the foundation charter for the college.[105] The Corpus accounts include several payments to messengers who travelled between Oxford and Winchester to see Bishop Fox in subsequent

---

[100] CCCO H/1/4/1, ff, 32r, 35r. The glass contributed to the comfort of the Fellows and students of Corpus.

[101] Julian Reid has suggested that imagery in the glass windows at Corpus was made by the glaziers who produced the windows at King's College, Cambridge; see J. Reid, 'The Founder's Textile', *The Pelican Record*, 48 (2012), 22. The scheme at King's was one that Bishop Fox helped to devise; see Angela Smith, 'Bishop Fox and Stained Glass in Early Tudor England', *Journal of Stained Glass*, 31 (2007), 35–52. Parker was not a glazier and presumably made stone windows and door surrounds.

[102] For Fox's itinerary, see Smith, 1988, 451–66. Until his resignation as Keeper of the Privy Seal, Fox was often resident in London, which was sixty miles from Oxford and took several days to travel. Winchester was marginally closer.

[103] In the 1370s, for example, the clerk of the works at Merton College library, visited its chief benefactor, the Bishop of Chichester, on several occasions; see E. A. Gee, 'Oxford Masons, 1370–1530', *Archaeological Journal*, 109 (1953), 54.

[104] Smith, 1988, 484.

[105] See Allen, 89.

months. In June 1517, for example, George Roper was paid 4 shillings for riding to Winchester two times over the course of the month.[106] In October 1518, the building accounts reveal that 7d was paid to an unnamed horseman, who delivered a letter from the bishop to Oxford.[107]

At the end of February 1517, Fox wrote to Claymond to inform him that a barge full of equipment for Corpus, 'kechyn stuff and other thingis', had recently left Westminster.[108] The goods were accompanied by Robert Bayly of the Savoy and were probably bound for Henley, whence they would be carried by cart to Oxford.[109] In his letter to Claymond, the Bishop promised to send additional equipment at a later date. Once the college became habitable, some articles were required immediately. A number of items, including a knife for the buttery, pans and a kitchen shovel, were purchased locally in Oxford and are therefore recorded in the building accounts.[110] The subsequent purchase of further items required for the college is recorded in the general college account books or Libri Magni, which start in 1521. The items bought for the college and listed in the first Liber Magnus, include plate, a candelabra, maps and an astrolabe, the latter costing 8s 8d.[111]

In common with his other building works, Fox ensured that Corpus was ornamented with his heraldic arms, pelican device and motto, *Est Deo Gracia*. These all functioned as visual prompts to remind those who saw them to pray for the Bishop's soul. Fox's heraldic arms adorn the fan vault over the college gateway.[112]

It is clear that Fox commissioned stained glass for some of the windows at Corpus, including the chapel. Only fragmentary remains of the early-sixteenth-century glass survive. Fragments featuring the Bishop's arms, for example, can still be seen in the westernmost window on the south side of the library vestibule. Two further examples of episcopal arms are mounted in the window of the tower room facing south over the Front Quad.[113]

---

[106] CCCO H/1/4/1, f. 10v. Roper continued to act as a messenger long after the college was finished. In 1532–3 he was paid for a trip to London on college business, CCCO C/1/1/1, f. 89r. Roper was described as a horseman in the *Valor Ecclesiasticus*, II (London, 1814) 249.
[107] CCCO H/1/4/1, f. 49r.
[108] Allen, 91.
[109] CCCO H/1/4/1, f. 3v.
[110] For example, CCCO H/1/4/1, f. 13r.
[111] An intriguing entry in the *Libri Magni* in 1532 regarding sacristy expenses records that 6d was paid for a picture (*pictura*) of the late, dearest (*carissimus*) founder. It is tempting to think that this payment was made for the delivery of the posthumous Tudor portrait of Fox by Jan Corvus at Corpus which would have been occasionally shown to students and Fellows of the college and most likely kept in the sacristy, CCCO C/1/1/1, f. 103v.
[112] The vault is undocumented but is almost certainly the work of William Vertue. It inaugurated a trend for similar fan vaults constructed in colleges at Oxford (Newman, 'The Physical Setting', 610).
[113] Fox was involved in several extensive glazing projects probably advising on subjects to be glazed; see Angela Smith, 'Bishop Fox and stained glass in early Tudor England', *Journal of Stained*

The quarries in the hall windows are filled with examples of Fox's device of a pelican vulning, which, though based on the early-sixteenth-century pelican to be seen on Fox's bosses and chantry chapel at Winchester, in fact date to the mid-nineteenth century (Plate 15).[114] A fragment of Fox's motto, *Est Deo Gracia*, is preserved in the college archive and another fragment, *Est Deo*, has been inserted in a north-facing window of the south range of the upper library at Merton College, which may have originated in Corpus.[115] Fox's motto can be seen painted on two of the corbels that ornament the hall (Plate 13). There are no records in the surviving college accounts concerning this work since all three examples were part of the work of the first phase of building and, presumably, were recorded in the earlier 'books and payments' of 1516, now lost. There is, however, an entry in the surviving accounts for a payment of 2 marks (26s 8d), made in 1518, to a carver, Edmund More of Kingston in Surrey, for making Oldham's heraldic arms.[116] This is the earliest known documentary reference to Edmund More who went on to work for Wolsey, carving the royal arms to adorn Hampton Court for the Cardinal.[117]

Bishop Fox chose John Claymond, his friend of many years, to be the first President of Corpus Christi College.[118] Claymond was President of Magdalen College and he also held the Mastership of the Hospital of St. Cross near Winchester but relinquished both these posts in order to take up the presidency of Corpus. On the foundation of the college, Claymond probably assumed full responsibility for its completion, a task originally intended to fall to the Prior and Convent of St. Swithun's. It is therefore Claymond's name that is to be found in some of the contracts that were drawn up and subsequently copied into the Corpus accounts. The accounts record, for example, that it was Claymond who contracted Robert Carow to obtain materials and supervise the internal work required in order to complete the work on the presidential lodgings at Corpus; the accounts reveal that these rooms were designed by Humphrey Coke.[119]

Glass, 31 (2007), 35–52. It is likely that the windows of the chapel at Corpus were glazed with a figurative scheme that included images of the saints Fox named in the college statutes and also his armorials and those of benefactors to the college including William Frost and Hugh Oldham.

[114] The quarries were made by James Powell and Sons (pers. comm. Tim Ayers of York University). Further fragments of early-sixteenth-century glass including part of Bishop Fox's motto are preserved in the college archive.

[115] This notion is put forward and the fragment illustrated in Tim Ayers, *Corpus Vitrearum Medii Aevi, Great Britain*, 6, Merton College, part 2 (Oxford, 2013), 439.

[116] CCCO H/1/4/1, f. 26v.

[117] See E. Law, *History of Hampton Court Palace*, I, 2nd edn. (London, 1885), 125.

[118] Claymond and Fox had known each other since 1486.

[119] CCCO H/1/4/1, f. 53.

As Fox's college in Oxford was nearing completion, the clerk of the works recorded numerous payments in the accounts for items such as fittings for doors and windows. A local smith called John Bankes supplied a number of locks, bars and hinges, the latter variously described in the accounts as *hengys*, *garnetts* or *gymmeys*.[120] Such items could often be comparatively expensive; a 'doble stokke locke' with keys for the treasurer's house, for example, cost 3s 8d.[121] In January 1518, eighteen dozen chains were bought for attaching books in the library.[122] Of particular interest is the fact that the Corpus accounts record a payment in September 1518, to a carrier for delivery of two *pypys* (barrel-like containers) of books of Greek to the college that were brought from London.[123] These books may have been amongst the large collection that Bishop Fox gave to Corpus, although an unnamed merchant is referred to in the accounts.[124] The load was clearly substantial, because the cost of carriage amounted to 11s 6d.

Prior to the opening of the Libri Magni, the building accounts incorporated expenses concerning the early administration of the college. One entry, for example, refers to the purchase of a paper book so that an inventory could be taken of the college chattels.[125] Another entry records that parchment was bought for documents of an official nature; 4d was paid 'for a skynne of parchment to wryght Mr. Frostys Indenture'.[126] The individual referred to in the entry, Mr Frost, was Bishop Fox's steward, William Frost, who endowed Corpus with the manor of Mapledurwell.[127] As a benefactor to the college, Frost and his wife Juliana were named in the college statutes; Bishop Fox ordained that prayers be said for the couple in the college chapel, to be named the 'Frost altar'. A further administrative detail found in the Corpus building accounts shows that the college was granted exemption from the jurisdiction of William Atwater, the Bishop of Lincoln, within whose jurisdiction it lay. By way of thanks, Bishop Atwater and his chancellor received gifts of gloves.[128]

---

[120] CCCO H/1/4/1, f. 43r.
[121] CCCO H/1/4/1, f. 7r.
[122] CCCO H/1/4/1, f. 34v. Entries in the Libri Magni show that further chains were purchased in the 1530s as the library holdings increased thanks to gifts from other donors.
[123] CCCO H/1/4/1, f. 47v.
[124] Liddell suggested that the books given by the Bishop were brought to Corpus on various occasions; see J. R. Liddell, 'The Library of Corpus Christi College, Oxford in the Sixteenth Century', *The Library*, 4th series, XVIII, 1937–8, 387.
[125] CCCO C/1/1/1, f. 13r. Separate inventories were made of the books in the library and of the jewels in the tower according to the college statutes (Ward, 186–7). These sixteenth-century inventories have been lost; the earliest to survive dates from the seventeenth century.
[126] CCCO H/1/4/1, f. 49v.
[127] Fox described Frost as a 'sadde, substanciall, feithfull man, and well lerned in the lawe'; see Allen, 113. For Frost, see Fowler, 32–4.
[128] CCCO H/1/4/1, f. 10v; Hearne, 287.

The surviving building accounts for Corpus end in November 1518. The sum recorded at the end of the accounts for the works undertaken during the final eighteen months of construction is £697 17s 8d. No further accounts for Corpus are known to exist until 1521, when the first entries were made in the Liber Magnus. The building project had provided employment for many skilled craftsmen and also unskilled local workers, and some of these men, including Humphrey Coke, William East and Robert Carow, were later employed by Cardinal Wolsey in the 1520s, in the building of Cardinal College. The first students were admitted to Corpus Christi College in July 1517 and within four years the numbers of students had doubled. The college buildings soon began to show signs of wear and tear and there are a number of entries in the Libri Magni recording payments for minor repairs to the fabric.[129] Some further works were undertaken at Corpus in the mid-1500s, though no major building work was carried out at the college until the early seventeenth century, when new presidential lodgings were constructed.[130]

THE MANUSCRIPT

The manuscript comprises the building accounts 2 March 1517 to 21 November 1518, ff. 1r–51v, followed by four further folios attached to guards. These comprise f. 52r, a smith's bill for metalwork, possibly the work of John Bankes, who features in the accounts; ff. 53r–53v, account of woodwork undertaken in the chapel, library and President's chamber; ff. 54r–54v, account of masonry work about various parts of the college, especially walls, including the length and height of sections built; and f. 55r, two contracts between John Claymond and 1. Robert Carow, carpenter, and 2. William Collyns and Nicholas More, carpenters, for carpentry in the cloisters and cloister chambers. Sewn into the accounts themselves, forming f. 43, is a bill of John Bankes, smith, for ironwork supplied from 2 June 1518. The original parchment cover, which has been preserved, is a bifolium of a fourteenth-century manuscript of the *Summa in foro penitentiali* of Berengar Fredoli.

The nineteenth-century tight-back binding measures 332 × 239 × 20 mm (height, width, thickness). The upper and lower endleaves are of cream wove paper, and the same paper has been used to create guards to which are adhered the original limp parchment wrapper (sewn to a guard before f. 1), and ff. 52–5 ult., at the end of the volume.

---

[129] The glass windows suffered frequent damage and were often subject to repair; see CCCO C/1/1/1, ff. 53r, 66v.
[130] Fowler, 73.

The text-block is made up of only two quires, one of which was probably originally sewn through the fold (stitched) into the limp parchment wrapper, which has been retained.

The first quire, ff. 1–28 plus 2 stubs, is made of a high-quality white laid (single-faced mould) paper with a serpent watermark and no countermark. The watermark is similar to Briquet 13824, dated to 1524, from Basel. The accounts begin with the year 1517, showing that the paper would have been made or bought and used in fairly quick succession. A single bifolium, ff. 6/25, is of a different paper stock, lower in quality with less even/fine chain and laid lines, and a different watermark (see below). Chain lines are vertical, and deckle edges are present on all sides; the bifolia have been put together with mixed wire/felt size and sheet orientation. Fol. 1 has been repaired with wove paper, at the time of the current binding. The final two leaves of the quire have been cut away, leaving only stubs. The heavy dirt layer on ff. 1r and 28v shows that this booklet was unbound for many years, and also that the final leaves had been cut away early on. From f. 14 on, the leaves are water stained, but ff. 1–13 are not affected.

Quire 2, ff. 29–51, are of lower-quality laid paper with wider chain and laid line spacing and less well beaten. Again, the chain lines are vertical and deckle edges are present on all sides; the entire quire is made of the same paper, with the open hand and flower/star watermark, similar to Briquet 10794, dated to 1532, from Ingolstadt, also similar to papers of the 1530s and 1540s from France, Navarre, etc. Fol. 43 is not a bifolium but a small piece of the same paper with a fold, sewn directly to f. 44 with an earlier thin, brown thread, which may date from the earlier binding in limp wrapper. Fols. 29r and 51v are very dirty, and there is water damage and mould staining/softening throughout.

Fol. 52 is adhered to a guard and has been cut down from a larger piece of paper; chain lines run vertically oriented. Fol. 53 is also adhered to a guard and retains a spinefold with earlier sewing holes; chain lines run horizontally. Fols. 54 and 55 are a bifolium sewn to a guard; chain lines are horizontally oriented. It is likely that ff. 53–5 were originally together as part of a stitched booklet. Fols. 52, 53, 55 have been repaired with wove paper (along fore-edge), f. 54 has not.

The limp parchment wrapper measures *c.* 384 × 500 mm (height × width), with turn-ins on all four edges ranging from 19 to 55 mm in width. There are numerous holes in the spinefold of the wrapper, but it was not possible to see into the spinefolds of the two quires.

The text-block has been sewn on four thin cords laced into millboards, covered with mid-brown tanned skin (sheep). The binding has been decorated in blind with a panel design on the boards, using a combination of single/double fillets, a foliate roll and corner fleurons. The spine is undecorated.

EDITORIAL NOTE

The building accounts together with ff. 53–5 are primarily written in a single clear secretary hand. A few phrases on ff. 44v–45r have been written in an italic script, although whether by the original clerk or by a later scribe is unclear. They are identified in the published text by an editorial footnote. Fol. 52r is written in a different secretary hand, with a distinctive phonetic spelling, especially in the use of 'v' for 'w', e.g. *veyng* and *vendos* for *weighing* and *windows*. The text is generally legible, with the exception of parts of f. 29r, which has suffered from staining and water damage. With the exception of standard phrases, such as *In primis, Item,* and *Summa,* the accounts are written in English.

The manuscript bears two sets of foliation. The first, in ink in the centre of the top margin of the recto, was possibly undertaken in the seventeenth century. It now begins at f. 4r, suggesting that three leaves are missing. The manuscript was later foliated in pencil, also in the top margin, normally a little to the right of the earlier foliation. This foliation was probably done in the twentieth century, possibly by Joseph Grafton Milne, librarian of Corpus Christi 1933–1946, who did much work sorting the college archives. Both numberings have been indicated in the printed text, in the form [*f. 1r; original f. 4r*].

As noted above, the accounts comprise a series of short *bokes* or books of payments and wages, each one generally of a fortnight's duration. Books of longer duration occur where several days' holiday were taken in one week due to a major Church feast, such as after Easter 1518, when the clerk accounted for three working days beginning Thursday 8 April, when work resumed, plus the two following weeks (f. 37v).

Each book is normally headed with the dates of the period being accounted for, although occasionally the clerk omitted to complete the date, as at the end of August 1518, where he wrote 'This booke made ffrom the ', but failed to fill in the details (f. 46v); he then failed to enter the start date of the next pay book.

Within each book, payments are broken down by type of material and craft or trade for which payment is being made, with related items grouped together, with a blank line normally left before the next set of entries. New subjects of payments are normally indicated by a brief description in the left-hand margin. Sums paid are recorded on the right-hand side of the page. Measurements and quantities of material are normally recorded in feet and inches. In some recording, particularly long sections of masonry for example, the clerk used the perch and also the tease, the latter a term applied to a measurement (of about seven feet) that was particular to Oxford. When writing numbers, whether for quantities, measurement or sums of money, the clerk generally used Roman numerals. Sometimes, but not consistently, he recorded the total of a page in Arabic numerals in the bottom right-hand corner of the page. These have sometimes been crossed out, rendering them wholly or partially illegible. At the end of each 'book', normally halfway across the page, the clerk has written the *Summa* or total for that pay period. Sometimes the clerk made a number of attempts at totalling either a page or a book, and occasionally made a mistake even in the final figure; where identified these have been footnoted. At seven irregular intervals the clerk recorded the sum paid over several pay periods. These occur on ff. 10r, 20r, 28v, 34r, 41r, 48r and 51v. The sum total for the full set of accounts is also given on f. 51v.

Daily payments to craftsmen and artisans follow a distinctive pattern, with the craftsman's name on the left-hand side, followed by two or, where appropriate, three columns of symbols used to indicate the number of days or half days worked, or not worked, in each week, with the total wages for each craftsman written at the right-hand side. The crafts and trades follow an order of seniority, with the carpenters and masons listed first, descending through, for example, joiners, layers and sawyers, and finishing with general labourers. Within these craft and trade groups precedence is maintained, beginning with the master craftsmen on the highest daily rate, followed by journeymen, and finishing with apprentices and 'laborars' or *servi*. Certain tradesmen were paid for piecework, such as paviors, who were paid for completing a defined quantity of paving, or sawyers, for slitting laths by the hundred. Payment was also sometimes made 'in prest'; that is, in advance.

The principal symbols were an open circle or o, to denote a full day worked; a half-circle to denote a half-day worked; a black dot or filled-in o, denoting a normal working day for some reason not worked, and a cross, +, denoting a day not worked because it was a holy day (holiday). Where a craftsman did not work at all during a given week, the clerk normally left the entire week blank; if the craftsman worked some days but not others, the scribe indicated all six days using the appropriate symbols.

Occasionally the clerk made a mistake or otherwise changed his mind. For example, he might mark a man down with a black dot, indicating he had not worked on a regular working day, but then realized that it had actually been a holy day, and so wrote a cross either above or over the black dot. On one or two occasions the clerk has written an o divided by a vertical line, which might indicate a change of mind, where he has altered a full day's

EDITORIAL NOTE

work to half a day. Rather than attempt to reproduce these symbols exactly, certain symbols have been employed as set out in the list of conventions printed below. One or two further symbols used only rarely have been identified, and explained where possible, in the footnotes.

The clerk was inconsistent in his use of capitals for proper names, such as the names of people, places and months of the year, and these forms are reproduced as they occur in the text. The original punctuation has similarly been retained; likewise, underlining of parts of the text.

Throughout the manuscript the clerk used standard Latin and English abbreviations, e.g. *It'm* for Item, and the regular omission of er/ar, e.g. corn' for corner, Rob't for Robert, etc. In most instances abbreviations have been expanded using italics, and a modern spelling favoured for the expansion, even where the clerk elsewhere provided evidence of alternative spellings, e.g. car*riage* rather than car*yage* and Wyll*iam* rather than Wyll*yam*. Exceptions to expansion are the Latin abbreviations Md' for *Memorandum* and di' for *dimidium*, i.e. half. The latter is often used in conjunction with quantities of material otherwise expressed in English, and is therefore undeclinable. The English word 'co'menanwntyd', and variations, for reasons set out in a footnote, could not with certainty be expanded.

The following conventions have been used in the preparation of this transcription:

[...	Text missing to the right of this point
[...]	Passage where text is missing or illegible; completed where possible
\<text thus\>	Text added in a different hand
\text thus/	Text written in above the line or added later
Text ~~thus~~	Text deleted in the original
[*sic*]	Entry in the text which may be an error by the writer
[*blank*]	No entry in the text where a word might be expected (usually with reference to sums of money)
(?)	Preceding reading uncertain
o	A day worked
c	A half-day worked
x	A regular working day not worked
+	A day not worked because it was a holy day
(+)	Original symbol overwritten or otherwise altered to indicate a holy day

For specimen pages from the manuscript, see below, Plates 7–10.

THE BUILDING ACCOUNTS
OF CORPUS CHRISTI COLLEGE,
1517–1518

MARCH 1517 3

[f. 1r; original f. 4r]

[Jhus mary........lady.....]
Townesend car*riage* from netylbed
In *pri*mis v^C xv footes and ij bordes off an other state
contaynyng xv^ti footes
It*em* [....] v^C lackyng ij footes

Jhus mary lady helpe am[*en dico vobis*.....]¹

[f. 1v; original f. 4v]

[Blank]

[f. 2r; original f. 5r]

regni regis henrici 8^vi 8vo/

<1517>

This boke made the viij yere off the Reigne off kyng
herry the eygth: ffrom the second day off March unto
the xvj day off the same moneth

In *pri*mis paid to Mast*er* Wotton² ffor v hundred off drye planch³ bord aft*er* iij s the hundred	xv s
It*em* paid to harry boseby ffor iij hundred off drye bord aft*er* ij s viij d the hundred	viij s
It*em* to the same harry ffor vij hundred off planch bord not seasonyd aft*er* aft*er* [sic] ij s vj d the hundred	xvj s vj d
It*em* paid to John locke ffor the caryage off thes iij loodes off bord aft*er* iij d the loode	ix d
It*em* paid to lawncelate the ~~Schater~~ Slater ffor too thowsond ~~bord~~ lathis aft*er* vj s iiij d the M¹	xij s viij d

---

¹ Text inside square brackets completed by comparison with similar invocation on f. 51v. Written vertically down the right-hand edge of the page.
² Probably the local carpenter Thomas Wotton, who is recorded working for Magdalen and Lincoln colleges in Oxford in the 1520s; see Salzman, 5, 30, 40.
³ The *planch* in this entry were seasoned wooden planks.

\prest xx s/ Md'[4] co'menawntyd[5] and agreyd wyth John Townesend pavyar to ffynd stone sande and pavyng off the cowrte off the college[6] a ta [sic]
\xlvj s viij d/ tease[7] and an halff in bred ffrom the wall rownd abowght the cowrt and the gate howse wyth a
\vj s viij d/ suffycyent chavett […] & corantt to voyd the water.
[8] and the said John to have ffor every tease fyndyng sond stone and workemanshypp xiiij d the summe off teasys lxxxj teasys   xx s

\iiij li xiiij s vj d/

Md' to the said John ffor pavyng off the wood yard to the kechyn to fynd hym stone and sond: and he to have ffor his labors vj d ffor every tease the summe off the teasys: liiij teasys

Md' to the said John ffor pavyng off halff the strette ffrom the wood yard gate by the wall off Merton college to the corner off the wall next unto canterbury college[9] iij score and ix teasys and ffrom the said corner to the garden gate by saynt ffrideswyde is[10] wall which conteynyth x[..]vij xlvij teasys to have found hym stonne and sand takyng ffor every tease vj d the summe off the hole v score xvj di teasys

Item paid to pytfeld for a lood & a halff off Tymber w^t the caryage off hytt to the college   ix s ij d

---

[4] The abbreviation Md' for *Memorandum* has been retained throughout.

[5] This word, together with the nominal form *co'menawntys*, occurs several times in the manuscript but is never expanded completely. The *Middle English Dictionary*, ed. H. Kurath (Ann Arbor, Michigan, 1959), records the Middle English word *covenaunt* together with several variants, including *cumnaunt*, *connaunt*, and *comenaunt*. As it is uncertain how the clerk might have expanded this word it has, contrary to regular practice, been left unexpanded wherever it occurs.

[6] This entry refers to a contract by which John Townesend agrees to supply the materials required for paving the college quad and for carrying out the work.

[7] The tease was a form of square measurement that regularly features in these accounts. It was specially used by paviors and was variously spelt, *teese*; see S. Walker, *Building Accounts of All Souls College, Oxford, 1438–1443*, OHS, 42 (2010), 258; also *teys* or *toise*; see Salzman, 147.

[8] This entry refers to the management of waste water. A *chavett* is the sharply angled cut of a gutter (cf. chevron) and *courant* is the current of water, especially heavy rain along that gutter, as indicated by the phrase 'corantt to voyd the water'.

[9] Canterbury College was a Benedictine house owned and managed by Christ Church Priory in Canterbury.

[10] The priory of St. Frideswide was an Augustinian house adjacent to Corpus Christi. It was dissolved in the 1520s and partially demolished to make way for Cardinal College, founded by Wolsey.

MARCH 1517

Item paid to John Matteson for xij plankes off asch
off xvij footes off lengyth and xx^{ti} ynchis in breddyth
ffor a knedyng trooffe pastery bordes and tables for
chambers at xviij d the pese   xviij s

[*f. 2v; original f. 5v*]

Item payd for ij hoopys on for a cowle an other for a payl	j d ob
Item paid ffor ij sevys for the masons and plasterers[11]	ijij d [*sic*]
Item paid to Robynson for a C off vj penny C v penny nayle[12] C iiij d nayle & a C iij d nayle	xviij d

naylys bowght att london

naylys bowght att london

Item ffor x M^l ij penny nayl att x d le M^l	viij s iiij d
Item ffor iij M^l iiij penny nayll att xv d le M^l	iij s ix d
Item ffor iij M^l iiij penny nayll at xix d le M^l	iiij s ix d
Item ffor iij M^l v penny nayll ij s le M^l	vj s
Item for iij M^l vj d penny nayll ij s viij d le M^l	viij s
Item for ij bagges off sprygg price ix s vj d le bagge[13]	xix s
Item for caryage off the same naylys to ye waterys syde to the barge	ij d

ffor Ragg from hedyngton[14]

In primis paid to Richard Knott ffor x lood caryage att vj d le lood	v s
Item to walton for vij loodes caryage	iij s vj d
Item to Roger haryson for xj lood caryage	v s vj d
Item to Thomas medam for xiij loodes caryages [*sic*]	vj s vj d
Item to Jasper wase for vij lood caryage	iij s vj d
Item paid to John ffrancleyn for the foresaid xlviij loodes off stone att the quarre after xiij s iiij d le C loodes	vj s iiij d

ffor sond lombe and lymbe[15] caryage

Item paid to Richard harne for v loodes off sond and iij loodes off lombe att iiij d the lood ~~caryage~~	ij s viij d

---

[11] Two hoops purchased for a cowl (a tub with handles) and a pail and also a sieve bought for the masons and for the plasterers.
[12] Nails.
[13] Sprygg or sprig was a type of small nail; see Salzman, 199, 313.
[14] Ragstone brought from the quarries at Headington. Ragstone is the generic term applied to stone of various sorts that was quarried in thin pieces.
[15] Sand, loam (clay), and lime.

	Item paid to John Tewnesend ffor iij loodes off sond after iij d le lood	ix d
	Item paid to Richard harne for ij quarterys off lyme caryage borowyd off Richard lewose[16]	ij d

[f. 3r; original f. 6r]

borowyd off magdaleyn college	Item paid to wylliam Clare for caryage off a lood off tymber ffrom magdalen college borowyd	iiij d
borowyd off Merton college	Item paid to the same clare for the caryage off v quarter lyme from holywell[17] to the college	iiij d
Smyth	Item paid to garratt Smyth ffor a payar off hengys[18] to the new dore y^t is broke in to the botery[19] wayng xj li save a quarter paying for every li j d ob qua	xviij d ob
lewose	Md' aggreid and co'menauntyd wt Rychard lewose for the makyng off a stone wall betwyxt the kechyn \yard/ and the garden ffor the dyggyng off the foundacion and workemanshypp	
prest xx s	off every foote upp ryght xviij a lengyth to the perche[20] paying ffor every perch xij d the summe off perchys in the same wall xxvijti	
Smyth	Item paid to Garrate Smyth ffor a new mattoke[21] made off old stoffe	xij d
Roger Morwent Joyner	Md' co'menawntyd and agreyd w^t Roger Morwentt[22] by humfrey cooke: ffor makyng off the ber benche in the Masteris parlower[23] the which is xviij footes in lengyth to be made suffycyant and clenly: Also ffor	

---

[16] Richard Lewis.
[17] Holywell in Oxford was less than half a mile from Corpus.
[18] Hinges.
[19] The buttery was a room where barrels were usually stored.
[20] The perch was a unit of measurement that could as it seems in this instance, be applied to the volume of masonry; one perch was 5.03m in length by 0.45m high and 0.30m thick. This entry refers to sections of boundary wall that Lewis built.
[21] A mattock, used for digging and chopping.
[22] This contract concerning an eighteen-foot bench to be made for the President's lodgings by carpenter Roger Morwent, was published in Salzman, 572–3. Morwent was a local carpenter and is not known to have been related to Walter Morwent, a Fellow of Merton College or Robert Morwent who was the first Vice-President and later President of Corpus Christi. For Roger Morwent, Harvey, 208.
[23] For Humphrey Coke, see Harvey, 64–5.

MARCH 1517

payde prest ~~vij s~~ xxvij s [~~....~~:s ~~......~~s ~~vj s..iij d~~ ~~ij s...ij d~~ ~~iij s iiij d~~ ~~vj s viij d~~ ~~x..ij s]~~ [28]	sealyng[24] off the said parlower wallys rownd abowght the wyndowys by neth and a bove in the said parlower and to make too portalles on in the parlower and a nother in the chamber above: And too cobertes[25] on by neth and a nother a bove off v footes in lengyth a pease and xx^{ti} ynchis brood clenly wrowght and hawnsyd:[26] And to seale the flower over the said parlower w^t panys glued and ffrett w^t well ynbowyd(?) batons off a yard square: And the said Roger moreover to make a dore att the stayar foote gluyd: And he to have fond hym all manner off stooffe y^t is to say waynscott[27] glew naylis broddes and sawyng: ffor his workmanshypp to have — v li	xxvij s

Summa istius solutionis ~~xj li xix s ij d~~ x li xvj s ij d

[f. 3v; original f. 6v]

Item for too loodes caryage off the kechyn stooff ffrom henley[29]	xvj s
Item paid to Thomas barnes and walter pownd for the caryage off ij loodes off waynscottes from henley	xvj s
Item pro expenses for the possessyon off the howse ut patet billa	iiij s iij d
Item paid to M^r wynsemore for the makyng off diverse instrumentes[30]	iij s iiij d

Summa xxxix s vij d

---

[24] Seallyng is the term used for panelling with wainscot.
[25] Cupboards.
[26] Salzman interprets *hawnsyd* as raised; see 572.
[27] Wainscot is a term that applies to the high quality sawn oak that was used for panelling rooms.
[28] Sums of money in this margin crossed out, partially illegible.
[29] This payment refers to kitchen utensils brought from London by barge and delivered to carriers at Henley-on-Thames, who then transported the goods a further twenty miles to Oxford.
[30] Richard Wynsemore is named in connection with payments made to Merton College in spring 1513 for a plot of land purchased by Fox for his college; see Fowler, 65–6.

[*f. 4r; original f. 7r*]

\regni regis henrici 8^{vi} 8vo/

This boke made ffrom the xvth day off March
unto the xxx^{ti} day off the same Moneth

lyme	In primis paid to larden and grene ffor ij loodes off lyme conteynyng viij quarterys and vj boschelles after xv d ob le quarter	xj s iiij d
paid	Md' co'menantyd and agreid w^t Elys larder [*sic*] for iiij loodes off lyme every loode conteynyng iiij quarters after xiiij d le quarter	
~~prest iij s iiij d~~	the summe off quarterys xvj att [?] the leest to be browght into corpus xpi'[31] college in oxfford the thorseday before palmis Sonday[32]: and this bargen to be done Richard leowse is suertye	iij s iiij d
	Md' co'menantyd and agreid wyth Cornell Clerke ffor the makyng off the dextis[33] in the liberary to the summe off xvj after the manner and fforme as they be in Magdaleyn college except the <u>popie</u> heedes off the seites thes to be <u>workmanly</u> wrowght and clenly and he to have all manner off stooff ffoond hym and to have ffor the makyng off on dexte x s the summe off the hole – viij li	
	Item borowyd att Magdaleyn college on C off v d nayle a Є C off vj d nayle di' C x d nayle	
Tymber from netylbed	Item to John Townesend ffor l~~j~~ footes \di'/ caryage	iij s iiij d
	Item to Jasper wase for lj footes	iij s iiij d
	Item to John knott for xlj footes	ij s viij d
	Item to John ~~dewe~~ \medam/ for xlviij footes	iij s ij d
	Item to haryson for xlvij footes	iij s
Ragg from hedyngton	In primis paid to Rychard knott for xv loodes caryage att vj d le lood	vij s vj d

---

[31] The Greek letters χ and ρ (chi and rho) are the first letters of the word Χριστός/Christos, and were regularly indicated using the Latin letters x and p for words beginning with Christ; such as Christi, indicated here, and the personal name Christopher, which occurs elsewhere in the manuscript. In each case the unexpanded version has been retained.

[32] Palm Sunday.

[33] An agreement with Oxford carpenter, Cornell Clerk for library presses (*dextis*). Clerk had previously carried out minor works at Magdalen College; see Harvey, 54. He was probably a specialist joiner.

MARCH 1517

	Item paid to Thomas medam for xix loodes	ix s vj d
	Item to Walton for […] \xiiij/ loodes caryage	vij s
	Item to Jasper for v loodes caryage	ijs vj d
	Item to Roger haryson for x loodes	v s
	Item to John Townesend for j lood	vj d
	Item paid to John francleyn for iij^{xx} and iij loodes after xiij s iiij d the hundred lood and for a lood off free stone[34]	viij s ij d
ffor sond and lome	Item paid to John Townesend for xvj loodes off ~~lome~~ \sond/ after iij d le loode	iiij s
	Item to the same John for iij loodes off lome after iiij d le lood	xij d
	Item to John March for ij loodes off loome	viij d
fre stone	Item for a lood off ffree stone	xij d
		3li 17s

[*f. 4v; original f. 7v*]

borowyd att quenys college	Item a M^l lath borowyd att Quenys college[35]	
borowyd att bayly college: paid to pytfyld for bord	Item paid to John Townesend ffor the caryage off v quarterys off lyme borowyd att bayly[36] college	iiij d
	Item paid to pytfeld for v C planch bord att ij s viij d le C	xiij s iiij d
	Item paid to Medam for the caryage off the same	ij d
waynscott caryage from henley	Item paid to John peerson for a lood off waynscott caryage from henly to oxfford	vj s viij d
	Item to Wylliam pownd for caryage off a lood off waynscottes from henly	viij s

Summa — ~~vj~~ v li v s vj d

28s 6d

---

[34] Freestone was a term applied to stone soft enough to be easily chiselled into shape and therefore suitable for mouldings.
[35] A thousand laths acquired from Queen's College.
[36] Balliol College, Oxford.

[*f. 5r; original f. 8r*]

This boke made from the xxx^{ti} day off March
unto the t ix day off Aprell

lyme	In primis paid to larden ffor for [sic] xxvj^{ti} quarterys and v boschelles after xiiij d le quartery off the which he receyvyd in prest iij s iiij d	xxxj s x d
	Item paid to grene for iiij quarterys lyme after xiij d le quarter	iiij s iiij d
lath	Item paid to launcelote the slatter for on M^l off long lath price vj s viij d and for ij M^l short lath an a C price le M^l vj d vj s	xix s ij d
tymber from	Item to John Townesend for xlviij footes di' caryage	iij s iiij d
netylbed	Item to the same John for xliiij xlviij footes di'	iij s iiij d
	Item to Chare for xlviij footes di'	iij s iiij d
	Item to wylshere for lj footes di'	iij s v d
Townesend	Md' paid to John Townesend for the pavyng off the quadrant takyn by the teerse as his apperyth in the fyrst lesse(?)	xlvj s viij d
Ragge from	In primis to Robert walton for xx^{ti} loodes caryage after vj d le lood	x s
hedyngton	Item to Thomas medam for xxiij^{ti} loodes	xj s vj d
	Item to haryson for for [sic] xxiij^{ti} di' loodes	xj s vj d
	Item to Richard knott for xxti loodes \xvij loodes/	viij s vj d
	Item to Jasper wase for vj loodes	iij s
	Item paid to francleyn for iiij^{xx ti} ix loodes off ragg after xiij s iiij d le C loodes	xj s
free ston	Item paid to the same ffrancleyn for a loode of free stone	xij d
lome	Item paid to John Townesend for x loodes off sond	
and sond	after iij d le lood	ij s vj d
	Item to the same John for a loode off lome	iiij d
	Item to harne for a lood off lome	iiij d
	Item to March for ij loodes off lome	viij d
	Item for bromys[37]	ij d
	Item for a hoope to the bukcate[38]	j d
	Item for the caryage off the carpenterys tooles	viij d

Summa viij li xvj s viij d

8li 16s 8d

---

[37] Brooms.
[38] A hoop for a bucket.

APRIL 1517

[*f. 5v; original f. 8v*]

This boke made ffrom the xv^th day off Apryll
unto the xxv^ti day off the same monyth

lyme	In primis paid to Richard horne ffor iiij quarterys and vj boschelles off lyme after xiij d le quarter	v s
	Item paid to Elys larden for xxij^ti quarterys off lyme att xiij d le quarter	xxiij s x d
Tymber from	Item paid to Richard chare for l footes caryage	iij s iiij d
netylbedd	Item to John Scharpe for lij footes di'	iij s iiij d
	Item to John wylshere for xlviij di' footes	iij s iiij d
	Item to John Myller for lj footes di'	iij s iiij d
	Item to John Townesend for for [*sic*] lj di' footes	iij s iiij d
	Item to John meden for lj footes	iij s iiij d
	Item to John Townesend for l footes	iij s iiij d
	Item to Thomas wylshere for lj footes di'	iij s iiij d
	Item to John bond for lj footes	iij s iiij d
	Item to John wase for xlviij footes di'	iij s iiij d
	Item to Jasper Wase for lj footes di'	iij s iiij d
	Item to Thomas Townesend for lj footes	iij s iiij d
fre stone	Item paid to John ffrancleyn for iij loodes off ffree stone after xij d le loode	~~iij s~~ iij s
	Item to Jasper wase for the caryage off the same	xviij d
lome	Item to John March for ~~vij~~ \ix/ loodes of lombe att iiij d le loode	iij s vj d
Cornell	Item delyveryd to cornell in parte off payment off hys bargeyn for the makyng off the dextys in the liberary	vj s viij d
gravell	Item paid to Townesend for x loodys off gravell att iij d le lood	ij s vj d
	Item to the same Townesend for iiij loodes off lome att iiij d le lood	xvj d

~~Summa iiij li vij s iiij d~~

~~58s 8d~~
4li 7s 4d

[*f. 6r; original f. 9r*]

rag from hedyngton	Item paid to Richard medam for xxiij^{ti} loodes cariage	xj s vj d
	Item to Robert walton for xviij loodes cariage	ix s
	Item to haryson for xxiiij^{ti} loodes car*riage*	xij s
	Item to Jasp*er* wase for xiij loodes car*riage*	vj s vj d
	Item to Richard knott for xviij loodes	ix s
	Item paid to ffrancleyn ffor iiij^{xx} xvj loodes off ragg att xiij s iiij d the hundred	xij s

Su*m*ma Tot*ali*s — vij li vij s iiij d

[*f. 6v; original f. 9v*]

<1517> This boke made from the xxvj^{ti} day of Aprell the ixth yere off the reigne off kyng herry the eyght unto the ixth day off May

lyme	In p*ri*mis paid to Elys larden for xxvj^{ti} quart*er*ys off lyme att xiiij d the quart*er*	xxviij s viij d
bord	Item to pye the carpent*er* for iij^C planch bord and iij^C quart*er* bord att ij s viij d le hundrid	xvj s
sprygg	Item for a bagg of sprygg	ix s j d
glew	Item for ij dosyn glew att ij d ob le pownd	v s
	Item to John Swetestarr ffor the carage off tymb*er* att netylbedd^{39}	iiij s
humfrey cooke	Item paid to M^r humfrey from the last day off ffebruary unto the xiijth day off March the which is xxij^{ti} days to be alowyd: And ffrom the xiijth day off Aprell unto the second day off Maii the which is xij days to be allowyd the some off days xxxij aft*er* xx d le daye^{40}	lvj s viij d
Carow	Item paid to Rob*er*t Carow in full payment off iij^{xx} xiij li xiij s iiij d as hytt apperyth by his indenture in ffull paymentt att this daye^{41}	xxviij s viij d
leyowse	Item paid to Richard leyowse for fendyng stone workmanshypp and settyng off the soyles off xiij dorys^{42}	xij s

---

[39] Nettlebed near Henley-on-Thames, where wood was sourced and where bricks and tiles were made; see Salzman, 230.
[40] Another entry recording two lengthy visits paid by Master Carpenter, Humphrey Coke.
[41] The entry concerns local carpenter Robert Carow whose previous work at the college is indicated by a payment of £73 13s 4d.
[42] The *soyl* in this entry refers to the stone sills at the base of each door. The term is usually

APRIL/MAY 1517

lome	Item paid to March for vij loodes off lome att iiij d le lood	ij s iiij d
	Item paid to Garratt Smyth for xvj[xx] broodes att iij d le score	iiij s
	Item for iiij payer hynges and hookes to the seller and botery dorys waying xliiij ll att j d ob qua le pownd	vj s v d
	Item ffor the mendyng off hengys for the wycatt[43]	vij d ob
	Item to swereers[44] ffor the queyre waying v li di'	viij d
	Item ffor to henges and too hookes to the wydraft dorys[45] waying ix li	xv d ob qua
	Item xij nayles for the plomber waying v li	viij d ob qua
	Item for pacthredd[46]	ij d

[f. 7r; original f. 10r]

tymber from netylbedd	Item to John Scharpe for l footes di' caryage	iij s iiij d
	Item to Richard chare for li l footes	iij s iiij d
	Item to Thomas wylshere for l footes di'	iij s iiij d
	Item to John Scharpe for xlix footes di'	iij s iiij d
	Item to Richard chare for xlviij footes	iij s iiij d
	Item to Thomas wylschere […] li footes di'	iij s iiij d
ragg from hedyngton	Item to John knott for vij loodes caryage att vj d le lood	iij s vj d
	Item to Robert Walton for vij loodes	iij s vj d
	Item to Medam for vij loodes	iij s vj d
	Item to haryson for x loodes	v s
	Item for a doble stokke lokke[47] to the tresowre howse dore wt ij keys price	iiij s viij d
	Item for iiij lockes wyth too keys a peese ij to the chaple dorres and too to the vestrye dorys price off iij off them iij s viij d the pece and the other locke ij s viijd	xiij s viij d
	Item for a locke to the botrye dore wyth too keys	ij s

Summa [blank]

---

used in connection with windows; see Salzman, 93–4.
[43] Hinges for a wicket, a small door set within a larger door; see Salzman, 254, 571.
[44] It is unclear what this term refers to; it seems to be some form of ironwork.
[45] Hinges bought for doors made from thick planks (*wydraft*).
[46] *Pacthredd* or packthread was a type of twine used for both measuring lines when building and also for tying materials; see Salzman, 340.
[47] This entry refers to the locks bought for the door to the college treasury, the chapel, vestry and buttery.

14 BUILDING ACCOUNTS OF CORPUS CHRISTI COLLEGE

from london	Item for <u>v lockes</u> Wyth ij keys the pece to <u>the masteris lodgyng</u>[48] att ij s iiij d le pece	xj s viij d
	Item for iiij payer of garnettes[49] for portalles at xij d le payer	iiij s
	Item for viij handels & loppys to the same portalles price the pece vj d	iiij s
	Item for iiij latchis & iiij catchys & crampettes[50] to the same portalles att vj d le pece	ij s
	Item for iiij dosyn rynges for dorys att iij s iiij d the dosyn off hert rynges & iij s viij d the dosyn off rownd rynges	xiij s
	Item for a locke and a payer off garnettes for a cobberd	xviij d
to walcar the caryar	Item paid to walkar the caryar for the caryage off lockes hengys and sprygg the which was iij^C wayght lakyng x pownd	iij s
	Item paid to wylliam collyn for his costes from london[51]	xij d

Summa ~~xiij li v s viij d~~

Summa ~~xiiij li xx d~~ xiij li xiij s iiij d

4li 17s

[f. 7v; original f. 10v]

This boke made from the ixth daie off maij
unto the xxiiij dai off the same monyth

lyme	Item paid to Elys larden for xxx^{ti} quarterys off lyme allowyng xxj quarterys ffor the score price the quarter xiij d	xxxj s v d
ragg	Item paid to francleyn for di' C lood off ragg	vj s viij d
herdelles	Item paid to wylliam hyxis for ij dosyn herdelles[52]	vj s
bast roopys	Item for iij cople off bast roopys[53] at j d ob le cople	iiij d ob
elme bord	Item paid to herry thycatt for iij quartery off elme borde[54]	xxj d

---

[48] Keys purchased for the President's rooms.
[49] A *garnett* is a hinge.
[50] Crampettes were a sturdy, iron fixing; see Salzman, 289.
[51] A William Collyn was apprenticed to Humphrey Coke.
[52] Hurdles.
[53] Ropes.
[54] Elm was often used for scaffolding.

MAY 1517

lath nayle	Item for iiij^C lath nayle	v d
	Item for a cowle	vij d
waynscott from henley	Item paid to Richard pownd for the caryage off ~~x~~ iij^{xx} x waynscottes from henly to oxford	xiij s iiij d
	Item to Richard veer for xxxiiij waynscottes caryage	vj s viij d
naylys	Item to John Smyth for v^C x penny nayle att vij d ob le C	iij s j d ob
	Item to the same John for v^C vj penny nayle att iiij d ob le C	xxij d ob
lath	Item paid to lawncelate for iiij^{ml} lath att vj s viij d le m^l	xxvj s viij d
carow for beddys	Item paid to Robert Carow for the makyng off xx^{ti} beddes after ij s the bed he fyndyng all manner off stooffe except nayles[55]	xl s
		6li 18s 10d ob

[f. 8r; original f. 11r]

tymber from netylbedd	1 John Knott for xlvij footes di' caryage	iij s iiij d
	4 Thomas wylshere for xlvj^1 footes / lij^2 footes / for lij^3 footes / and ^{4}xlix footes	xiij s iiij d
	4 Richard chare for l footes di' / l footes di' / xlvij footes di' / l footes di'	xiij s iiij d
	4 John sharpe for l footes di' / lj footes / l footes / and l footes	xiij s iiij d
	3 John chare for l footes di' / l footes / and liij footes di'	x s
	1 John welman for xlix footes di'	xiij s iiij d
	Item payd to pye the carpenter for iij^C planch bord and iij^C quarter bord after ij s viij d le hundred	[...~~5..8d~~]
		xvj s

Summa x li xj s vj d ob

3li [~~7s~~] \12s/ 8d

---

[55] Carow is paid for making twenty beds at 2s a piece. The beds were probably for the Fellows; see Newman in Mc Conica, 611.

16   BUILDING ACCOUNTS OF CORPUS CHRISTI COLLEGE

[*f. 8v; original f. 11v*]

This boke made from the xxiiij^{ti} daye off maij
unto the xxxj^{ti} daij off the same monyth

Tymber from	In primis paid to Richard Chare for xlvij footes caryage	iij s
netylbed	Item to John Chare for xlj footes	iij s
	Item to Thomas wylshere for lj footes	iij s iiij d
ragg from	Item paid to walton for xxxix^{ti} loodes off ragg caryage	
hedyngton	att vj d le lood	xix s vj d
	Item to Jasper wase for xxx^{ti} loodes	xv s
	Item to haryson for xxxiiij^{ti} loodes	xvij s
	Item to John knott for xxiij^{ti} loodes	xjs vj d
	Item to kelham rede for xiiij loodes	~~vij d~~ vij s
	Item to John medam for xxxv loodes	xvij s vj d
	Item to John hart for xxxj loodes	xv s vj d
	Item paid to francleyn ffor ij hundred loodes \& vj/ off ragg after xiij s iiij d le hundred	xxvj s viij d
lyme	Item paid to Elys larden for xliij quarterys off lyme price the quarter xiij d alowyng xxj^{ti} for xxj^{ti}	xliiij s v d
sond	Item paid to John Townesend ~~pa~~ ffor iij^{xxti} and xiiij loodes off sond after iij d le loode	xviij s vj d
	Item paid to bankes for lockes and yorne[56] worke	xiij s iiij d

Summa x li xv s iij d

[~~9li~~ …s …d]

[*f. 9r; original f. 12r*]

This boke made from the thyrd day off June
unto the xxij^{ti} day off the same monyth

waynscott	Item primis paid to John Cockes for xxxiiij^{ti}	
caryage	waynscottes caryage from henley	vj s viij d
from henley	Item to Thomas lemesley for xxxiiij^{ti} waynscottes	vj s viij d
	Item to Richard grene for xxxiiij^{ti} waynscottes	vj s viij d
	Item to John Coterell for xxxij^{ti} waynscottes	£vj s viij d
	Item Robert devyn for xxxij waynscottes	vj s viij d
	Item to Wylliam Pownd for xxxiiij waynscottes	vj s viij d
ragg from	Item paid to Robert walton for xxix^{ti} loodes off ragg	
hedyngton	caryage att vj d le lood	xiiij s vj d

[56] Iron.

JUNE 1517

	Item to Medam for xviij loodes cariage	ix s
	Item to haryson for xxiiij^ti loodes cariage	xij s
	Item to Jasper for xxxij^ti loodes cariage	xvj s
	Item to John hart for xxiiij loodes	xij s
	Item to John knott for xxj^ti loodes	x s vj d
	Item paid to francleyn for an hundred and an hallff off ragg att xiij s ~~vj d~~ \iiij d/ le hundrid	xx s
freston	Item to the same francleyn ffor iij loodes off free ston	iij s
	Item to Jasper for the cariage off the same	xviij d
sond	Item paid to John Townesend for lvij loodes off sond att iij d le lood	xiij s iiij d
	Item paid to the same Townesend for a lood off stone	vj d
lome	Item paid to March ffor iiij loodes off lome att iiij d le lood	xvj d
lyme	Item paid to Elys larden for xxxviij^ti quarterys off lyme att xiij d le quarter allowing xxj for xx^ti	xlj s
lath nayll	Item ffor lath nayll	xijd
planch bord	Item to Robert carow for ij^C planch bord for the lyberary att iij s le hundrid	vj s
waynscott	Item paid ffor ij^C di' waynscottes	xj li iiij s viijd
	Item paid to John Matheow ffor the caryage off the same from london to henley att ~~iij~~ xiij s iiij d le hundrid	xxxiij s iiij d
		[~~22li..s..13s~~]

[f. 9v; original f. 12v]

naylys from london	Item for a M^l vj penny nayle	ij s x d
	Item for a M^l v penny nayle	ij s iiij d
	Item for a M^l iiij penny nayle	xix d
	Item for a bagg off sprygg	x s vj d
to w vertue and humfray cooke for theyr labors	Item for the coostes of wylliam vertue[57] att the xxij day off June for the space off viij days	xiij s iiij d
	Item for the coostes off humfrey cooke att the xxij day off June for viij days	xiij s iiij d
	Item paid to Wylliam care for rydyng forward	x d
	Item paid for ruschis to lay the stooff on[58]	vj d
	Item paid to lawncellatt the slatter for iij^Ml lath price the thowsand vj s viij d	xx s
	Item to the same lawncelate	iij s iiij d

---

[57] For William Vertue, see Harvey, 307–10.
[58] Rushes purchased to cover and protect building materials.

18   BUILDING ACCOUNTS OF CORPUS CHRISTI COLLEGE

	~~Item to John Abankes~~	
prest	Item delyv*er*yd to John a bankys Smyth	xx s
\x/John ward	It*em* paid to John ward in prest for his bargayn takyng by grett ffor the makyng off the wyndoys abowght the cloyst*er* as his [*sic*] apperyth by hys co'menawntys[59]	xl s
	It*em* to the ~~th~~ said John in prest for ~~ijC~~ xx[ti] loodes off square stone	iij s iiij d

[*f. 10r; original f. 13r*]

Est	Md' co'menawntyd and agreid w[t] wyll*ia*m Est for vij[C] and iij[xx] footes off cresse table and seve*r*all table att iiij d the foot ~~ffe~~ hytt to be made off the stone[60] off taynton[61] and browght home to the college att his p*ro*pre coostes and charges whereoff he hath receyvyd in ernyst	vj s viij d
	It*em* paid to Will*ia*m broke for xiiij foote cariage of taynton stone	ij s
	It*em* to wyll*ia*m Sawnd*er*ys xiiij foote	ij s
	It*em* to Rog*er* Phelyppys xvij footes	ij s
	It*em* to wyll*ia*m popley xiiij footes	ij s
	It*em* to wyll*ia*m broke xvj foote	ij s
	It*em* to wyll*ia*m Sawnd*er*ys xvij foote	ij s
	It*em* to John locke for xvj footes di'	ij s
	It*em* to John ward xv footes & di'	ij s
	It*em* to John Slatter xv footes	ij s

~~Su*mma* vj li xv s viij d~~
Su*mma* To*tali*s xxix li xv s ~~viij d~~ iiij d
S[...]
~~Su*mma* o*mn*iu*m* E*m*ptoru*m* iiij[xx] li xiiij li xiij s ob~~
Su*mma* hucusq*ue* xcix li viij d ob 1.[62]

~~99 li 9s ob~~(?)

[~~5 li..7s 8d~~]

---

[59] John Ward of Little Barrington in Gloucestershire is named here as the mason responsible for making the windows of the cloister.
[60] The entry refers to stonework carried out by master mason, William East or Est. The *cresse* table could refer either to steps or '*greses*', also called *grass table* which was used at the base of an external wall; see Salzman, 89; for *greses*, ibid., 488.
[61] This entry records a payment to William East for the stone he had prepared. For East, see Harvey, 89–90. The quarries at Taynton had been in operation since the 12th century and produced a fine limestone that was used for ashlar.
[62] The total of ff. 2r to 10r.

JUNE/JULY 1517

[*f. 10v; original f. 13v*]

This Boke made ffrom the xxij[ti] day off ~~Julii~~ June to the iiij day off Julij

elme borde	In primis paid to Robert Gely ffor iiij[C] elme bord att ij s iiij d le hundrid	ix s iiij d
rag from	Item to Robert walton ffor xx[ti] loodes carriage att vj d le lood	x s
hedyngton	Item to John Townesend for vj loodes	iij s
	Item to Jasper ffor xx[ti] loodes	x s
	Item to haryson for xj loodes	v s vj d
	Item to thomas medam for xvij loodes	viij s vj d
	Item to kellham redde for xvij loodes	viij s vj d
	Item to knott for xxj loodes	x s vj d
	Item paid to francleyn ffor an hundred loodes and a quarteryn off ~~kechyn see this~~ ragg after xiij s iiij d le hundrid	xvj s viij d
\x/ Mr Cambye	Item delyveryd to M[r] Cambye for hys expensys and other coostes as concernyng my lord off lyncon is seale and the chapter is seale for the exempcion off corpus xpi'[63] college owght off hys dyosisse[64]	iiij li xj s
	Item to the same master Cambye for hys labors and rewardes	xl s
glovys to my lord off lyncon	Item for glovys gevyn to my lord off ~~wynchester~~ \lyncon/ and his chaunceller[65]	ij s viij d
	Item to George Roper his expensys for twys rydyng to wynchester[66]	iiij s v d
the caryars off ffre ston from Taynton	Wylliam Broke for xviij footes caryage off taynton stone	ij s
	Item to Roger broke for xvij footes caryage	ij s
	Item to John warde for xix footes	ij s
	Item to John slatter for xv footes di'	ij s
	Item to Roger Phyllyppys for xviij foot	ij s
	Item to Wylliam broke for xix footes	ij s
	Item to Thomas Chedwell for vx footes	ij s
	Item to John ward for xvj footes	ij s

[63] See fn.30 to f. 4r.

[64] Diocese. This entry refers to a Mr Cambye, who negotiated the exemption of Corpus from the jurisdiction of the Bishop of Lincoln. This may have been John Cambye, a resident of Oxford in the early sixteenth century, who gave his name to a group of buildings in Oxford; see A. Chalmers, *A History of the University of Oxford* (Oxford, 1810), 423.

[65] The Bishop of Lincoln's chancellor. William Atwater was Bishop of Lincoln from 1514 until his death in 1522.

[66] A messenger named George Roper who was paid for riding to Winchester, presumably to carry news to Bishop Fox.

	Item to Roger broke for xviij footes caryage	ij s
	Summa xj li xviij s j d	
		11li 18s 1d

[f. 11r; original f. 14r]

This boke made from the iiij day of Julij
unto the xviij day off the same monyth

lyme	In primis paid to Elys larden for xliiij^ti quarterys off lyme at xiij d le quarter	xlviij s ij d
	Item to townesend for x loodes off gravell att iij d le loode	ij s vj d
ragg from hedyngton	Item to townesend for xvij loodes off ragg cariage att vj d le lood	viij s vj d
	Item to John hart for xviij loodes cariage	ix s
	Item to kelham rede for x loodes	v s
	Item to Jasper wase for xvj loodes	viij s
	Item to ffrancleyn for xj loodes	v s vj d
	Item to haryson for xiij loodes	vj s vj d
	Item to Robert Walton for xxij loodes	xj s
	Item paid to francleyn for iiij^xx ix loodes off ragg	xj s x d
	Item paid to Nicholas herne for iij loodes off pold ragg[67]	xxj d
borde	Item to Richard pytfyld for ij^C planch bord ij^C quarter bord	x s
	Item to Robert carow for a hundrid di' off planch bord	iiij s vj d
	Item paid to townesend in part off paymentt for the cariage away off the stooff thatt lay agaynst the college	vj s viij d
Smyth	Item delyveryd to John Abankes in part off payment off a byll which conteynyth iij li vj d ob	xxx s
	Summa viij li viij s xj d	
		8li 8s 11d

[f. 11v; original f. 14v]

This boke made from the xviij^th day off Julii
unto the second day off August

borde	In primis paid to Richard Pytfyld for C di' off planch bord	iiij s
	Item to Thomas waltar for a C planch bord	iij s

---

[67] The pold ragg is probably polled ragstone, meaning stone that has been carefully trimmed and smoothed.

JULY/AUGUST 1517

lyme	Item to Elys larden for xxiiij^{ti} quarterys off lyme att xiij d le quarter	xxiiij s xj d
ffreston from taynton	Item to John warde for xxj loodes off ffree stone ~~from~~ \off/ taynton att xviij d le loode whereoff he receyvid iij s iiij d in prest	xxviij s ij d
	Item paid to John Phylyppys for xviij footes cariage	ij s
naylys	Item for a M^l vj penny nayle	iij s
	Item for iij^C x penny nayle	xxij d
	Item for a thowsand lath nayle	ij s ij d
tynne	Item for viij li off tynne[68] att iiij d le pownde	ij s viij d
	Item to the sexten off new college for a C planch bord	iij s iiij d
gravell	Item to Townesend for xiiij loodes off gravell	iij s vj d
ragg from hedyngton	Item to Robert walton for xxij loodes cariage att vj d le lood	xj s
	Item to John Townesend for vjj loodes cariage	iij s vj d
	It [sic] to Jasper wase for xv loodes	vij s vj d
	Item to kelham rede for xij loodes	vj s
	Item to John francleyn for xxij loodes	xj s
	Item to haryson for viij loodes	iiij s
Smyth	Item paid to John abankys for iij lockes x hooke bondes and v gymmeys for the <u>chest in</u> the <u>tresar howse</u>[69]	xiiij s iiij d
M^r pantry payd	Md' borowyd off Thomas pantrye bedyll iij^C lackyng a foot off planch borde	borowyd
stooff from london	Item a stocke locke and a spryng locke in on for the vestery dore wt two keys	ij s viij d
	Item ffor two lockes to the ~~vestery dore~~ Tresar howse dore	iij s iiij d
	Item a spryng locke to the barbarhowse dore	x d
	Item a locke to the pastery dore	xx d
	Item a locke off yorne to the chaple dore	iij s iiij d
	Item a bolte ffor an ambery[70]	~~v d~~ vij d
	Item for a dosyn payer off garnettes	x s iij d
	Summa	vij li xviij s iij d
		7li 18s 3d

---

[68] Tin.
[69] The gymmys noted here and elsewhere in the accounts were probably *gemel* or *gemews*, a type of hinge comprising an identical pin plate and hanging plate but without a strap; see Salzman, 298.
[70] An aumbry in which the items required for the performance of the Eucharist were kept.

[*f. 12r; original f. 15r*]

This boke made from the second day off August ~~tt~~ to the xvj day off the same monyth

Smyth	Item paid to John Abankes for vij li wayght after j d ob qua le pownd in boltes and hengys to the botery dore	xj d ob
	Item ffor ij^C broddys att iij d le scole	ij s vj d
	Item ffor a stocke locke ffor the powltery dore	viij d
	Item ffor mendyng off too lockes	iiij d
	Item ffor ij grattes waying xij powndes	xxj d
	Item ffor too lachys and too stapulles for the botery dorys[71]	vj d
tymber from netylbed	Item to haryson for xlvij footes di' caryage	iij s iiij d
	Item to John Townesend for xlviij footes di'	iij s iiij d
	Item to kelham rede ffor xlviij footes caryage	iij s iiij d
	Item to Jasper wase xlvj footes	iij s iiij d
	Item to Robert walton for xliiij footes	iij s iiij d
lyme	Item paid to Elys larden for xxxix quarterys off lyme after xiij d le quarter	xlij s ij d
	Item ffor an hundred lath	viij d
	Item ffor ij^C slate stone	ij s
bord from netylbed	Item paid to John Townesend for the caryage off vj^C di' xxxj footes off planch bord ffrom netylbed	iij s iiij d
	Item for a doble stocke locke for the kechyn dore w^t ij keys	ij s viij d
	Item a locke for the larder dore w^t ij keys	xx d
	Item di' dosyn stocke lockes	iiij s
	Item for iij spryng lockes	ij s
	Item for di' a dosyn lockes for the kappys	iiij s
	Item for wyne gevyn to Mr Almosyner[72]	viij d

Summa iiij li vj s vj d ob

4li 6s 6d ob

---

[71] Latches and side-pieces (*stapulls*) for the door of the buttery. For *stapulls*, see Salzman, 258.

[72] Mr Almosyner probably refers to the Lord Almoner, Richard Rawlins, Warden of Merton College, who, according to Anthony Wood, *Athenae Oxonienses* (Oxford, 1691), 573, was made almoner to Henry VIII in succession to Cardinal Wolsey in 1514.

AUGUST/SEPTEMBER 1517

[*f. 12v; original f. 15v*]

This boke made from the xvj day off august
unto the xxx^{ti} day off the same monyth

lyme	Item paid to Elys larden for xxvij^{ti} quarterys off lyme att xiij d le quarter	xxviij s ij d
rag from	Item to Jasper for xxvj loodes caryage	xiij s
hedyngton	Item to Reede for xvij loodes	viij s vj d
	Item to Robert walton for xxxj^{ti} loodes	xv s vj d
	Item to harison for xx^{ti} loodes	x s
	Item to John francleyn for viij loodes	iiij s
	Item to townesend for vj loodes cariage	iij s
	Item paid to John francley [*sic*] for ij^C lakyng vij loodes	[*blank*]
~~tymber~~ bord from	Item paid to John townesend for the cariage off v^C iij^{xxti} and a xj footes off di' off bord [*sic*]	iij s iiij d
netylbed	Item to the same for the cariage off vj^C xxij footes	iiij s iiij d
	Item to the same for xxij loodes off pold stone	xiiij s
gravell	Item to the same Townesend for iij^{xxti} loodes vij off gravell	xvj s ix d
naylys	Item for di' thowsond iij penny nayle	xj d
	Item for x penny nayle	xvj d
	Item for bromys	v d

Summa vj li ij s iij d

6li 2s 3d

[*f. 13r; original f. 16r*]

This boke made ffrom the xxx^{ti} day
off August unto the xiij day off September

bord from netilbed	Item paid to John Townesend ffor xj^C xxvij^{ti} di' footes off planch bord	vj s viij d
	Item ffor the wryttyng off a payer off Indenturs	iij s iiij d
	Item ffor vj queyre off paper att ij d ob le queyre[73]	xv d
	Item ffor a boke off paper for to wryght yn the ymplementes off the college[74]	viij d
	Item ffor the byndyng off a boke off parchement	vj d

---

[73] A quire of paper comprised four sheets folded to form eight leaves.

[74] The entry refers to a book of paper purchased for writing ymplements. It is unclear whether this was an inventory of items acquired for the college or directives of some kind.

Smyth	Item to John A banckes for xxxij[ti] li off yorn ffor the wellys	iiij s viij d
	Item ffor iiij[C] broddys	vj s
ragg from	Item to bowdon ffor stone	xij d
hedyngton	Item to Townesend for ij loodes off ragg	iiij d
	Item to Jasper for xvij loodes carriage att vj d le loode \ij/[75]	~~viij s~~ ix s vjd
	Item to walton for xviij loodes	ix s
	Item to haryson for xviij loodes	ix s
	Item to knott for ij loodes	xij d
	Item paid to francleyn for xxxv[ti] loodes off ragg	iiij s vj d
	Item to the same francleyn for ij[C] loodes att xiij s iiij d le hundrid	xxvj s viiij d
freestone	Item ffor iiij loodes off ffreestone	iiij s
stooff from	Item ffor vj poyter[76] pottes wayng xxiiij[ti] pownd	
london	att v d le pownd	x s
	Item ffor a botery knyff[77]	xij d
	Item to the cariar for a C wayght cariage	xvj d
	Item a shovell for the kechyn[78]	xij d
naylys	Item ffor two thowsand di' off iij penny nayl	iiij s ij d
	Item ffor di' a thowsand off x penny nayll	iij s iiij d

Summa v li viij s xj d[79]

[~~4li 18s…~~]
5li 4s 11d

[f. 13v; original f. 16v]

This booke made from the xiij day off
September to the xxvj[ti] day off the same

lath	Item to lawcellatt for iij[Ml] lath att vj s viij d le M[l]	xx s
	Item to the same lawncellate ffor coveryng off the oven w[t] slate att x s the perch	ix s iiij d
bord from	Item paid to Townesend for the caryage off xj[C] xxviij[ti]	
netilbed	footes di' off planch bord	vj s viij d

---

[75] This 'ij' indicates an extra two loads, i.e. a total of nineteen loads.
[76] Pewter.
[77] Further items purchased for the kitchen namely pots and also a knife for the buttery.
[78] A shovel for use in the kitchen.
[79] This figure disagrees with the total in the bottom right-hand corner of the page by 4 shillings. The correct total is £5 4s 11d.

september 1517 / march 1517 (wages) 25

pavyar	Item paid to the same Townesend for the pavyng off the kechyn yard the which is xlij^ti perchis att vj d le perch[80]	xxj s
	Item to the same Townesend for the ryddyng off the strett	x s
gravell	Item to the same for xxvij^ti loodes off gravell	vj s viij d
rag from	Item to Jasper for xx^ti loodis off ragg cariage att vj d le lood	x s
hedinton	Item to Robert walton for xxij^ti loodes cari\a/ge	xj s
	Item to haryson for xiiij loodes caryage	vij s
	Item to banyster for x loodes caryage	v s
	Item to John ffrancleyn for di' hundred lood off ragg att xiij s iiij d le hundrid	vj s viij d
	Item to Townesend for xlvj^ti loodes off pold ragg	xxvij s ij d
	Item paid to bowdon for viij loodes off ragg	xiiij d
Smyth	Item for mendyng off the bokett	vj d
	Item for too polys off yorne	vj d
	Item for vj payer off gymmoys for the coope	iij s
	Item for iiij^C broddys di' att iij d le score	vj s ix d
	Item for mendyng off the saw	viij d
	Item for a newe bolt[81]	vj d
	Item ffor the byndyng off a parchment booke	vj d

Summa vij li xiiij s j d

[f. 14r; original f. 17r]

<1517>

This paymentt made ffrom the second day off March the viij yere off the Reigne off kyng herry the eygth unto the xv day off the same monyth

Carpenters	7[82]	Rychard threder		000000	iij s vj d
	7	John Browne for		000000	iij s vj d
	7	Cornell Clarke for	xxx000	000000	v s iij d
	7	Garratt bustard for		000000	iij s vj d
	6	Nicholas more		xx0000	ij s
	6	Thomas Mylton for		xx0000	ij s
	6	Jamys lenche for		x00000	ij s vj d
	6	John Smyth for	xxx000	c00000	iiij s iij d

---

[80] John Townesend is paid for paving the kitchen yard.
[81] Entries recording the mending of a bucket and a saw.
[82] These Arabic numerals in the margin represent the daily rate of pay.

~~prest~~ \paid/ vj s viij d	Item paid to Thomas lytyll and his fellow for sawyng off waynscott by the carffe att x s the C carves[83]				vj s ~~viiij~~ d[84]
sawyars	Item paid to Richard pytfed for slyttyng worke[85] by the C att xij d the C the sume off a C & iij q*uarter*				xxj d
row3ht mason	6	John Malowse for		oooooo	iij s
laborars	4	Symon holman for	xxoooo	oooooo	iij s iiij d
	4	harry horneclyff for	xxoooo	oooooo	iij s iiij d
	4	John Makyns for	xxoooo	oxoooo	iij s
	4	Nicholas herne for	xxxooo	xooooo	ij s vij d
	4	Cristofor Sexten for		oooooo	ij s
	4	John hobbys		xooooo	xx d
plast*er*ars	8	Wyllyam warleton for		oooooo	iiij s
	8	Gerrard Bodkyn for		oooooo	iiij s
	5	Roger whytte ther laborar for		oooooo	ij s vj d

Su*mm*a iij li ~~4s~~ iiij ~~d~~s[86]

Su*mm*a 3li 4s

[*f. 14v; original f. 17v*]

\r*egni* r*egis* h*enrici* 8^{vi} 8vo/

This payment made from the xv day off
March unto the xxx^{ti} day off the same monyth

Carpent*er*ys	:– 8	Thomas Threder	oooooo	oo(+)ooo[87]	vij s iiij d
	:– 7	John Browne	oooooo	oo(+)ooo	vj s v d
	:– 7	Cornell Clarke	o(+)oooo	oo(+)ooo	v s x d
	:– 7	Garratt bustard	oooooo	oo(+)ooo	vj s v d
	:– 7	Nicholas More	ocxxxx	xx(+)ooo	ij s vij d

---

[83] A carf denoted a cut in timber (*OED*). The reference to carffe or carves in this and subsequent entries, refers to the specialist cutting of timber in preparation for making scarf joints.

[84] The Roman v has been partially scratched out and altered to i, reducing the amount from 8d to 4d and accounting for the alteration in the Sum at the bottom of the page from £3 4s 4d to £3 4s.

[85] The process of *slyttyng* in this and subsequent entries refers to the slitting or splitting of wood into thin pieces.

[86] This sum was originally written iij li 4s iiij d. The 4s has been crossed out and the d overwritten as s.

[87] Threder and all the other workers on site rest on Wednesday 25 March, since this was a holy day, the feast of the Annunciation.

MARCH 1517

	:– 6 Thomas Mylton	ocxxxx	oo(+)ooo	iij s iiij d
	:– 6 James lench	oxoooo		ij s vj d
	:– 6 John Smyth	oxoooo		ij s vj d
	:– 6 Roger wryght	ooxooo	oo(+)ooo	v s
	:– 6 Richard makegood		oo(+)ooo	ij s vj d
	:– 6 wylliam kelly	oxoooo	oo(+)ooo	v s
	:– 6 John Avenell		oo(+)ooo	ijs vjd
Mason	John Smyth	xxoooo	oo(+)ooo	v s x d
plasterers	:– 8 wyllyam whorlton	oooooo	oo(+)ooo	vij s iiij d
	:– 8 Garratt bodkyn	oooooo	oo(+)ooo	vij s iiij d
leyars	:– 6 John Malow	oooooo	oo(+)ooo	v s vj d
	:– 6 david Eger		ccxxxx	vj d
	:– 6 Richard leyowse		oxxxxx	vj d

Sawyers :– Item paid to Thomas lytyll and his fellow for on
days labor   xij d
Item to the said Thomas for slyttyng worke att xij d le
hundred the summe off hundredes vj^C   vj s
Item payd to the same Thomas lytyll for C and di'
carfes off the which ~~is~~ he was paid vj s viiij d in prest   viij s viij d

Slatter   Rychard Ryley   xo   [blank]
   Rychard warner servus   xo   [blank]
Md' leyowse Item paid to Richard leyowse for his bargen before
wherein he receyvid xx s in prest \and for the makyng
off too dorys/   xiij s iiij d
   5li 7s 10d

[f. 15r; original f. 18r]

laborars	:– 5 Roger whytte	oooooo	oo(+)ooo	iiij s vij d
	:– 4 John Makyns	oooooo	oo(+)ooo	iij s viij d
	:– John Symons	oooooo	oo(+)ooo	iij s viij d
	:– Nicholas herne	oooooo	ox(+)ooo iij s ~~viij d~~ iiij d
	:– Xp'ofer Sexten	oooooo	oo(+)xoo	iij s iiij d
	:– Thomas yorden	oooxxx		xij d
	:– Wyllyam hobbys	oooooo	oo(+)ooo	iij s viij d
	:– Wylliam Sawnders	oooooo	oo(+)ooo	iij s viij d
	:– Wylliam Brytton	oooooo	oo(+)ooo	iij s viij d
	:– John Bull	ooxxx	co(+)ooo	ij s vj d
	:– John Smyth	oooooo	oo(+)ooo	iij s viij d
	:– John hobbys	oooooo	oo(+)ooo	iij s viij d

28   BUILDING ACCOUNTS OF CORPUS CHRISTI COLLEGE

    :— Mathewe owhen   xo(+)oxx   viij d

Item paid to Roger Morwentt ffor hys bargayn off v li for the sealyng off the parlower whereof he receyvid before vij s   xx s

Summa viij li ix s[88]

[7li..s..d] 8li 9s

[*f. 15v; original f. 18v*]

This paymentt made from the xxx[ti] day off March unto the ix[th] day off Aprell

carpenters	8	Thomas Threder	oooooo	oooo[89]	vj s viij d
	7	John Browne	oooooo	oooo	v s x d
	7	Nicholas More	oooooo	oooo	v s x d
	6	Richard makegood	oooooo	oooo	v s
	6	John Avenell	oooooo	oooo	v s
	6	Thomas Mylton	oooooo	oooo	v s
					\33s 4d/[90]
fremason		John Smyth	ooooxx		ij s vj d
leyars	6	Richard leyowse	xxoooo	oooo	iiij s
	6	John Malowse	oooooo	oooo	v s
	6	David Eger	oooooo	oooo	v s
	6	Richard heys	xxooxx	oooo	iij s
	5	harry perpoynt	xooooo	oo	ij s xj d
	6	John bond	xxoooo		ij s
	6	w hamond	oooooo	oooo	v s
	5	John stanley	xxoooo	oooo	iiij s[91]
	6	John spyllisby	xxoooo		ij s
plasterers		wylliam whorlton	oooooo	oooo	vj s viij d
		Garrate bodkyn	oooooo	oooo	vj s viij d
		Roger whyght	ooooooo	oooo	iiij s ij d
laborars		Symon holman	oooooo	ooooo	iij s viij d
		John Makyns	oooooo	oooo	iij s iiij d

[88] This total of ff. 14v and 15r is out by 1d and should actually be £8 8s 11d.
[89] Works appear to come to a standstill on Maundy Thursday, 9 April, 1517.
[90] Total for the carpenters, written in the right-hand margin.
[91] According to the number in the left-hand margin John Stanley was paid 5d a day, which would make a total of 40d, whereas he was paid 48d (4s). Perhaps he was paid a bonus for extra hours worked.

APRIL 1517

	Nycholas herne	oooooc	xxoo	ij s vj d
	Xpofor sexten	oooooo	oooo	iij s iiij d
	wylliam hobbys	oooooo	oooo	iij s iiij d
	John Smyth	oooooo	oooo	iij s iiij d
	wylliam brytter	oooooc	xxoo	ij s vj d
	Matheow owen	oooooo	oooo	iij s iiij d
	John wrykysham	oooooo	oooo	iij s iiij d
	Robert grove	xxooox	oooo	ij s iiij d
	Thomas yordan	xxoooo	oooo	ij s viij d
5li 19s 11d				[......d]

[f. 16r; original f. 19r]

sawyars	Item paid to thomas lytyll and his fellow for a C carffe off waynscott sawyng	xs
	Item to the same Thomas for ij^C slyttyng worke att xij d le C	ij s
Richard leyowse	Item paid to Richard leyowse ffor the making off the masteris wood howse by the perch att xij d le perch the summe off perchis xxiij^{ti}	xxiij s
Joyner	Item delyverid to Roger Morwentt the ixth day of Aprell for hys bargeyn off v li for the sealing off the masterys parlower whereoff he hath receyvid att too tymys xxvij s	xl s

Summa ix li xiiij s xi d

3li 15s

[f. 16v; original f. 19v]

This paymentt made from the xv day off
Aprell unto the xxv day off the same monyth

carpenterys	Richard Threder	ooo^{92}	ooo(+)o(+)^{93}	iiij s viij d
	John Browne	ooo	ooo(+)o(+)	iiij s j d
	Nicholas More	oox		xiiij d
	Thomas Mylton	oox	ooo(+)o(+)	iij s
	Richard makegood		ooo(+)o(+)	ij s

---

[92] Work on site resumes on Wednesday 15 April after Easter.
[93] The feast of St. George, patron of England, is celebrated on 23 April and the feast of St. Mark the Evangelist on 25 April. The holy days were originally marked with a black dot to indicate a day not worked, above which a cross was written to indicate it was not worked because it was a holy day/holiday.

30   BUILDING ACCOUNTS OF CORPUS CHRISTI COLLEGE

	John Avenell	ooo(+)o(+)	ij s
			\16s 11d/[94]
fremason	John Smyth	ooo(+)o(+)	ij s viij d
Joynerys	Item delyveryd to Roger Morwentt ffor the bargayn off sealyng off the masterys parlower whereoff he hath receyvid iij li vij s		ix s
rowyth layars	R leyowse	ooo	ooc(+)o(+)	iij s iij d
	w hamond	ooo		xviij d
	Davyth Eger	ooo		xviij d
	John Malowse	ooo	ooo(+)o(+)	iij s vj d
	John Spyllysby	ooo	ooo(+)o(+)	iij s vj d
	John Bond	o		vj d
plasterers	Garratt bodkyn	ooo	ooo(+)o(+)	iiij s viij d
	Thomas Tayler	ooo	ooo(+)o(+)	iiij s viij d
	John whorlton servus	ooo	ooo(+)o(+)	ij s xj d
sawyars	Item to Thomas lytyll and his fellow for vij^C slyttyng worke att xij d le C			vij s
	Item paid to John whyght and his fellow for vj^C slyttyng worke			vj s
pavyar	Item paid to Townesend for his bargen off the pavyng off the cowrte as hytt apperyth in the fyrst pay the which commyth to iiij li xiij s vj d whereoff he received iiij li vj s viij d			vj s viij d

[5..s..d]
3li 14s 3d [3li...3d]

[f. 17r; original f. 20r]

laborars	Symon holman	ooo	ooo(+)o(+)	ij s iiij d
	John Makyns	xoo	ooo(+)o(+)	ij s
	Nicholas herne	ooo	ooo(+)o(+)	ij s iiij d
	Xpofor sexten	ooo	ooo(+)o(+)	ij s iiij d
	w hobbys	ocx	ooo(+)o(+)	xxij d
	J Smyth	ooo	ooo(+)o(+)	ij s iiij d
	John brytton	ooo	ooo(+)o(+)	ij s iiij d
	Matheow owen	ooo	ooo(+)o(+)	ij s iiij d
	John ᵹ wrykysham	ooo	ooo(+)o(+)	ij s iiij d
	Richerd grove	oox	ooo(+)o(+)	ij s

[94] Total for the carpenters, written in the right-hand margin.

April/May 1517

Thomas iordan	ooo ooo(+)o(+)	ij s iiij d
Richerd Stevyns	ooo	xij d
wylliam whyght	ooo	xij d
		26s 6d[95]

Summa v li ix d

[*f. 17v; original f. 20v*]

<1517>   Thys paymementt [*sic*] made from the xxvj^{ti} day off Aprell
the ixth yere off the reigne off kyng henry the eyght
unto the ixth day off maij then nextt ensuyng

carpenterys	Richard Threder	oooo(+)o[96]	oooooo	vij s iiij d
	wylliam Colyns	oooo+o	oooooo	vij s iiij d
	John browne	oooo+o	oooooo	vj s v d
	Richard Makegood	oooo+o	oooooo	v s vj d
	Thomas Mylton	oooo+o	oooooo	v s vj d
	John avenell	oooo+o	oooooo	v s vj d
	John steyle	xooo+x		xviij d
				\29s 1d/[97]
Joyners	Robert Clerke		oooooo	iij s vj d
	peter vanderbye		oooo	ij s iiij d
	wylliam [*blank*]		oooo	ij s iiij d
rowyth layars	Richard leyowse	oo		xij d
	John Malowse	oooo+x	oooooo	v s
	John Spyllysbye	oooo+x	xoooxx	iij s vj d
sawyars	Item to Thomas lytyll and his fellow for the sawyng off a C carffe off waynscott			x s
	Item to the said Thomas for iij^C slyttyng worke di'			iij s iiij d
playsterers	Garratt bodkyn	oooo+o	oooooo	vij s iiij d
	Thomas Tayler	oooo+o	oooooo	vij s iiij d
	John whorlton	oooo+o	oooooo	iiij s vij d
Cornell	Item delyvered to cornell for his bargayn for the liberary as hytt apperyth on the backe of his Indenture			xiij s iiij d

---

[95] The total of this page, written in the right-hand margin.
[96] The feast of Ss Philip and James is celebrated on 1 May.
[97] Total for the carpenters, written in the right-hand margin. This sum is incorrect and should be 39s 1d.

R leyowse Item delyveryd to Richard leyowse for the makyng off the wall for the gloyster [sic] taskyd by the perch every perch being xviij footes in lengyth and a foote uppryght in part off payment[98]   ix s

5li 20d[99]

[f. 18r; original f. 21r]

laborars	Symon holman	oooo+o	oooooo	iij s viiij d
	wylliam brytton	oooo+o	oooooo	iij s viij d
	John makyns	oooo+x	oooooo	iij s iiij d
	Nicholas herne	oooo+o	ooox oo	iij s iiij d
	Xp'ofor sexten	oooo+o	oooooo	iij s viij d
	wylliam hobbys	oooo+o	ooox oo	iij s iiij d
	4 ob John Smyth	oooo+o	oooooo	iiij s
	4 ob wylliam wrykysham	oooo+o	oooooo	iiij s
	Robert grove	ooox+o		xvj d
	Matheow owen	oooo+o	oox ooo	iij s iiij d
	Thomas yorden	oooo+o		xx d

the dyggars Item paid to Nycholas herne and wylliam brytton for the
off the   dyggyng off lij perch for fowndacion att iij d le perch   xij s vj d
fowndacion

57s[⋯]10d
57s 10d[100]

Joynerys Item delyverid to Roger Morwentt for hys bargayn off v li for the sealyng off the masterys chamber   x s

~~Summa vijj li vij s x ix s~~

Summa viij li ix s vj d[101]

8li 9s [⋯]10d

---

[98] An entry recording a payment to Richard Lewis, for building the cloister wall.
[99] This total is incorrect because of the error under 'carpenterys' noted above and should be £5 11s 8d.
[100] The total for this page, both written in the right-hand margin.
[101] The total of ff. 17v and 18r. This total is correct, notwithstanding the error on f. 17v.

MAY 1517 33

[*f. 18v; original f. 21v*]

This payment made from the ix^(th) day off maij
unto the xxiiij^(ti) day off the same monyth

Carpenterys	R Threder	000000	000(+)oo[102]	vij s iiij d
	W Collyn	000000	000+oo	vij s iiij d
	J browne	000000	000+oo	vj s v d
	R makegood	ooxooo	000+oo	v s
	Item Avenell	ooxooo	000+oo	v s
	Thomas Mylton	000000	000+oo	v s vj d
	Nicholas more for viij dayis att ~~henly~~ netylbed			iiij s
				40s 7d[103]
rowyth layars	John Malowse	000000	ooc+oo	v s iij d
	wylli*a*m hamond	000000		iij s
	John Spyllysbye	000000	ooc+oo	v s iij d
plasterers	Garratt bodkyn	000000	000+oo	vij s iiij d
	Thomas Tayler	000000	000+oo	vij s iiij d
	J whorlton *servus*	000000	000+oo	iiij s vij d

sawyars	Item to Thomas lytyll and John Shyrt for iij q*ua*rter*ys*	
	off an hundred waynscottes sawyng aft*er* x s the hundred	vij s vj d
	Item to the said Thomas and his fellow for v^C slyttyng worke	v s
	Item to John whyght and Thomas whytakars for xv^C	
	slyttyng worke att xij d le hundred	xv s

laborars for the foundacion off the cloyster	Item paid to Nicholas herne and wylli*a*m Brytton for the dyggyng off the ffoundacion for the cloyster[104] by the perch ev*er*y p*er*ch co*n*teynyng xviij footes long and a foote depe havyng for ev*er*y perch iij d the su*m*me off perchys att this pay p*er*formyd […] xlvij^(ti)	xj s ix d

Richard leyowse	Item delyv*er*yd to Richard leyowse for the makyng off the towne wall and the wall abowght the ~~college~~ gloyst*er* taskyd in grett by the p*er*ch havyng for ev*er*y perch xij d and all man*ner* off stooff fond hym so delyv*er*yd this day as hytt apperyth by hys byll off co'menawnt	xxxj s

---

[102] The feast of the Ascension was celebrated on Thursday 21 May in 1517.
[103] Total for the carpenters, written in right-hand margin.
[104] Nicholas Herne and William Brytton are paid for digging the foundations of the cloisters.

34 BUILDING ACCOUNTS OF CORPUS CHRISTI COLLEGE

[*f. 19r; original f. 22r*]

laborars	Symon Holman	oooooo	ooo+oo	~~iij s iij d~~
				iij s viij d
	Xp'ofor sexten	oooooo	ooo+oo	iij s viij d
	John Makyns	ooxooo	ooo+oo	iij s iiij d
	Matheow owen	oooooo	ooo+oo	iij s viij d
	John wrykysh*a*m	oooooo	ooo+oo	iiij s j d ob
	John Smyth	ooooox	ooo+oo	iij s ix d
	John Maryn*er*	oooooo	ooo+oo	iij s viij d
	Thomas iordan		ooo+cx	xiiij d
				\~~8li 11d ob~~/[105]
pavyar	Item paid to John Townesend pavyar in ffull paymentt			
	off hys bargayn ffor the pavyng off the cowrte			xxj s ij d

Su*m*ma ix li ~~xj s vij d ob~~ xij s j d ob
9li ~~9s 4d ob~~ ix li xij s j d ob [..li...d ob]

[*f. 19v; original f. 22v*]

This paymentt made from the xxiiij[ti] daye off
maij unto xxxj[ti] day off the same monyth

carpent*ery*s	Richard Threder	oooooo	iiij s
	wyll*ia*m Colyn	oooooo	iiij s
	John browne	oooooo	iiij s
	Thomas Mylton	ooooc	ij s ix d
	John Avenell	ooooc	ij s ix d
	Richard makegood	ooooc	iij s ij d
rowth	John Malowse	ooooc	ij s ix d
layers[106]	Wyll*ia*m hamond	ooooc	ij s ix d
playst*er*ers	Garratt Bodkyn	oooooo	iiij s
	Thomas Taylor	oooooo	iiij s
	John whorlton s*er*vus	oooooo	ij s vj d

yoyn*er*s Item delyv*er*ed to Rog*er* Morwentt Robert More and
Rog*er* Gryffyth in p*ar*t off paymentt off theyr bargayn
for the sealyng off the chapell the lyb*er*ary and the

---

[105] Written in right-hand margin.

[106] *Rough layers*, also known as rough masons, were those masons who carried out some of the rough work and were somewhat less skilled than the freemasons. For the medieval rough layer or mason, see D. Knoop and G.P. Jones, *The Mediaeval Mason* (Manchester, 1933), 67.

MAY 1517   35

	masterys chamber according to theyr Indentyre	iij li
cornell	Item dedit to cornell the xxx^{ti} day off maij as hytt apperyth on the backe off hys Indenture	xiij s iiij d
Richard leyowse	Item delyveryd to Richard leyowse the xxx^{ti} day off maij for the makyng off the ~~gl~~ cloyster wall taskyd in grett by the perch	xl s
sawyars	Item paid to Thomas lytyll and his fellow for viij hundred slyttyng worke after xij d the hundred	viij s
	Item paid to John whyght and his fellow for iiij hundred slyttyng worke	iiij s

[f. 20r; original f. 23r]

laborars	Simon Holman	ooooo c	xxij d
	John makyns	ooooo c	xxij d
	Xp'ofor Sexten	ooooo x	xx d
	John Maryner	ooooo c	xxij d
	John Smyth	ooooo c	ij s
	John wrykysham	ooooo c	ij s
	Matheow owen	ooooo c	xxij d
	Thomas fforster	ooooo c	xxij d
dyggar off the foundacion	Item paid to Nicholas herne and wylliam Brytton for the dyggyng off the fowndacion off the cloyster by the perch every perch being xviij footes in lengyth and one foote depe the sume off perchis performyd att this pay be xlij^{ti} after iij d le perch		x s vj d

Summa ix li vij s iiij d[107]

\~~xviijs~~/

Summa Cv li xiiij s viij d[108] 2.

9li 7s 4d
8li 4s 10d

---

[107] The total of ff. 19v and 20r.
[108] The total of ff. 10v to 20r.

[*f. 20v; original f. 23v*]

This paymentt made from the thyrd day
off June unto the xxij day off the same monyth

carpenter*y*s	Richard Threder	ooo[109]	ooo+oo[110]	oooooo	ix s iiij d
	wyll*i*am Colyn	ooo	ooo+oo	oooooo	ixs iiij d
	John browne	ooo	ooo+oo	oooooo	viij s ij d
	Richard makegood	ooo	ooo+oo	oooooo	viij s ij d
	Thomas Mylton	ooo	ooo+oo	oooooo	vij s
	John Avenell	ooo	ooo+oo	oooooo	vij s
					\49s/[111]
rowyth layers	John Malowse	ooo	ooo+oo	oooooo	vij s
	John Schelman	ooo	ooo+oo		iiij s
plaste*r*ers	Garratt bodkyn	ooo	ooo+oo	oooooo	ix s iiijd
	Rog*er* whyght	ooo	ooo+oo	oooooo	ix s iiijd
	George wyllyngton	ooo	ooo+oo	oooooo	v s xd
	Simon holman	ooo	ooo+oo	oooooo	iiij s viij d
	John Makyns	ooo	ooo+oo	oooooo	iiij s viij d
	Xp'ofor Sexten	ooo	ooo+oo	oooooo	iiij s viij d
	Matheow owen	ooo	ooo+oo	oooooo	iiij s viij d
	John whrykysh*a*m	ooo	ooo+oo	oooooo	iiij s viij d
	John Smyth	ooo	ooo+oo	oooooo	v s iij d
	Nicholas herne	ooo		oooooo	iij s
	George Alye	ooo		oooooo	iij s
	wyll*i*am whyght	ooo	ooo+xo	oooooo	iiij s iiij d
	John yoyn*er*		ooo+oo	ooxxxo	ij s viij d
	Thomas yorden	xoo	ooo+xx	xxooxx	ij s iiij d

dyggars off the founacion [*sic*]	Item paid to the diggars off the foundac*i*on by the p*er*ch	vjs viij d
R*i*chard leyowse	Item delyv*er*ed to leyowse for the makyng off the walles abowght the college taskyd by the p*er*ch	iiij li

---

[109] Work on site resumed on Thursday 4 June after the holy days associated with the feast of Pentecost (Whitsun) on Sunday 31 May.
[110] Corpus Christi Day was celebrated on Thursday 11 June in 1517.
[111] Total for the carpenters, written in the right-hand margin.

[*f. 21r; original f. 24r*]

Cornell	Item paid to Cornell xxiiij day off June for his taske for the makyng off the lyberary as hytt apperyth by his indenture	xxvj s viij d
sawyars	Item paid to John whyght and Thomas whytakars for xj^C off slyttyng worke att xij d le C	xj s
	Item to Thomas lytyll and his fellow for x^C slyttyng worke	x s
	Item for xxv carves off waynscottes	ij s vj d

Summa xiij li ~~ix s iij d~~ v s iij d[112]

Summa omnium stipendiorum [...

~~14s~~

.3.[113] 118li 13s 1d   8s   13li 2s ..d

10s[114]

[*f. 21v; original f. 24v*]

This paymentt made ffrom the xxij day off
June to the iiij day off Julye

carpenterys	Richard Threder	00+000	+000000[115]	vj s viij d
	wylliam Colyn	00+000	+00000[116]	vj s viij d
	John Browne	00+000	+00000	v s x d
	Richard makegood	00+000	+00000	v s x d
	Thomas Mylton	00+000	+00000	v s
	John Avenell	00+000	+00000	v s
rowyth layers	Wylliam hamond	00+000	+0	iij s
	David Eger	oc		ix d
	John Malowse	00+000	+00000	v s
	John Gossopp	ox+		vj d

[112] The total for f. 20v and f. 21r.
[113] The third long accounting period starts at this opening.
[114] The numbers in these two rows clearly form part of a calculation but elude interpretation. It may be that the £118 13s 1d is an attempt to add the current pay period to the preceding long accounting period. If that is the case then the clerk has made a mistake as the total would be £118 19s 11d.
[115] Apparently entered in error and subsequently deleted.
[116] The feast of St. John the Baptist is celebrated on 24 June and the feast of Ss Peter and Paul on 29.

	Garrate bodkyn	oo+ooo	+ooooo	vj s viii d
	George wyllyngton	oo+ooo	+ooooo	iiij s ij d
	Simon holman	oo+ooo	+ooooo	iij s iiij d
	John makyns	oo+ooo	+ooooo	iij s iiij d
	Xp'ofor sexten	oo+ooo	+ooooo	iij s iiij d
	Matheow owen	öo+ooo[117]	+ooooo	iij s ij d
	John wrykysham	oo+ooo	+ooooo	iij s ix d
	John Smyth	oo+ooo	+ooooo	iij s iiij d
	Nicholas herne	oo+xoo	+ooooo	iij s
	w whyght	oo+ooo	+ooooo	iij s iiij d

sawyars   Item paid to Thomas lytyll and his fellow for a C waynscottes sawyng   x s

Item to the said Thomas for ij^C di' slyttyng worke att xij d le C   ij s vj d

Item to wylliam poys and his fellow for ij^C di' off slyttyng worke   ij s vj d

[f. 22r; original f. 25r]

Joynerys   Item paid to the Joyners the ~~x~~ iiij off July for ther bargain as hytt apperyth on ther Indenture   xxvj s

Cornell   Item paid to Cornell the iiij off ~~Jun~~lij att [sic] as hytt apperyth by hys Indenture   xx s

leyowse   Item paid to Richard leyow for hys co'menawnt off making off all manner off walles abowght the college by the perch havyng for every perch as hytt aperyth by hys co'menawntt   iij li

slatter   Item paid to lawncelatt the slatter for coveryng off the ij drawghtes the poltery howse and Mr Presydentes wood howse in grett by the perch prest   iij li

Item to the same slatter for dyverse reperacions don abowght the howse att [sic] hytt apperyth by a byll   xviij s vj d

dyggars off the fowndacion   Item paid to the dyggars off the fowndacion for iij^{xx} ij perchys att iij d the perch wheroff they receyvid vjs viijd   viij s x d

Summa xiiij li ~~xv s~~ x s

14 10s   14li 10s

---

[117] ö is used at this point in the original, apparently to indicate a half-day worked. It is the only occurrence of this symbol.

JULY 1517 39

[f. 22v; original f. 25v]

This pay made ffrom the iiijth day off Julij
unto the xviijth day off the same monyth

carpenterys	Richard Threder	0+0000	00+000[118]	vj s viij d
	Wylliam Colyn	0+0000	00+000	vj s viij d
	John Browne	0+0000	00+000	v s x d
	Richard makgood	0+0000	00+xoo	v s iij d
	John Avenell	0+0000	00+xxo	iiij s
	Thomas Mylton	0+0000	00+000	v s ij d
	Thomas gyttens	0+0000	00+000	v s
rowth layers	John Malowse	0+0000	00+xoo	iiij s vj d
	wylliam hamond	0+0000	xx	ij s vj d
plasterers	Garratt bodkyn	0+000x\o/	00+000	vj s viij d
	George Wyllyngton	0+0000	00+000	iiij s ij d
laborars	Symon holman	0+0000	00+000	iij s iiij d
	John Makyns	0+0000	00+000	iij s iiij d
	Xp'ofor Sexten	0+0000	00+000	iij s iiij d
	Matheowe owen	0+0000	00+xoo	iij s iiij d
	John wrykysham	0+0000	xx+oxo	ij s iiij d
	wylliam whyght	0+0000	ox+ooo	iij s
	John Smyth	x+0000	ox+oox	ij s iiij d
	Nicholas herne	0+xooo	xx+xoo	ij s
	George alye	x+xooo	oo	xx d
	wylliam brytton	x+oooo		xvj d

Sawyars Item to Thomas lytyll for a hundrid waynscottes carfys sawyngx s
Item to Richard Pyttfyld for vij^C slyttyng worke   vij s
More Item delyveryd to Rychard morere [sic] for bord
sawyng att netylbed and for drawyng off tymber to the pytt   x s
Joyners Item delyveryd to the yoyners the xv day off Julij as
hytt apperyth by ther Indenturys   xx s

---

[118] The feast of the Translation of St. Thomas of Canterbury was celebrated on 7 July and the feast of St. Swithun on 15th of that month.

40 BUILDING ACCOUNTS OF CORPUS CHRISTI COLLEGE

[*f. 23r; original f. 26r*]

leyowse	Item delyveryd to Richard leyowse for the makyng off all manner off rowy3ht warke abowght the college \by the perch/	~~xxxvj~~ s viij d
cornell	Item delyveryd to cornell the xviij day off Julij	xx s

Summa viij li xvj s j d

8li 16s 1d

[*f. 23v; original f. 26v*]

Thys pay made from the xviij[th] day off
July unto the second day off August

Carpenterys	Richard Threder	oo+xx+	xooooo[119]	v s
	wylliam Colyn		xcoooo	iij s ij d[120]
	John Browne		xxoooo	ij s iiij d
	Thomas Gyttens	oo+oo+	oooooo	v s
	Richard makegood	oo+ox+	xxoooo	iiij s j d
	Thomas Mylton	oo+oo+	oooooo	v s
	John Avenell	oo+ox+	xxoooo	iij s vj d
	John Grymshave		xooooo	xij d
rowyth masons	John Malowse	oo+xo+	xxoooo	iij s vj d
	wylliam hamond		xxoooo	ij s
laborars	Symon holman	oo+oo+	oooooo	iij s iiij d
	John Makyns	oo+oo+	oooooo	iij s iiij d
	X'pofor Sexten	oo+oo+	cxoooo	ij s x d
	Matheow owen	oo+oo+	oooooo	iij s iiij d
	John wrykysham	oo		viij d
	John Smyth	oo+oo+o		xx d
	wylliam whyght	oo+oo+	oooxxx	ij s iiij d
	George Alye		ooooc	xviij d
sawyars	Item Richard Pytfyld for iiij[C] slyttyng worke ~~ax~~ att xij d le hundred			iiij s

[119] The feast of St. Mary Magdalen is celebrated on 22 July and St. James the Great on 25 July.

[120] Richard Threder and William Colyn were normally paid 8d per day, but the figures in this column do not equal the sum of days worked at the rate of 8d per day, so they would appear to have been paid a bonus or a slightly higher day rate. Richard Threder was paid 5s (60d) for seven days' work instead of 4s 8d (56d), and William Colyn 3s 2d (38d) for four and a half days' work instead of 3s (36d).

JULY/AUGUST 1517

	Item for di' a hundrid carvys	v s
	Item to Thomas lytyll for ~~di' a~~ iij^C slyttyng worke	iij s
	Item to the same for di' a hundrid carvys	v s
leyowse	Item delyveryd to Richard leyowse the fyrst day off August as hytt apperyth by hys letter off cowenawnt for the makyng off the walles by the perch	xl s
	Item paid to Roger Morwent for the sealyng off the neyther study in the masterys logyng by the yard att vj d the yarde the some off yardes xxvj	xiij s

[*f. 24r; original f. 27r*]

Cornell	Item delyveryd to Cornell the fyrst day off August for hys bargayn as hytt apperyth by hys indenture	vj s viij d
the dyggars off the foundacion	Item paid to the dyggars off the fowndacion by the perch att iij d the perch the summe off perchys ~~x~~ iij^{xx} ij	xv s vj d
slatter	Item paid to lawncellate the slatter for xiiij teerse and an halffe off slattyng he fyndyng all manner off stoof every teerse beyng x footes square havyng for every teerse x s whereoff he receyvid iiij li before	iiij li v s

Summa xj li x s ix d

11 li 10s 4d
8d

[*f. 24v; original f. 27v*]

Thy paymed [*sic*] made from the second day off August
unto the xvj day off the same monyth

carpenterys				
	Richard Threder	oooooo	+oooo(+)[121]	vj s viij d
	w Colyn	oooooo	+oooo+	vj s viij d
	J browne	oooooo	+oooc+	v s vj d
	R makegood	oooooo	+oooc+	vs vj d
	Thomas gyttens	oooooo	+oooc+	iiij s ix d
	Thomas Mylton	oooooo	+ooox+	iiij s vj d
	J Avenell	oooooo	+oooc+	iiij s ix d

---

[121] The feast of St. Lawrence is celebrated on 10 August and the Assumption of the Virgin Mary on the 15 August. Against Richard Threder's name on the feast of the Assumption the clerk originally marked a black dot, to indicate a normal day not worked, which he overwrote with a cross, to change it to a holy day.

rowyth	John Malowse	oooooo	+oooc+	iiij s ix d
masons	wyll*i*am hamond	oooooo	+oxxx+	iij s vj d
	It*e*m paid to Colyn for his coostes to netylbed			viij d
	Garratt bodkyn	xxxxxo	+oooc+	iij s viij d
laborars	Symon holman	oooooo	+oooc+	iij s ij d
	John Makyns	oooooo	+oooc+	iij s ij d
	Xp'ofor sexten	oooooo	+oooc+	iij s ij d
	wyll*i*am whyte	oooooo	+oooc+	iij s ij d
	John Smyth	xxxxoo	+oooc+	xxij d
	Nicholas herne	o	+oooc+	xviij d
	George Alye	oc	+oooc+	xx d
	wyll*i*am bryttayn	oc	+ococ+	xviij d
slatt*er*	lawncellate	oooo		ij s
	wyll*i*am looder	oooo		xvj d
More to the sawyars att netylbed	It*e*m delyv*e*ryd to the sawyars att netylbed for sawyng off bord			xiij s iiij d
sawyars	It*e*m paid to John whyte for vj^C slyttyng worke att xij d le C			vj s
	It*e*m to the same John ffor q*uarter* \off/ a hundrid carvys off waynscottes			ij s vj d
the dyggars off the foundac*i*on	It*e*m paid to the dyggars off the fowndac*i*on for xxix^{ti} p*er*ch taskyd in grett by the perch iij d for a p*er*ch			vij s iiij d

[*f. 25r; original f. 28r*]

leyowse	It*e*m delyv*e*ry [*sic*] to Richard leyowse for hys bargayn off makyng off all man*ner* off rowyth worke by the perch	xl s
warde	It*e*m delyv*e*ryd to John ward the xv day off august ffor the makyng off the wyndoys off <u>the cloyster</u> and <u>off the chamber</u>ys as many as nede to the same worke taskyd by grett	xx s
Joyn*e*rys	It*e*m delyv*e*ryd to the yoyn*e*rys the xv day off august	xx s

S*umm*a ix li ✖ ij s vij d

8li 21d
[..li..8s..5d]^{122}

---

[122] Both these entries are faint and may represent earlier attempts to total these two pages.

AUGUST/SEPTEMBER 1517 43

[*f. 25v; original f. 28v*]

Thys pay made from the xvj day off August
unto the xxx^{ti} day off the same monyth

carpenterys	Richard Threder	oooooo	+oooooo[123]	vij s iiij d
	w Colyn	oooooo	+ooooo[124]	vij s iiij d
	R makegood	oooooo	+ooooo	vj s v d
	J browne	oooooo	+ooooo	vj s v d
	T Mylton	oooooo	+ooooo	v s vj d
	J Avenell	oooooo	+ooooo	v s vj d
	Antony	oooooo	+ooooo	v s vj d
	J Malowse	oxxxoo	+ooooo	iiij s
laborars	S holman	oooooo	+ooooo	iij s viij d
	Nicholas hernene [*sic*]	oooooo	+xoooo	iij s iiij d
	w brytton	oooooo	+ooooo	iij s viij d

Richard   Item delyveryd to Richard leyowse the xxix^{ti} day
leyowse   off g agust [*sic*] ffor his bargayn taskyd by grett   xxxiij s iiij d
sawyars   Item to John whyte for sawyng di' C cawnt carves   v s
     Item to the same John for v^C slyttyng work   v s
Joyners   Item delyveryd to the ioyners the xxix^{ti} day off august
     as hytt apperyth on theyr byll off co'menawntt   xxxvj s viij d
\More/
sawyars att   Item sent to the sawyars att netylbed   xiij s iiij d
netylbed

Summa vij li xij s

~~7li 12s 4d~~
7li 11s 6d

[*f. 26r; original f. 29r*]

Thy [*sic*] pay made ffrom the xxx^{ti} day off
august unto the xiijth day off September

carpenterys	Richard Threder	oooooo	o+oooo[125]	vij s ~~viiij~~ d
	wylliam Colyn	oooooo	o+oooo	vij s iiij d
	John Browne	oooooo	o+oooo	vj s v d

---

[123] Apparently entered in error and subsequently deleted.
[124] The feast of St. Bartholomew is celebrated on 24 August.
[125] The feast of the Nativity of the Virgin Mary is celebrated on 8 September.

44   BUILDING ACCOUNTS OF CORPUS CHRISTI COLLEGE

	Richard Makegood	000000	0+0000	vj s v d
	Thomas Mylton	000000	0+0000	v s vj d
	John Avenell	000000	0+0000	v s vj d
	Antony	000000	0+0000	v s vj d
	John Malowse	000000	0+0000	v s
laborars	Symon holman	000000	0+0000	iij s viij d
	Nicholas herne	000000	x+0000	iij s iiij d
	wylliam brytton	000000	0+0000	iij s viij d

leyose Item delyverid to Richard leyowse the xiijth day off September xl s
yoyners Item delyvered to the ioyners the same day as hitt
   apperith by ther indenturs   xl s
sawyars Item to Richard pytfyld for a C di' off waynscott
   carvys sawyng att x s the hundred   xv s
   Item to the same for an hundred slyttyng worke xij d
   Item to John sawyar for vij^C di' xvj footes off slyttyng
   worke   vij s viij d
   Item for di' a hundred carves off waynscott   v s

    Summa viij li viij s iiij d

                  ~~8li~~ 7s 11d
                  8li 8s 4d

[f. 26v; original f. 29v]

  Thys payment made ffrom the xiij day off September
   to the xxvj^{ti} daye off the same monyth

Carpenterys	Richard Threder	0(+)0000[126]	0+0000	~~vij s iiij d~~ vj s viij d
	wylliam Colyn	0(+)0000	~~0+0000~~	~~vij s iiij d vj s viij d~~
				iij s iiij d[127]
	John browne	0(+)0000	0+0000	~~vj s v d~~ v s x d
	Antony	0+0000	0+0000	v s
	John Malowse	0+0000	0+0000	v s
laborars	Simon holman	0+0000	0+0000	iij s iiij d
	Nicholas herne	0+0000	0+x000	iij s
	wylliam brytton	0+0000	0+0000	iij s iiij d

[126] The second day of this week in the entries for Richard Threder, William Colyn and John Browne originally marked with 'o' to indicate a working day and then overwritten with a cross to indicate a feast day. The feasts of the Exultation of the Holy Cross and St. Matthew are celebrated on 14 and 21 September respectively.

[127] Written in right-hand margin.

SEPTEMBER/OCTOBER 1517 45

Richard leyowse	Item delyveryd to Richard leyowse in part off paymentt for the makyng off the wallys abowght the ~~cloyster~~ college	xl s
edmond more	Item paid to Edmond more for the makyng off my lord off Exciterys armys	vj s viij d
sawyars	Item paid to Richard Pytfyld and hys servant for a hundred a halff off waynscott carves sawyng att x s the hundred	xv s
	Item to John whyght and his fellow for iij^c slyttyng worke	iij s
Joyners	Item delyveryd to the Joyners ffor ther bargayn off seallyng off the chapell and the lyberary	iij li

Summa viij li ij d

8li 2d

[f. 27r; original f. 30r]

This Booke made from the xxvj day off
September to the xth day of October

carpenterys	Richard Threder	0+0000[128]	000000	vij s iiij d
	wylliam Colyn	0+0000	000000	vij s iiij d
	John Browne	0+0000	000000	vj s v d
	Antony	0+0000	000000	v s vj d
	John Malowse	x+0000	000000	v s
laborars	Simon holman	0+0000	000000	iij s viij d
	Nicholas herne	0+0000	0c0000	iij s vj d
	William Brytten	0+0000	000000	iij s viij d
R leyowse	Item to Richard leyowse for the makyng off the walles by the perch			iij li
Joyners	Item delyverid to the Joyners as hytt apperyth by ther Indenture			iij li
Sawyars	Item to Richard pytfyld for a C di' off waynscott carvys sawyng att x s the hundrid			xv s
ragg from hedyngton	Item to Jasper for xxj loodes cariage off ragg att vj d le lood			x s vj d
	Item to John wase for vij loodes cariage			iij s vj d
	Item to haryson for xj loodes			v s vj d
	Item to walton for xvij loodes			viij s vj d
	Item to banyster for ix loodes			iiij s vj d

[128] The feast of St. Michael the Archangel (Michaelmas) is celebrated on 29 September.

	Item to Townesend for viij loodes off pold ragg	v s
	Item to bowdon for stone from magdaleyn college pytt	ix d
tymber from netylbed bord from netilbed	Item to Townesend for a lood tymber caryage off li footes di' delyveryd att magdaleyn college	iij s iiij d
	Item to the same for the caryage off vj^C xxvj footes off bord	iij s iiij d
gravell	Item to Townesend for ix loodes off gravell att iiij d le loode	ij s ~~ix d~~ iij d
beddes	Item to Robert Carow for vij beddes att ij s the peese[129]	xiiij s
		11li 18s 7d

[*f. 27v; original f. 30v*]

Smyth	Item for hoopes to the barell off the well	xij d
	Item for iij stapulles	iij d
	Item for byndyng off the bokett w^t the cheyne	ij s iiij d
	Item for thre plates to the chaple dore	iij d
	Item for ij hookes and hynges waying vj li di'	xj d ob
	Item for iij gymnois(?)[130] for the dresser	ix d
	Item for a bolt to the chapell dore	iiij d
	Item for xxiij li di' off yorne worke	iij s xj d
	Item for xx boltes and stapulles for wyndoys	iij s
	Item for Roopys to the well	xijd

Summa xij li xij s iiij d ob

[~~..s..d..ob~~]
13s 9d ob

[*f. 28r; original f. 31r*]

This boke made from the xth day off Octobre to the xxiiij day off the same

Carpenter	Richard Threder	0+0000	+00000[131]	vj s viij d
	w Colyn	0+0000	+00000	vj s viij d
	John Browne	0+0000	+00000	v s x d
	Antony	0+0000	+000xx	iiij s

---

[129] Carow is paid for making a further seven beds at 2s each.
[130] Hinges for a dresser.
[131] The feast of St. Edward the Confessor is celebrated on 13 October and the feast of St. Frideswide is celebrated on 19 October.

OCTOBER 1517

	J Malowse	0+0000	+xxcoo	iij s ix d
laborars	Simon holman	0+00x0	+00000	iij s
	Nicholas herne	0+x000	+00000	iij s
	William Brytton	0+0000	+00000	iij s iiij d

leyowse	Item delyveryd to Richard leyowse for the making off the wallys by the perch att xij d the perch	iij li
sawyars	Item to ~~Jasper~~ Richard Pitfyld for di' C waynscottes carvys	v s
	Item to the same for ij^C slyttyng worke	ij s
lyme	Item paid to Elys larden for xxxvijj^{ti} quarteris off lyme att xiij d le quarter allowyng xxj for xx	xxxix s
	Item to Jasper for xij loodes off ragg caryage att vj d le lood	vj s
	Item to walton for xiij loodes caryage	vj s vj d
	Item to banyster for v loodes	ij s vj d
	Item to haryson for xj loodes	v s vjd
	Item to Johon [sic] wase for xvj loodes	viij s
17 debet 8(?)	Item paid to John ffrancleyn for a hundrith loodes off ragg	xiij s iiij d
	Item to the same John for iiij loodes off ffreeston	iiij s
gravell	Item paid to John Townesend for xlvj loodes off gravell att iij d le loode	xj s vj d
		9li 19s 7d

[*f. 28v; original f. 31v*]

tymber from netilbed	Item to John Townesend for the cariage off xliiij footes off tymber	iij s iiij d
	Item for xvij loodes off pold ragg	ix s iiij d
	Item for a bawdryke and a roope for the bell[132]	iiij d
Smyth	Item for vj stapulles	vj d
	Item for xxxj boltes and stapulles for wyndoys	vj s ij d
	Item for iiij hookes and too hengys	vj d
	Item for v lachys and kachys[133]	xx d
	Item for ij^C broddys di'	iij s ix d
	Item for a cheyne[134] to the chapell bell	ij s vj d
	Item for ij peesys off yorne to the same	iij d
	Item to the cooper for too bokettes and the mendyng off an old bokett	xvj d

---

[132] A baldric is a leather strap for connecting a clapper to the inside of a bell.
[133] Latches and catches.
[134] Chain.

48 BUILDING ACCOUNTS OF CORPUS CHRISTI COLLEGE

More	Item delyveryd to more for the sawyars att netilbed	xviij s iiij d
	Item ffor naylis	ij s vj d
Smyth	Item paid to John A bankes for the parcelles conteynyd in thes too byllys to the summe off iiij li xiiij s ob off the which he receyvid in prest the xviij day off Julye xxx s as hytt apperith in this boke and now for the full payment off this	iij li iiij s

Summa xv li xiiij s j d

.3.
x   xx d[135]

.3.   Summa C ix li xj s vij d ob[136]

5li 14s 6d[137]

[*The stubs of two folios follow between this and the following folio. There are remains of writing on the verso of the first stub.*]

[*f. 29r; original f. 32r*]

This boke made from the xxv day off october
unto the vijth day off november

	Richard Threder	oo(+)xxx[138]	+xoooo[139]	iiij s
	wylliam Colyn	oo+ooo	+ooooo	vj s iiij d[140]
	John Browne	oo+xxx	+ooooo	iij s vj d
	John Malowse	oo+ooc	+ooooo	iiij s ix d
laborars	Simon holman	oo+ooc	+ooooo	iij s ij d
	Nicholas herne	oo+ooo	+ooooo	iij s ij d
	George Aley	[oo+ooo][141]	+ooooo	xx d
	Robert wyld	xx+xxx	+xxxoo	viij d
Sawyars	Item Richard pytfyld for di' C waynscottes sawyng			v s
	Item to the same for ij^C di' off slyttyng worke			ij s ~~vj~~ vj d

---

[135] These figures elude interpretation.
[136] The total of ff. 20v–28v, Thursday 4 June to Saturday 24 October 1517.
[137] The total for this page.
[138] The top half of this page is heavily stained but largely legible with the assistance, in places, of ultraviolet light. The original, indeterminable, symbol on the third day of this week overwritten with a cross to indicate a holy day; the feast of Ss Simon and Jude.
[139] The feast of All Souls is celebrated on 2 November.
[140] William Colyn was normally paid 8d a day. It is possible that he worked nine and a half days during this period, when he would have been paid 6s 4d (76d).
[141] This reading is uncertain due to staining of the paper. If George Aley worked five days this week, then he was paid only 2d a day over the fortnight.

OCTOBER/NOVEMBER 1517

Cornell	Item to cornell for the makyng off the~~xys~~ \dextes/ in y^e liberary	x s
More	Item to Richard more for the sawyars att netylbed	v s
rag from hedyngton	Item to Robert walton for xij loodes caryage off ragg att vj d le loode	vj s
	Item to the same for iij loodes off freeston caryage	xviij d
	Item to Jasper wase ffor xj loodes cariage	v s vj d
	Item to haryson ffor v loodes caryage	ij s vj d
	Item to John wase for vij loodes caryage	iij s vj d
	Item paid to John francleyn for halffe a hundryth loodes off ragg	vj s viij d
	Item to the same John for iij loodes off ffree stone	iij s
ferne	Item to Jasper for ij loodes off ferne to cover the walles	ij s
	Item to walton for a loode of ferne[142]	xij d
	Item to John Townesend for iiij loodes off pold ragg	ij s iiij d
gravell	Item to the same John for iij loodes off gravell	ix d
	Item to Jasper waase [sic] for xliiij footes off tymber caryage from netilbed	iij s iiij d
tymber from Netilbed	Item to John Townesend for xlvij footes caryage	iij s iiij d
	Item to John wase for xlv^{ti} footes caryage	iij s iiij d
bord from netilbed	Item to John Townesend ffor v^C xlij^{ti} footes di' off bord caryage	iij s iiij d
dryppyng pans	Item ffor ij dryppyng pannys[143]	ij s iiij d
	Item ffor a frying pan	xiiij d
paper	Item ffor a reame off paper	ij s iiij d

.4.

[*f. 29v; original f. 32v*]

lyme	Item paid to Elys larden for xxxviij^{ti} quarterys off lyme att xiij d le quarter allowyng xxj for xx^{ti}	xxxix s
John ward	Item paid to John warde free mason for the makyng off the wyndoys off the cloyster and the chamberys as hytt apperith in a byll off cowenawnt	iij li
Smyth	Item for iij^C broddys att xviij d the hundrith	iiij s vj d

---

[142] Fern purchased to cover and therefore protect the upper parts of the incomplete walls from frost.

[143] Pans purchased for the kitchen, including two dripping pans to catch the drips from meat roasting on a spit.

	Item a bolt and a stapull to M^r presydent is wod howse	
	waying iij li att j d ob qua le pownd	v d
	Item ffor a staple to the aple howse	j d
	Item ffor iij lachis and kachis	x d
ffrom the	Item ffor xx^{ti} payer off tynnyd garnettes	
Smyth	price the payer viij d	xiij s iiij d
att london	Item ffor the Joynterys to ~~ley cooper~~ y^e triangle	v s x d
Carver	Item delyveryd to humfrey cooke to pay the carver off	
off the	the knottes ffor the chaple att <u>xvj d</u> le peese carvyng	
knottes	the some of knottes an <u>hundrith xij in prest</u>	
	\off the summe off vij li ix s iiij d/[144]	iij li
	Item paid ffor waynscottes to carve them on	xvj s viij d
	Item ffor a coote cloth gevyn to John ward fremason	viij s
w vertue	Item to M^r vertue for vj dayis being here and rydyng	
	to the quarre off taynton att xx d le day	x s
h Cooke	Item to humfray Cooke for viij days att xx d le day	xiij s iiij d
	Item ~~a grett~~ for the horse heyre y^t he roode on for wood	iiij d
R leyowse	Item delyveryd to Richard leyowse the xxviij da off octobre	v li
Joyners	Item to the Joynerys as hytt apperith on ther indenture	vj li

Summa xxvij li xvj s

[f. 30r; original f. 33r]

This booke made from the vijth day off novembre
unto the xxij day of the same moneth

Carpenterys	Richard Threder	oooooo	oxoooo	vij s iiij d
	wyllyam Colyn	oooooo	oooooo	viij s
	John Browne	oooooo	oxoooo	vj s vj d
	John Avenell		oooo	xx d
laborars	Simon holman	oooxxx	oxoooo	ij s iij d
	Nicholas herne	oocxxx	oxoooo	~~xij~~ xxij d ob
	william Brittayne		xxxooo	xj d
	Xp'ofor sexten	oocxxx	oxoooo	xxij d ob
	Robert wyld	oocxxx	oxoooo	xxij d ob
	George Alye	oocxxx	oxoooo	xxij d ob

[144] The knotts referred to in this entry are the wooden bosses that were made to ornament the ceiling in the college chapel.

NOVEMBER 1517

Sawyars	Item to Richard pittfeld for a qu*arter* of a hundrith off waynscottes sawyng	ij s vj d
More	Item to Richard More for the sawyars att netilbed	xx s
ragg	Item to Jasp*er* wase for xiij loodes of ragg car*riage*	vj s vj d
	Item to John wase for xiiij loodes of ragg and on fre	vij s vj d
	Item to Rob*er*t walton for xij loodes of ragg	vj s
	Item to haryson for x loodes caryage	v s
	Item to townesend for iiij loodes	ij s
	Item to John ffrancleyn for a quar*ter* off hundrith ragg	iij s iiij d
	Item to the same for on loode of fre	xij d
	Item to townesend for vij loodes of pold ragg	iiij s iiijd
Cornell	Item paid to cornell for a small end of hys bargayn for the makyng of the dextes in the lib*er*ary	xiij s iiij d
	Item for candellys for carpent*er*ys[145]	viij d
	Item for seallyng nayle	ij s viij d
	Item for roopys bowght of the clarkes of M*er*ton college[146]	xij d

[*f. 30v; original f. 33v*]

Smyth	Item v^C broddys att xviij d the hundrith	vij s
	Item for iij Stapullys	iij d
	Item for makyng off iiij payer of pott hookes	ix d
	Item for vj spykyns	vj d
Richard leyowse	Item to Ric*hard* leyowse rowyth mason	xx s
Joyn*er*ys	Item to the Joyn*er*ys the xxij day of novembre	xl s
	Item delyv*er*yd to Rob*er*t Carowe att the seallyng off his Indenture made for the makyng off halff the cloyst*er* w^t the chamb*er*ys over the same as hitt apperyith by hys Indenture	x li

Su*mm*a ~~xix li vj s j d~~ xviij li xviij s vj d

20 5s 1d

~~1242~~li 13s 5d ob[147]   18li 18s 6d

---

[145] Candles purchased for the carpenters at work inside the college buildings.
[146] Ropes bought from the clerk of Merton College, which is adjacent to Corpus Christi.
[147] Apparently originally written 122li then the first 2 overwritten as 4, to produce 142li, although it has not been established as to what it refers.

[*f. 31r; original f. 34r*]

This booke made from the xxij^{ti} day off nevember [*sic*] unto the vth day off Decembre

Carpenterys	Richard Threder	oo+ooo	+ooooo[148]	vj s viij d
	william Colyn	oo+ooo	+ooooo	vj s viij d
	John Browne	oo+ooo	+ooooo	v s x d
	John Avenell	oo+ooo	+ooooo	iij s viij d
laborars	Simon holman	oo+ooo	+ooooo	ij s vj d
	Nicholas herne	oo+oxx	+ooooo	ij s
	william bryttayn	oo+ooo	+ooooo	ij s vj d
	George Alye	oo+ooo	+ooooo	ij s vj d

	Item to Richard pyttfeld for a quarter off a hundrith carvesij	s vj d
	Item ffor a hundrith slyttyng worke	xij d
ragg from	Item to Jasper wase for ix loodes caryage att vj d le lood	iiij s vj d
hedyngton	Item to John wase for x loodes caryage	v s
	Item to walton for iiij loodes caryage	xviij d
	Item to haryson for iiij loodes and on of free ston	ij s vj d
leyowse	Item delyveryd to Richard leyowse	xx s
	Item to John Townesend for vij loodes off pold ragg	iiij s
gravell	Item to the same John ffor viij loodes off gravell	ij s
Smyth	Item paid to the Smyth ffor a hundrith wayght off yorn ther be viij barrys[149] and off that he is owyng xxiiij li	xvj s iiij d
Joynerys	Item delyveryd to the Joynerys as hytt apperyth by hys Indenture	iij li
	~~Item to the same Joynerys~~	~~xx s~~
	Item hys rydyng y^t rode for warde	vj d
lockys from	Item oon locke for the <u>bowsery</u> dore w^t iij keys price	iij s
london	Item oon locke for the <u>ynner</u> dore off the bowsery	xx d
	Item too lockes for the tresar howse dore price	iij s iiij d
	Item for iiij stock lockes at viij d le peese	ij s viij d
More	Item delyveryd to william Colyn and Nicholas More	
Colyn	att the seallyng off ther Indenture made for the frame off halffe the cloyster as hytt apperyth in the same Indenture	iij li

Summa xj li ij s ~~xj~~ d

---

[148] The feast of St. Catherine is celebrated on 25 November and the feast of St. Andrew on 30 November.

[149] Iron bars probably used to keep glass in place in windows; see Salzman, 292.

DECEMBER 1517

[*f31v; original f. 34v*]

This booke made from the vth day off december unto the xx^ti day off the same monyth

carpenterys	William Colyn	o+oooo[150]	oooooo	vjj s iiij d
	Richard Threder	o+oooo	oooooo	vij s iiij d
	John Browne	o+oooo	oooooo	vj s vij d
	John Avenell	o+oooo	oooooo	iiij s
rowyth mason	John hamond		oooooo	ijs vj d
laborars	Simon holman	o(+)oooo[151]	oooooo	ij s viij d
	Nicholas herne	o+oooo	oooooo	ij s viij d
	william Britten	o+oooo	oooooo	ij s viij d
	George Alye[152]	o+oooo	oooooo	ij s viij d

Sawyars   Item to Richard pyttfyld for the sawyng off hallfe a hundrith and xvj carvys after x s the hundrith   vj s iiij d

Item to the same for a hundrith slyttyng worke   xij d

carver off the knottes   Item sent by william Colyn to Thomas Rossell the carver off the knottes ffor the chaple[153]   xl s

Item for on locke to the tresar howse dore price   xx d

Item for ij dosyn ryngges for the cappys   iij s

warde   Item delyveryd to ward fremason as hytt apperith by his byll \ffor the makyng off all manner off wyndoys off taynton stone/   xl s

Richard leyowse   Item delyveryd to Richard leyow the xix^ti day off december ffor the ffynall end off hys bargayn ffor the makyng off rowy3th wall att xij d le perch the some off xxxvij^ti score perchis and three where off he hath receyvid xxxv li   xliij s

Item ffor the <u>remevyng off the woode</u> howse wall in the cloyster   v s

Joynerys   Item to Robert More Roger Morwent and Roger Gryffith Joynerys for all soch [...] co'menawntes as they be bownd in a Indenture

---

[150] The feast of the Conception of the Virgin Mary is celebrated on 6 December.
[151] The original symbol of the second day is indeterminable, overwritten with a cross.
[152] Labourers were normally paid at 4d a day, and so we would expect these four to be paid 3s 8d (44d) for eleven days work when in fact they were paid 2s 8d (32d).
[153] This entry reveals that the carver who made the bosses for the college chapel was Thomas Roossell or Russell; see Salzman, 217.

        made betwyxt humfrey Coke and then which comyth
        to the su*m*me off \xxxiij li xxij d whereoff they have
        receyvid as hytt apperyth by ther Indenture on the
        backe xxvij li ij s viij d/   v li xix s ij d
        Item for candelles   x d
                15li 18s 5d

[*f. 32r; original f. 35r*]

        16
rag from   2 Jasp*er* wase for xvj loodes off ragg and too off frestone[154]   ix s
hedyngton 18
        2 Item to John wase for xviij loodes off ragg and too off free x s
        6
        1 Item to lawrence banyst*er* for vij loodes cariage
        on off them free   iij s vj d
        5
        Item to walton for v loodes caryage   ij s vj d
        11
        7 Item to haryson for xj loodes ragg vij loodes off free   ix s
        Item to Townesend for ij loodes carriage   xij d
        Item paid to John ffrancleyn ffor iiij score loodes off
        ragg aft*er* xiij s iiij d th [*sic*] hundrith loodes   xj s
ffre stone Item to the same for xiij loodes off freston att xij d le loode   xiij s
gr*a*vell   Item to John Townesend for xiiij loodes off sond   iij s vj d
        Item to the same John ffor vij loodes off pavyng stons   iiij s ij d
pavyng in the Item paid to the same John ffor xxvj ~~perch~~ teerse
kechyn yard off pavyng in the kechyn yarde att vj d the perch   xiij s
naylys   Item ffor a thowsond x penny nayle   vj s ~~viij d~~ iiij d
        Item ffor ij thowsond vj penny nayle   vj s viij d
        Item ffor ij thowsond v penny nayle   vj s
        Item ffor oon thowsond off iiij penny nayle   ij s ij d
        Item ffor halfe a thowsond off lath nayle   iiij d
wyll*i*am Est Item delyve*r*yd to wyll*i*am Est fremason ffor the
        makyng cariage and settyng
        att his p*ro*pre coostes and charge all man*n*er off grasse
        table[155] and seve*r*all table as schalbe necessary to the
        college aft*er* iiij d the foote as hytt apperyth by his
        co'menawnt made the xxij[ti] day off June   iiij li

---

[154] The numbers in the left margin indicate the number of loads of free stone and the superscript numbers, the number of loads of rag stone.

[155] *Grasse table* was the stone used at the base of an external wall; see Salzman, 89.

JANUARY 1518

glasyar   Item paid to Robert Glasyar for lvij[ti] footes off glas
after v d le foote[156]   xxijj s ~~ix d~~ viij d

Summa xxv li iij s ~~v s~~ iij d[157]

~~9li 4s 10d~~[158]

[*f. 32v; original f. 35v*]

anno domini 1518 \regni regis 8[vi] 9[no]/

This booke made ffrom the ffyrst day off Januarii
the ix[th] yere off kyng henry the viij[th] unto the
xxiij[ti] day off the same monyth

carpenterys	Richard Colyn	xx(+)ooo	oooooo	oooooo	x s
	John Avenell	xx+ooo	oooooo	oooooo	vj s iij d
laborars	Simon holman	oooooooo	oooooo	oooooo	v s
	Nicholas herne	oooooooo	oooooo	oooooo	v s
	William Britten	ooooooooe	oooooo	oooooo	v s j d
	George alye	oooooc	oooooo	oooooo	iiij s vij d

More   Item paid to Nicholas more to pay the sawyars off
netylbed and for to paie ffor the caryage off tymber
the xij[th] day off January   xlvj s viij d

ragg from   Item to Jasper wase for the caryage off xij loodes off ragg   vj s

hedyngton   Item to John wase for the caryage off xxij[ti] loodes \&/
on off ffree   xj s vj d

Item to haryson for the caryage off xxij loodes and iij
off ffree   xij s vj d

restat xij d   Item to Robert walton for the caryage off iiij loodes   ij s

[…]   Item to John Townesend for ij loodes   xij d

Item delyveryd to John ffrancleyn the xxij[ti] day off
Januarij ffor the foresaid ragg ~~for~~ di' C   vj s viij d

ffreestone   Item to the same for iiij loodes off ffree stone   iiij s

Smyth   Item for ij[C] broodes and xxviij[ti] att xviij d the hundrith   iij s iiij d

Item ffor the handle off the wycatt[159]   ij d

Item ffor a candlestykes [*sic*] off yorn to the botrye   vj d

Item ffor a key to the coole howse dore[160]   ~~iij~~ d

---

[156] Robert Glasyer is paid for 57 feet of glass at 5d a foot.
[157] The, incorrect, total of ff. 31v and 32r. The correct total should be £26 3s 3d.
[158] The, incorrect, total of f. 32r. It should be £10 4s 10d.
[159] The handle of a wicket door.
[160] The door to the coalhouse.

56 BUILDING ACCOUNTS OF CORPUS CHRISTI COLLEGE

~~prest~~ \paid/ to ffrancleyn	Item delyveryd to John ffrancleyn in preest owyng hym butt for xij loodes	xx s
Townesend	Item to John Townesend for xxv^{ti} loodes off gravell	vj s iij d
gravell	Item ffor a loode off stone	v d
	Item ffor candell	v d
Smyth	Item to John a banckes ffor xiiij barrys waying ij^C xv li [...] and owyng hym off old ffor xxiiij li whereoff remaynyth now to the next paye xxxix li unpaid	xxxij s viij d [~~..li 10s~~][161]

[*f. 33r; original f. 36r*]

R leyowse	Item delyveryd to Richard leyowse rowyth mason the xxij day off January ffor the makyng off all manner off wallys abowght the college perteynyng to hys craft: off whatt so ever thykenes they be att [sic] hytt apperyth by hys indentures havyng for every perch a which is a foote uppryght and xviij footes long xij d	xl s
	Item payd for the byndyng off a paper boke	v d
	Item ffor scafold cordys[162]	vj d
	Item Sir wylliams for hys coostes goyng to netylbed	xviij d

Summa xj li xij s v d[163]

42s 5d

[*f. 33v; original f. 36v*]

This Booke made ffrom the xxiij^{ti} day off M[...][164]

carpenterys	Wylliam Colyn	ooooo	ø+oooo[165]	vij s
	John Avenell	ooooo	ø+oooo[166]	iiij s iiij d
fremason	John Chayney	ooooooo	c+oooo	viij s

---

[161] Presumably £9 10s, the sum of this page.
[162] Cords used in connection with scaffolding.
[163] The total of ff. 32v and 33r should be £11 12s 8d.
[164] The rest of the date left blank, but this book covers the period 23 January to 6 February.
[165] ø represents a symbol in the manuscript that is a circle divided vertically, the left side white and the right side filled in black. It is possible that this represents a half day, where the clerk has written 'o' by mistake, indicating a full day's work, and then crossed out half to indicate only half a day. Several of the fortnightly wages on this page do not relate to the normal day rates of pay and so may represent either bonuses or stoppages.
[166] The feast of the Purification of the Virgin Mary (Candlemas) is celebrated on 2 February.

JANUARY/FEBRUARY 1518 57

rowyth	Richard leyowse	oooo	c+oooo	iiij s iij d
masons	wyll*i*am spyllisbye		x+oooo	ij s
laborars	Simon holman	oooooo	ø+oooo	iij s
	Nicholas herne	oooooo	ø+oooo	iij s
	wyll*i*am Brytton	oooooo	ø+oooo	iij s
	George Alye	oooooo	ø+oooo	iij s
	wyll*i*am Myllett		x+xooo	xij d

More	Item delyv*er*yd to Nicholas more *v* the vj day off februarij ffor the sawyars off netylbed	xx s
rag from hedyngto*n*	Item to Robert walton for viij loodes off ragg caryage & oon off fre att vj d le loode caryage	iiij s
	Item to John wase for xiijj loodes off ragg car*r*iage	vij s
	Item to haryson for xj loodes off ragg and iiij off ffree	vij s vj d
	Item to Jasp*er* for vij loodes off ragg cari*age*	iij s vj d
ffreestone	Item to John ffrancley for the foresayd v loodes off ragg att xij d le lood	v s
cordys	Item ffor scafold cordys	iiij d
	Item for george is coostys rydyng to taynton quarrie	v d
	Item for xviij dosyn Chaynys to the lyb*er*arye[167] att xviij d le dosyn	xxvij s
the carv*er* off the knottes	Item to the carv*er* off the knottes	xl s
	Item ffor to dosyn courtyn rynges for hangynges to the altarys[168]	iiij d
		[4̶l̶i̶ ̶.̶.̶s̶ ̶4̶.̶.̶.̶d̶][169]

[*f. 34r; original f. 37r*]

	Item ffor a mort*ar* and a pestell[170]	v s viij d
	Item ffor ij dosyn Rynges for cappys	iij s
	Item for too lockes for the almorys in the kechyn	xvj d
barelles	Item to John Raynold for barellys for ale	ix s v d ob

Cochyn

Item for iiij Casementes	v s iiij d
Item for a feyer schovyll[171]	xvj d

---

[167] Eighteen dozen (216) chains, purchased for the library.
[168] Curtain rings acquired to attach hangings around the altars in the college chapel.
[169] Although these figures have been crossed through and are partly illegible, the first number is clearly £4. We would expect this number to be the total for this page, but the correct total for this page is £7 13s 8d, which is the amount carried over to the sum on the following page.
[170] A mortar and pestle for use in the college kitchen.
[171] A shovel for the fire in the kitchen.

58   BUILDING ACCOUNTS OF CORPUS CHRISTI COLLEGE

Item for a feyer pyke to the kechyn	xij d
Item for a peyll[172]	xiiij d
Item for a flesch hooke[173]	iiij d
Item for iij gymmeys and iij barrys to the kechyn	xx d
Item for a locke	xij d
Item for hengys and a locke for a coofer in the botery	xviij d

Summa ix li vj s v d ob[174]

4   Summa Ciij li xix s v d ob .4.[175]

9li 6s 5d ob[176]

[f. 34v; original f. 37v]

\Anno regni regis henrici 8^{vi} 9no/

Thys ~~Indenture~~ \booke/ made ~~th~~ ffrom the ~~x~~ vj day
off ffebruarie unto the xxj day off the
same monyth

Carpenterys	Wyllyam Colyn	oooooo	oooooo	viij s
	John Avell [sic]	ooooooo	oooooo̶	v s
fremason	Rychard Parker		oøooooo̶	iij s iiij d
Rowyth	Richard leyowse	øooooo		ij s ix d
masons	John spyllysby	oooooo		iij s
	Robert Jonson	ooooxx		ij s
laborars	Simon holman	oooooo	oøoooo	iij s x d
	Wyllyam brytton	oooooo	oøoooo	iij s x d
	Nicolas herne	oooooo	oøoooo	iij s x d
	George Alye	oooooo	oøoooo	iij s x d
	John Myles	oooooo	xxxxxx	ij s

	Item paid to John hynton ffor graffyng stockes	viij d
1	Item paid to Jasper for xiij loodys off ragg carriage and on off fre	vij s
	Item to John wase for xvij loodes off ragg	viij s vj d
3	Item to haryson for xiiij loodes off ragg ~~and~~ iij off ffree	viij s vj d

---

[172] A baker's peel, used for extracting loaves of bread from a hot oven.
[173] A meat hook for hanging meat or for extricating hot meat from a pot.
[174] The total of ff. 33v and 34r.
[175] The total of ff. 29r to 34r, Monday 26 October 1517 to Saturday 6 February 1518.
[176] The total of f. 34r.

FEBRUARY/MARCH 1518

1̶0̶9̶	1 Item to walton for xiij loodes off ragg and oon off ragg [sic]	vij s
	Item restat in manubus [sic] francleyn xlj loodes off ragg	
free stone	Item paid to the sayd John francleyn for v loodes off free stone	vs
Richard	Item delyveryd to Richard leyowse the xxj day off februarij	xx s
leyowse	Item paid to the caryar for the caryage off letterys	iiij d
candelles	Item for candelles	v̶i̶i̶ iiij d

[f. 35r; original f. 38r]

Smyth	Item ffor iiij stapullis	iiij d
	Item the mendyng off the locke and a new key to the closett dore	iiij d
	Item ffor an ax to the kechyn[177]	x d
	Item ffor a plate and wardys to the locke off the vestery dore	iiij d
	Item for a handle to the chaple dore	viij d
	Item for a handle on the backsyde off the wycatt	iiij d
	Item for iiij barrys ffor the lyberary and a peese of yorne to the bell waying a hundrith wayght	xvj s viij d
caryage off	Item to John warde for the caryage off iiij loodes off	
free stone	ffreeston from taynton price the lood caryage ij s iiij d	ix s iiij d
ward	Item delyveryd to John ward ffremason for the makyng off the wyndoys for the cloyster off taynton stone as hytt apperyth by hys co'menawntes	iiij li

Summa x li vij s vij d

10li 7s 7d   1̶0̶l̶i̶ 7̶s̶ v̶i̶j̶ 7̶d̶

[f. 35v; original f. 38v]

Thys booke made from the xxj[ti] day off ffebruarij unto the vij day off March

Carpenterys	Wylliam Colyn	oo(+)ooo[178]	oooooo	vij s iiij d
	John Avenell	oo+ooo	oooooo	iiij s vij d

---

[177] An axe for use in the kitchen.
[178] We might have expected the feast of St. Mathias, Thursday 25 February, to have been kept as a day of rest rather than Wednesday 24th. It is possible that Wednesday was kept instead as it was the first of the spring ember days. *Ember Days* were three days (Wednesday, Friday and Saturday) of prayer and fasting, which fell in four roughly equal seasons. The spring ember days began on the Wednesday between the first and second Sundays of Lent.

60 BUILDING ACCOUNTS OF CORPUS CHRISTI COLLEGE

fremason	Richard parkar	oo+ooo	oooooo	vj s viij d
	Richard leyowse	oo+ooo	oooooo	v s vj d
	wylliam Spyllysby	oo+ooo	oooooo	v s vj d
laborars	Simon holman	oo+ooo	oooooo	iij s vj d
	Nicholas herne	oo+ooo	oooooo	iij s viij d
	wylliam Brytton	oo+ooo	oooooo	iij s viij d
	George Alye	oo+xoo	oooooo	iijs ~~viijd~~ iiijd

Robert Carow More	Item delyveryd to Robert carow as hytt apperyth by hys Indenture: the vj day off Marche			x li
	Item to Nicholas More the vj day off March ffor pay the sawyars and swetestare[179] for the bryngyng off tymber to the pytt[180] to be sawyd			xxxiij s iiij d
Richard leyowse ~~prest~~\paid/	Item to Richard leyowse as hytt apperyth by hys byll			xx s
to larden	Item to Elys larden in prest for lyme			x s
	Item for scafold cordys			ij d

Summa xv li vij s iij d

15li 7s 3d   ~~12~~5li 7s 3d

[f. 36r; original f. 39r]

Thys boke made ffrom the vij[th] day
off March to the xxij[ti] day off the same

Carpenterys	Wylliam Colyn	oooooo	oooooo	viijs ij d[181]
	John Avenell	oooooo	oooooo	v s
	Richard parkar	oooooo	oooooo	vj s viij d
laborars	Simon holman	oooooo	xxxooo	iij s
	Nicholas herne	oooooo	ooooox	iij s viij d
	wylliam Brytton	oooooo	xoooox	iij s iiij d
	George Alye	oooooo	xooooo	iij s viij d
sawyars	Item to John Benett and hys fellowe for a hundrith and xlij footes off slyttyng worke			xvij d

[179] John Swetestare mentioned on f. 6v.
[180] A saw pit or open pit over which logs were lain and then sawn into timber boards by a two man team of sawyers.
[181] William Colyn's normal pay rate of 8d a day would have resulted in a fortnight's pay of 8s (96d). Presumably the additional 2d was a bonus or overtime payment.

MARCH 1518 61

ragg from	Item Jasper for xvij loodes caryage att vj d le loode	viij s vj d
hedyngton	1 Item to banystar for xiij loodes off ragg and on fre	vij s
	3 Item to Robert walton for vij loodes ragg iij ffree	v s
	1 Item to John wase for xx loodes ragg and oon ffree	x s vj d
	Item to haryson for xiij loodes off ragg	vj s vj d
	unpayd /19 loodes	
	Item to John ffrancleyn for for [sic] v loodes off ffree stone	v s
	Item to the caryar for letterys carying	iiij d
bord off	Item to Jasper wase for the caryage off iiij^C di' xxxvj	
netilbed	footes off off [sic] planch bord ffrom netylbed	iij s
	Item to haryson for the carriage	
	off iiij^C di' xxxix^{ti} footes off borde	iij s
	Item to John Townesend for vj^C and one footes carriage	iij s
	Item to Richard chare for vj^C ij footes off planch bord	
	caryage	iij s iiij d
gravell	Item to John Townesend ffor iiij loodes off gravell	xij d
	Item to George ffor hys costys rydyng to blewbery[182]	v d
Colyns	Item to Colyns and Nicholas more for ther bargayn	xl s
and more		
More	Item to Nicholas more for the sawyars off netylbed	xiij s iiij d
Smyth	Item ffor xij lockes and hengys for the hole dexis in	
	the lyberarye att xx d the peese	xx s
	Item for iiij lockes for the halffe dexys	iiij s

[f. 36v; original f. 39v] [Blank][183]

fremason	Richard parkar	oooooo[184]	oooo+	v s iiij d
laborars	Nicholas herne	oooooo	oooo	iij s iiij d
	George Alye	oooooo	oooo	iij s ij d[185]
	wylliam brytton	oooooo	oooo	iij s iiij d
	Simon holmon	oooooo	oooo	~~iij~~ iij s iiij d
rowyth layers	Richard leyowse	oooooo		~~ij~~ iij s
	wylliam syllysbye [sic]	oooooo		iij s

---

[182] George [Roper?] is paid for riding to Blewbury near Didcot, though no reason is recorded.
[183] No dates are given for this period, but it covers the working days Monday 22 March to Maundy Thursday, 1 April.
[184] Thursday 25 March was worked by all the craftsmen in spite of it being the feast of the Annunciation. Perhaps because it was close to the Easter close-down the following week.
[185] Labourers were normally paid at the rate of 4d per day. George Alye is recorded as working the same number of full days during this fortnight as his fellows but was paid 2d less. Perhaps his wages had been stopped for arriving late, or for inferior workmanship.

	wyll*i*am stanley	00000000 [*sic*]	iiij s
	Richar [*sic*]	0000	ij s
Ric*hard*	Item d*edit* to Richard leyowse the second day off apryll		xx s
leyowse	Item to pet*er* for xxxj stapulles and settyng		ij s vjd
	Item to John for iiij dosyn stapulles and settyng		vj s
bord from	Item to John Townesend for iiij^C xxx footes		
netilbed	off planch bord caryage from netilbed		~~iij[..]~~ iij s
g*ra*vell	Item to John Townesend for ix loodes off sond		ij s iij d
	Item to the same for ij loodes off bord from netylbed		v s viij d
	2 It*em* to Rob*ert* walton oon loode of ragg ij free		xviij d
	2 Item to haryson for ij loodes of free		xij d
	3 Item to banyst*er* for iiij loodes of free ij ragg		ij s vj d
	Item to Jasp*er* for ij loodes caryage of ragg		xij d
fre ston	Item to John francleyn for vij loodes off ~~ragg~~ free ston		vij s
	Item \to/ the same John francley for a q*ua*rt*er*yn of ragg		iij s iiij d
Est	Item to wyll*i*am Est the second day of Apryll		xx s
	Item to the smyth for iij li halff to the well		v d
	Item for iiij hookes and hengys waying viij li		xiiij d
	Item for a rake		iiij d
	Item for a payer of hengys to the closet dore \viij li/		xiiij d
p*re*st to	Item to John townesend for the caryage off xj loodes		
~~Townesend~~	off bord from netylbed att iij s the loode		~~xiij s iiij d~~

[*f. 37r; original f. 40r*]

Item for a locke to the wyne seller dore		xij d
Item for the seallyng of hys co*m*posytion		vj viij d
S*um*ma xiiij li v s x d		
14li 5s 10d		[*14li 5s 10d*]

[f. 37v; original f. 40v]

APRIL 1518

This booke made from the vij^th day
off Aprill unto the xxv^ti day off ye same monyth

laborars	Simon holman	ooo[186] oooooo	oooo+o[187]	iiij s viij d
	Nycholas herne	ooo xxoooo	oooo+o	iiij s
	William bryttayn	ooo oooooo	oooo+o	iij s viij d
	George Alye	ooo oooooo		iij s

	Item to John Phylyppys	xviij d
ragg from	.1. Item Jasper for vij ragg oon ffree	iiij s
hedyngton	.1. Item to walton x ragg oon ffree	v s vj d
	Item to haryson x loodes off ragg	v s
Richard leyowse	Item to Richard leyowse	xl s
	Item to John Townesend for xxxj^ti loodes gravell att iij d le lood	vij s viij d
Est	Item paid to John Jonys ffor the Caryage off iij loodes off Cresse table	vij s iiij d
	~~Item to Richard chare for the caryage off v^c iiij^xx xij loodes off quarter bord~~ -	~~[ij s iiij d]~~
	Item for a Thowsond x penny nayle	vj s iij d
	Item ij^Ml iiij penny nayle	iiij s iiij d
naylys	Item a thowsond v penny nayle	iij s
	Item for iij penny nayle	xij d
		xiiij s vij d
prest to	~~Item to Elys larden in prest~~	~~xx s~~
larden	Item to Elys larden ffor xlvj^ti quarterys off lyme att xiij d le quarter	l s iiij d

Summa vij li xij s iij d

7li 12s 3d

---

[186] Work resumed on Thursday 8 April following the Easter holiday.
[187] The feast of St. George is celebrated on 23 April.

[f. 38r; original f. 41r]

\Anno regni regis henrici 8 10mo/

<1518> Thys Booke made ffrom the xxv^ti day off
Aprill unto the ix^th day off Maij

laborars	Simon holman	oooox+	(+)oooo(+)[188]	iij s
	Nicholas herne	oooo~~x~~x+	(+)oooo+	iij s
	Wylliam Bryttayn	oooox+	+ooooo	iij s

ragg from   .1. Item to Jasper Wase for xviij loodes off ragg
hedyngton   carriage oon free   ix s vj d
                                                                    18
            .3. Item to haryson for xvij loodes off ragg carriage iij free   x s
                                                                    17[189]

            .1. Item Walton for xv^tene loodes off ragg carriage
            and oon ffree   viij s
            Item to John ~~hart~~ \wase/ for x loodes off ragg   v s
            Item to John hart for xx^ti loodes off ragg   x s
            .1. Item to kenelme rede for on loode of rag an other
            off ffree   xij d

[...] .8.   Item payd to John ffrancleyn for a hundrith loode off ragg xiij s iiij d
ffre stone Item to the said John for viij loodes off ragg   viij s
~~Elys prest~~ ~~Item to Elys larden in prest~~   ~~vj s viij d~~
Smyth   Item ffor too barrys to the lyberary wayng xxxiij li att
            j d ob qua   iiij s ix d
            Item ffor a candi\l/styke   iij d
            Item ffor a payer off Jemoys   iiij d
            Item ffor ij new keys   vj d
            Item ffor the mendyng off the rackes   xviij d
the cariar Item to the caryar off london ffor a hundrith wayth carriage xv d
ward   Item to John ward the ~~iiij~~^th \last/ day off Apryll   iij li
~~prest~~ \paid/ Item to wylliam Samson for the caryage off stone
            from taynton   xiij s iiij d
~~prest~~   ~~Item to John Jonys for carriage off stone from taynton~~ ~~xiiij s~~

                    Summa vij li xv s ix d

~~132li 13s 8d ob~~[190]   7li 15s 9d   ~~8li 16s 5d~~

---

[188] The feast of Saints Philip and James is celebrated on 1 May and the feast of the Invention of the Holy Cross is celebrated on 3 May.

[189] 18 and 17 written in the right-hand margin against their respective entries, to indicate the number of loads of ragstone.

[190] This figure eludes interpretation.

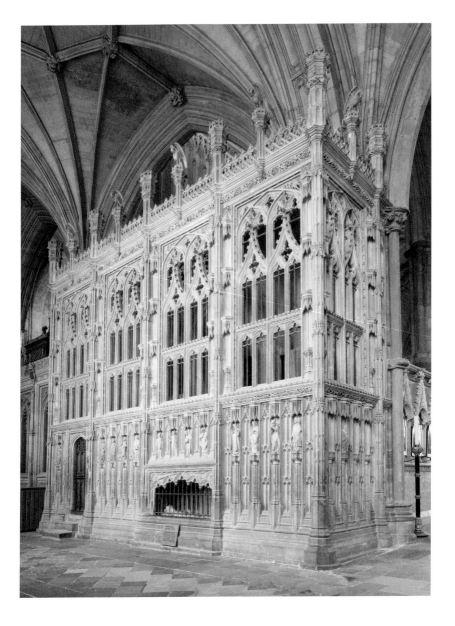

1. Fox's chantry chapel in Winchester Cathedral (photo: John Crook)

2. The hall at Corpus Christi College, with its hammerbeam roof, completed in 1516 (photo: Nicholas Read)

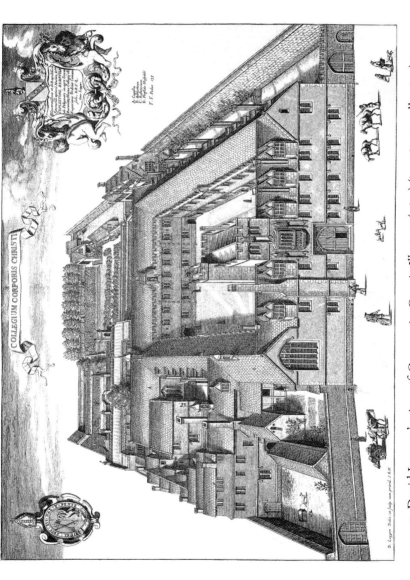

3. David Loggan's view of Corpus, in *Oxonia Illustrata* (1675) (in private collection)

4. Oriel window above Corpus gate, with the arms of St. Swithun's Priory in Winchester (left) and Bishop Fox's personal arms (right), flanking the sculptural detail of angels holding the eucharistic cup, a reference to Corpus Christi (photo: Angela Smith)

5. Detail of the fan vault designed by William Vertue over the main entrance to Corpus (photo: Angela Smith)

6. Detail of woodwork in the library at Corpus (photo: Julian Reid). Rodney Thomson, in his Lowe Lectures in 2017, suggested that timber from the original desks of 1517 was reused when the library was refitted in 1604, particularly the hour-glass-shaped supports under the shelves.

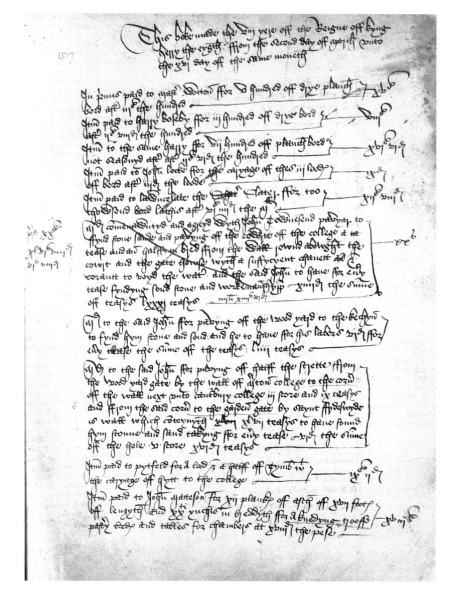

7. The account for 2–16 March 1517 (f. 2r from CCCO MS H1/4/1). For transcript see p. 3.

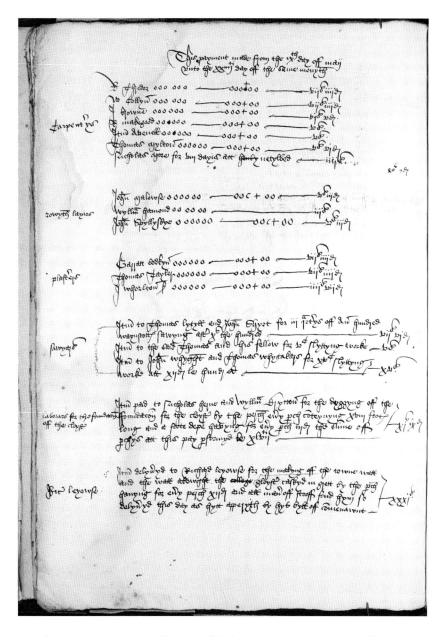

8. Fol. 18v. Payments to craftsmen of daily wages, 9–24 May 1517, illustrating the variety of symbols used to indicate time worked. For transcript see p. 33.

9. Fol. 44v. The entries in the margin for 'waynscott from Henley' and 'borde from netylbed' are in a slanted humanist cursive hand. For transcript see pp. 74–5.

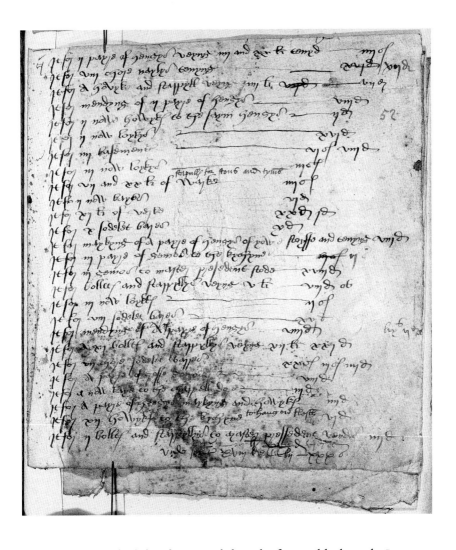

10. Fol. 52r. A schedule of ironwork bought from a blacksmith. It is in a different hand and employs distinctive spelling conventions. For transcript see p. 86.

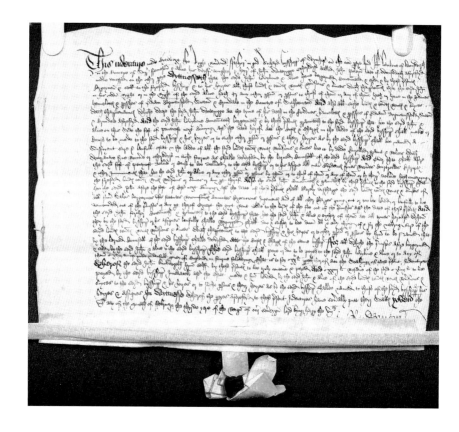

11. Agreement of 1512 concerning the sale of land, between Bishop Fox and the freemason, John Lebons (CCCO C5/Cap.11/Ev.109). For transcript see pp. 104–5.

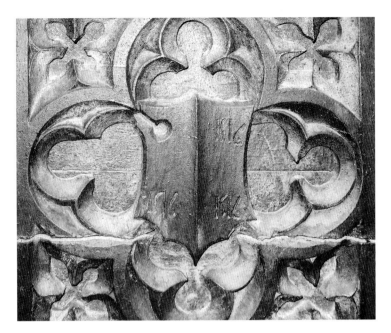

12. The date 1516 carved on a shield in a quatrefoil of the frieze beneath the hammerbeam roof in the hall at Corpus (photo: Angela Smith)

13. Corbel in the hall at Corpus with partial view of Bishop Fox's motto (photo: Angela Smith)

14. Corbel in the hall at Corpus showing the heraldic arms of Winchester Cathedral, the initials T.S.P. for Prior Thomas Silkstede, and part of the dedication to Saint Swithun (photo: Angela Smith)

15. Fox's pelican device in the nineteenth-century glass in the north window of the hall at Corpus (photo: Angela Smith)

16. Details of the frieze in the hall (photos: Angela Smith)
a. Bishop Fox's device of a pelican vulning
b. A different treatment of the pelican vulning, showing that at least two craftsmen carved the details

c. A heart within the crown of thorns, and an episcopal mitre
d. A pomegranate for Katherine of Aragon

17. More details of the frieze in the hall (photos: AngelaSmith)
a. The heraldic arms for the Huddleston family
b. Monogram with two 'V's for *Virgo Virginis* against a stylized rose (?)

c. Monogram featuring the letter M for Mary set against a spear and nails suggesting the Sorrows of the Virgin
d. A third monogram referencing Mary, featuring the letter R (for Regina), a V, and an inverted V

MAY 1518

[*f. 38v; original f. 41v*]

This booke made from the ixth day of Maij
unto the xxiij^{ti} day off the same monyth

Carpenter	Item Richard parka	ooo	oooooo	~~iij s iiij d~~ iiij s
	Thomas Stonie		ooooo c	ij s ix d
	John barkar		ooooo c	ij s ix d
	Simon holman	ooo+oo[191]	ooooo c	iij s viij d
	Nicholas herne	ooo+oo	ooooo c	iij s iiij d
	w brytton	ooo+ooo	ooooo c	iij s iiij d

More	Item delyvered to Nocholas [*sic*] More the xviij day off Maij	xx s
Richard leyowse	Item to Richard leyowse the xxj day off Maij	xl s
bordys from netylbed	Item to cholsey and mede for 514 ffootes bord	ij s viij d
	Item to Richard chare for v^C xv footes carriage \off bord/	iij s viij d
	Item John chare for ~~vC for~~ vj^C x footes carriage	iij s
	Item to Thomas wylteschere for v^C xv footes carriage	iij s
	Item to Richard Chare for vj^C viij footes di'	ij s viij d
	Item to John chare for for [*sic*] v^C xix footes	ij s viij d
	Item to Thomas \Mede/ for vj^C iij footes	ij s viij d
	Item to Richard Chare for vj^C iiij footes di'	ij s viij d
	Item to John Wylteshyre vj^C xij footes	ij s viij d
	Item Rychard Chare for iiij^C xxxvj^{ti} footes	ij s viij d
leedbord	Item to Thomas wylshyre for a lood off leede bord and for ~~x~~ lvj footes di' off shellys	ij s viij d
	Item to John Chare for a loode leed bord caryage	ij s viij d
	Item to John Chare for the caryage off iij^C di' vj footes di'	ij s viij d
	Item to Thomas \mede/ for ij^C di' xxix footes di'	ij s viij d
Schellys from netylbed	Item to Thomas Wylschyre for iij^C a foote and a halff	ij s viij d
	Item to ~~John wylschyre~~ \~~Thomas mede~~/ for oon hundrith di' vj footes di'	ij s viij d
	Item to Thomas Mede for iij^C xxiiij footes	ij s viij d
	Item to John harme for a lood off shellys	ij s viij d
Jeistes for the Cloyster from netylbed	Item to Thomas Mede for a lood off geistes \carriage/	ij s viij d
	Item to kenelme Rede for a lood off jestys carriage	ij s viij d
	Item to John ~~wylschyre~~ \harme/ for a lood off jestys carriage	ij s viij d

[191] Ascension Day, the fortieth day after Easter, fell on Thursday 13 May 1518.

	Item to Thomas wylschyre for a lood off gestes	ij s viij d
	Item to John wylschyre for a loode of gestes	ij s viij d

[*f. 39r; original f. 43r*]

		\l s ij d/
lyme	Item Elys larden for xlvj quarterys off lyme and vj boschelles att xiij d the ~~boschell~~ quarter	~~xlix s iiij d~~
frestone	Item to wylliam Samson for iij loodes caryage	viij s
from	Item to John Jonys for vij loodes caryage	
taynton	~~att~~ ffrom taynton quarry att ij s iiij d le quarter	
	~~whereoff he hath receyvyyd~~	viij s iiij d
	Item to Thomas archar for ij loodes	iiij s viij d
	Item to John branne a loode	ij s iiij d
	Item to cheyney for a days worke	viij d
	Item to Sir wyllyams for hys costes to netylbed	xiiij d
John chester	Item to John chester ffor the makyng off ix dosyn stapullys ffor the cheynys in part off payment	vj s
	3 Item to Jasper wase for xvij loodes off ragg and iij off ffre	x s
	2 Item to John wase for xxij^{ti} loodes off ragg and ij ffree	xij s
	4 Item to haryson for for [*sic*] vij loodes off ragg and iiij free	v s vj d
	Item to John francleyn for di' a hundryth loodes off ragg	~~viij s viij d~~
		~~vj s [...] d~~
		\vij s/
	Item to John francleyn for ix loodes off ffre stone	ix s
	Item ij sevys a bokett and a boll	viij d
	Item thomas desford iij days	xviij d
	Item to hys laborar iij days	~~x d~~ viij d
	Item for ij^C lath nayle	ij d
	Item to John Townesend for xlvj loodes off gravell att ~~ij~~ iij d le lood	xj s vj d
Smyth	Item for a feyer shovell to the vestery	ij s
	Item for too botoms to sensors	x d
	Item for a hooke to the rowygh castes(?)	ij d
	Item for iiij hookes waying xiij li for dorys in the cloyster	xxij d ob

Summa xiiij li vij s ob

14li 6 7s ob

MAY/JUNE 1518   67

[*f. 39v; original f. 42v*] [*Blank*][192]

	Item Richard parkar for iiij days worke			ij s iiij d
	John Malowse	ooxooo		~~iij s~~ ij s vj d
	Richard heyse	oooooo		iij s iiij d
	w hamond	oooooo		iij s
	Thomas Stone	oooooo		iij s
	John barkar	oooooo		iij s
Sawyars	Item to thomas whytakare and hys fellow for vj^c footes saw			vj s

	Simon holman	ooo	ooo+oo[193] oooooo	~~iiij s~~ iiij s vj d
	Nicholas herne	ooo	ooo+oo oooooo	iiij s viij d
	wylliam brytton	ooo	ooo+oo oooooo	iiij s vj d[194]
	Christofor sexten		ooo+oo oooooo	iij s viij d

Richard leyowse	Item the xiiij day off June to Richard leyowse	xl s
~~prest~~ Elys lyme	\Item/ Inprest to Elys larden for lyme	iij s iiij d
	Item to Elys larden for xlviij quarterys off lyme att xiij d le quarter whereoff he receyvyd iij s iiij d	xlv s v d
	4 Item to Jasper for xvij loodes off ragg and iiij free carriage	x s vj d
	Item to haryson for xvj loodes ragg carriage	viij s
	Item to John wase for xxiiij loodes of ragg carriage	xij s
	Item to John Cooke for xiij loodes off ragg carriage	vj s vj d
~~prest~~ ~~francleyn~~	\Item/ delyveryd to John ffrancleyn quarryman ~~in prest for ragg~~ \for di' a hundrith ragg/	vj s viij d
	Item to the sayd John francleyn for iiij loodes off fre	iiij s
	Item to the sayd francleyn for a quarteyn of ragg	iij s iiij d
\payde/ ~~prest~~ Bankes	Item to John Bankes in prest	liij s iiij d
hyrdylles	Item ffor xxj^ti hyrdylles	iij s vj d
	Item for iij hyrdylles	vj d
the gyldyng off the knottes	Item dd to humfry Cooke for the gyldyng off iiij^xx and xviij hole knottes and xiiij halff knott att iij s viij d the peese off the hole knottes and xxij d	

---

[192] No dates are given for this period, but it covers the working days Thursday 27 May to Saturday 12 June. Monday 24 to Wednesday 26 May were probably taken as holiday following the feast of Pentecost (Whitsunday), 23 May.
[193] The feast of Corpus Christi fell on Thursday 3 June in 1518.
[194] Labourers were normally paid at the rate of 4d per day. Simon Holman, Nicholas Herne and William Brytton all worked 14 full days. Herne received the full sum of 4s 8d (56d) but Holman and Brytton received 4s 6d (54d), so perhaps had 2d stopped from their wages for some offence or for working fewer hours.

	the halff knott[195]	xix li v s
parkar	Item Richard parkar for settyng off wyndoys by the grett as hytt apperyth by hys covenantes	xiij s iiij d

[f. 40r; original f. 43r]

tymber	Item to Thomas Mede	ij s viij d
	Item to John harme for a lood of tymber from netylbed	ij s viij d
	Item to thomas barnys a loode carriage	ij s viij d
	Item to Thomas Wilteschyre for a lood off tymber carriage	ij s viij d
	John Chare for a loode off tymber carriage	ij s viij d
	Item to Richard chare for a loode of tymber carriage	ij s iiij d
	Item to John Alam for a loode of tymber carriage	ij s viij d
	Item to John chare for a lood carriage	ij s viij d
	Item to Thomas wylschyre for a loode	ij s viij d
	Item to John harper a loode	ij s viij d
	Item John Mede a loode carriage	ij s viij d
	Item to John harper a loode carriage	ij s viij d
warde	Item to John ward the ix[th] day off June	xl s
planckes	Thomas Me\de/ a loode off planckes ij[C] di'	ij s viij d
	Item to Thomas mede a loode carriage	ij s viij d
	Item to Thomas barnys a loode carriage	ij s viij d
frame	Item to Richard chare a loode carriage	ij s viij d
	Item to John Chare a loode carriage	ij s viij d
	Item to Thomas mede a loode carriage	ij s viij d
	Item for maylyng cord	iiij d
	Item for a payle	iiij d
	Item for mosse[196]	viij d
	Item to John Townesend for lij[ti] loodys off gravell	xiij s iiij d
More	Item to Richard More for the sawyars	xx s
	Item for iij ons goyns [sic] to baryngton quarry and for horse heyer[197]	v s
Est	Item to Thomas damaske for a loode carriage for est[198]	ij s
	Item to sampson for iij loodes carriage	vij s

---

[195] Humphrey Coke is paid for gilding ninety-eight large bosses at 3s a piece and fourteen small bosses at 22d each.

[196] Moss was acquired probably for use as a protective layer between the unseasoned roof structure and the lead above; see Walker, 259.

[197] Three men paid for going to Barrington quarry and a payment for horse hire.

[198] Damaske is paid for a load of stone carried to William East.

JUNE 1518

Summa xxxviij li xij s vij d[199]

38li 12s 7d

[f. 40v; original f. 43v]

This booke ffrom the xij[th] day off June unto
the xxvij[ti] day off the same monyth

John Malowse	000000	000+00[200]	v s iij d[201]
Richard hayse	[blank]	[blank]	x̶i̶x̶ d
John barkar	[blank]	[blank]	vj d
Simon holman	000000	00c+00	iij s vj d
W bryttayn	000000	00c+00	iij s vj d
N herne	000000	00c+00	iii j s iiij d
Christopher Sexten	000000	00c+00	iij s vj d
W Sawnders	000000	00c+00	iij s vj d

Richard leyowse	Item to Richard leyowse the xxvij[ti] day off June	xl s
lyme	Item to Elys larden ffor lvj quarterys off lyme att xiij d le quarter	lvij s vj d
Richard parkar	Item to Richard parkar for settyng off wyndoys and Coynnys by the grett	xiij s iiij d
naylys	Item for a M[l] off vj penny nayle	iij s viij d
ston from berryngton	Item to Sampson for the caryage off iiij loodes off baryngton stone	viij s
	Item to Jasper wase for xxiij loodes off ragg and v free	xiiij s
	Item to John wase for xxiiij loodes off ragg and iij free	xiij s vj d
	Item to haryson for viij loodes off ragg	iiij s
	~~Item to John Cooke~~	[blank]
	Item to John francleyn for viij loodes off ffree	viij s
	Item to the same for halffe a hundrith ragg	vj s viij d
	Item to John Townesend ffor xxxvij[ti] loodes off gravell att iij d the loode	ix s iij d

[199] The incorrect total of ff. 39v and 40r. The correct total of the figures for this period is £38 12s 3d. This might have arisen from Richard Chare having been paid 2s 4d for the carriage of one of the loads of timber while the standard price for the carriage of a load of timber was 2s 8d; the clerk might have calculated the carriage of twelve loads of timber at 2s 8d instead of eleven loads at 2s 8d and one at 2s 4d.

[200] The feast of St. John the Baptist is celebrated on 24 June.

[201] John Malowse was regularly paid at the rate of 6d per day, so that we would expect his total wages for this period to be 5s 6d.

sawyars	Item to John whytacars and hys fellow for xj^C sawyng	xj s
	Item for wax and rosyn[202] for Symon	viij d
	Item for on goyng bercott[203]	iij d
	Item for scafold cordys	vj d

[*f. 41r; original f. 44r*]

wyllyam Morys for xlviij footes off tymber caryage from netylbed	ij s viij d
w Morys ffor lj footes caryage	ij s viij d
Thomas barnys for xlix footes di' carriage	ij s viij d
t barnys for lj footes	ij s viij d
John harme for xlvij footes di'	ij s viij d
t Mede for xlviij footes di'	ij s viij d
John harme for xlviij footes	ij s viij d
Thomas mede for l footes di'	ij s viij d
J harper xlix footes di'	ij s viij d
W Morys for xlvj footes di'	ij s viij d
T Mede for xlvij footes di'	ij s viij d
T barnys for xlviij footes	ij s viij d
J harme for xlix footes	ij s viij d
T Mede for xlvj footes	v̶i̶ ij s viij d
T barnys for xlvij footes	ij s viij d
W Morys for xlij footes	ij s viij d
T Mede for xlvij footes	ij s viij d
W ffrancleyn for xlix footes di'	ij s viij d
t barnys for xlvij footes	ij s viij d
J harper for a lode of borde	ij s viij d

Summa xiij li ix s v d[204]

.5.   Summa cxxj li xvij s vij d ob[205].5.

13li 9s 5d

---

[202] Wax and resin was commonly mixed to make a water-resistant plaster that could be used instead of the usual mortar on areas of masonry that were prone to getting wet; see Salzman, 153.

[203] Probably Burcot in Oxfordshire, which lies close to the River Thames.

[204] Total of ff. 40r and 41r.

[205] The total of ff. 34v to 41r, Monday 8 February to Saturday 26 June. The sum is out by 1d and should be £121 17s 8½d.

JUNE/JULY 1518

[*f. 41v; original f. 44v*]

This boke made from the xxvij^{ti} day off June unto the xjth day off August [*sic*]

Richard makegood	0+0000	00+0000[206]	vj s ij d[207]
w carter	0+0000	00+0000	v s vj d
John Malowse	0+0000	00+000	v s
John ~~bene~~ spyllysby	0(+)0000		ij s vj d
John Gossupp	0+0000	00	iij s vj d
Simon holman	0+0000	xo+ooo	iij s
Nicholas herne	0+0000	o\o/(+)xoo	iij s iij d
w brytton	0+0000	00+000	iij s iiij d
Chistofor [*sic*] sexten	0+0000	00+000	iij s iiij d
w barons	0(+)0000	xo+ooo	iij s

More	Item to ~~Richar~~ Nicholas More the xv day off June by the hondys off chare	xx s
ward	Item to John warde the vth day off Julij	xxvj s viij d
Ito Richard parkar	~~Ito to Richard parkar the day off Julj for the settyng off wyndoys and chymneys~~	~~xiij s iiij d~~
Richard leyowse	Item to Richard leyowse the xth day off Julj	xl s
sawyar	Item to Thomas whytakars for vij^C sawyng	vij s
hyrdylles	Item to John byschopp for ~~ij~~ \on/ dosyn hyrdylles	ij s ij d
Robert Carow	Item dedit to the sayd Robert the xth day off Julij	vj li

[*f. 42r; original f. 45r*]

1	Item to Jasper wase for xxj loodes off ragg: and on free	xj s
1	Item to John wase for xxij loodes ragg on fre	xj s vj d
1	Item to Robert walton for iij off rag on free	~~iii~~ ij s
	Item to John Cooke for vij loodes off ragg	iij s vj d
	Item to John ffrancleyn for di' a hundrith ragg	vj s viij d
3	~~Item to the same John for iij lood's off ffree~~	~~iij s~~
naylys	Item to wylliam hoogys for a M^l vj penny nayle	iij s viij d
	Item to Thomas forest ij M^l ~~and a halff~~ off vj penny nayle	vj s iiij d

---

[206] The feast of Saints Peter and Paul is celebrated on 29 June and the feast of the Translation of St. Thomas of Canterbury on 7 July.

[207] Elsewhere Richard Makegood was paid 7d a day, which would have given total pay of 6s 5d (77d).

72 BUILDING ACCOUNTS OF CORPUS CHRISTI COLLEGE

caryar	Item to gamson caryar for iij^C wayght	iij s viij d
	Item to John harper ffor xlvij footes di'	ij s viij d
	Item to Thomas Mede ffor ~~x~~ l footes	ij s viij d
	Item to Thomas barons for a loode off tymber	ij s viij d
	Item to John chare for a loode	ij s viij d
	Item to Thomas mede for a lood off geystes	ij s viij d
	Item ffor oon goyng twyse to netylbed and twyse to baryngton	iij s x d

Summa xvij li xj d

17li 11d

[f. 42v; original f. 45v] [Blank][208]

	Richard Makegood	000+00	000+00[209]	vj s viij d
	Wylliam Carter	000+00	000+00	v s
	John Bond	000+00		ij s vj d
	Simon holman	00x+xo	000+00	ij s viij d
	wylliam herne	000+00	000+00	iij s viij d
	wylliam Bryttayn	000+00	000+00	iij s iiij d
	Xp'ofor Sexten	000+xo	000+00	iij s
	wylliam Myllwell	000		xiij d[210]
sawyars	Item to John whyttakars for viij^C slyttyng worke			viij s
wylliam plomer	Item dd to wylliam Thomas plomer in prest as hytt apperyth in hys byll off cowenauntes			xx li
Richard parkar	Item to Rychard parkar for makyng off ~~chymnys and dorys by ger grett~~ \iiij small wyndoys for the [blank]/			iiij s
lyme	Item to Elys larden for xix quarterys at xiij d le quarter			xix s vj d
Richard leyowse	Item dd to Richard leyowse the xxiijj day off Julij			xl s
Richard parkar	Item to Richard parkar for makyng off \v/ chymneys and settyng \in the chamberys over the cloyster In fre stone/[211]			xx s

[208] No dates are given for this period, but it covers the working days Monday 12 to Saturday 24 July.
[209] The feast of St. Swithun is celebrated on 15 July and the feast of St. Mary Magdalen on 22 July.
[210] We would expect William Myllwell to be paid 12d for three days work, at a rate of 4d per day; perhaps he got paid 1d extra for working longer days.
[211] Richard Parker is paid for making and erecting five chimneys for the rooms above the cloister.

JUNE/JULY 1518

	Item ~~so~~ to the same for on dore makyng	viij s
tymber from	Item to Thomas barons for a lood of tymber carriage	ij s viij d
netylbed	Item to mede for iij loodes carriage ~~for a~~	viij s
	Item to John Chare for ij loodes off tymber	v s iiijd
	Item to sampson for iiij loodes caryage	~~x s viij d~~ viij s

[*Stub of f. 43r, which is a smaller single sheet of paper bound into the gathering. The figures here were written in the left-hand margin of f. 43r and equate with the figures in the right-hand margin of that folio.*]

32
21
23
25
72
209
32
43
<u>6</u>
3

[*f. 43r; original f. 46r*]

[*The figures in the right-hand margin equate with the figures on the preceding stub*]
Thys byll beryth wyttnesse off all manner off Iron worke receyvyd
off John bankes Smyth ffrom the second day off June the \x^(th)/ yere
off o^r soverayn lord the kyng henry the eigh [*sic*]

In primys receyvyd the xiiij day off June for ~~iiij~~ \five/ wyndoys off the woodhowsys and vicys	xxxij li
Item the fyrst barre ffor the cloyster wyndoo[212]	xxj li
Item the second barre	xxiij li
Item the thyrd barre	xxv li
Item iij barrys	~~iiij~~ lxxij li
Item for x barrys	ij^C ix li
Item for the barrys off iij wyndoys to <u>the vyce</u>	xxxij li
Item for vj wegys	xliij li
Item for the mendyng off an ax	iiij d
Item to the lowyst wyndo off the vyce next the well	vj li
Item for a new stone sawe	v s
Item for iij^C braddys[213]	iiij s vj d

---

[212] Bars, for the windows of the cloister.
[213] The *braddys* in this entry refer to a small, headless nail known as broddes or brads; see. Salzman, 305.

74 BUILDING ACCOUNTS OF CORPUS CHRISTI COLLEGE

[*f. 43v; original f. 46v*]

[*Blank*] The reverse of John Bankes' bill.

[*f. 44r; original f. 47r*]

Smyth	Item payd to John a barkes [*sic*] for the contentes in thys byll wheroff he hath receyvyd liij s iiij d	xxvj s xj d
ragg from hedyng	Item to Jasper wase for xj ragg and iij free	vij s
	Item to John wase for xv ragg and on free	viij s
	Item to haryson for v loodes off ragg	ij s vj d
	Item for to [*sic*] francleyn for a quarten off ragg	iij s iiij d
	Item to the same for vij loodes of free	vij s
	Item to bowdon for dynggyng [*sic*] of iij loodes of freeston	xij d
	Item for expenses for Rydyng to walton in warwykeshyre to ~~se~~ vewe a parcell of lond[214]	ij s viij d

Summa xxx li viij s x d[215]

30li 8s 10

[*f. 44v; original f. 47v*]

This booke made from the [*blank*] day off ~~August~~ \Julij/ unto the ~~ix~~ \viij th/ day off August

	John Malowse	+00000[216]	000	iiij s
	Simon holman	+00000	000000	iij s vj d
	Nicholas herne	+0000x	000000	£iiij s
	wyllyam brytton	+0000x	000000	iij s iiij d
	Xp'ofor Sexten	+0000c	000000	iij s vj d
	wylliam ~~M~~ Kechynroffe	+0000	000000	iij s iiij d
naylis	Item ffor ij[Ml] off vj penny nayle			vj s viij d
sawyars	Item to Thomas wyttakars for x[C] off slyttyng worke			x s
	Item for here for the altarys in the chaple conteynyng xiij yardes di'			v s iiij d
	~~Item to John Raynold~~ for barelles			[*blank*]

---

[214] Walton in Warwickshire.
[215] The, incorrect, total of ff. 42v and 44r. The sum should be £30 9s 10d.
[216] The feast of St. Anne, mother of the Virgin Mary, is celebrated on 26 July.

july/august 1518

\waynscott from henley/	Item to Robert Nichols for caryage off a loode off waynscott from henly	vj s viij d
stone from baryngton	Item Archar for a loode caryage	ij s
	Item to Wyllyam Broke ffor the caryage off a loode off ston	ij s
	Item to henry broke for the caryage off a lood	ij s ~~viij d~~
Richard leyowse	Item to Richard leyowse the vij day off August	xl s
\borde from netylbed/[217]	Item to Thomas mede for a loode off borde caryage conteynyng [blank]	ij s viij d
	Item to Thomas barons for a loode off bord caryage conteynyng [blank]	ij s viij d
	Item to Thomas mede for a loode off bord caryage conteynyng [blank]	ij s viij d
	Item to Thomas barons for a loode off borde caryage conteynyng [blank]	ij s viij d

[f. 45r; original f. 48r]

\tymber from netylbed/	Item to Thomas mede for ij loodes caryage off tymber	v s iiij d
	Item to Thomas barons for ij loodes caryage off tymber	v s iiij d
	Item to Thomas Marvyng ffor a lood caryage	ij s viij d
waynscottes	Item ffor a hundryth off waynscottes bowght off the Mayster off the Savoy[218]	iiij li
	Item to the same for a dore	viij s
parkar	Item to Richard parkar for making off dore	viij s
	Item to the same ffor an other dore makyng	viij s
	Item to Thomas bowdon for drawyng off ij loodes off ffre and ~~on~~ v off rag	xiij d
stone from hedyngton	Item to haryson for ix loodes off ragg on fre ~~on~~ \iij too fre/ from bowdon	~~v s vj d~~ vj s vj d
	Item to John wase for xviij loodes ragg iiij fre ij rag ragg [sic]	xj s vj d
	Item to Jasper wase for xviij loodes off ragg	ix s
	Item Robert walton for v loodes off ragg: and ij loodes of ragg	iij s vj d

---

[217] This marginal note, together with 'waynscott from henley' above, and 'tymber from netylbed' on the following page, is written in a slanted cursive hand. They might have been inserted later, but it is possible that they were written by the original clerk, for some reason trying out a different hand.

[218] Wainscot purchased from William Holgill, Master of the Savoy Hospital in London, probably left over from the building works.

	Item to John francleyn ffor di' a hundryth ragg	vj s viij d
	Item to the same for iiij loodes off ffree	iiij s
prest to	Item to John francleyn in prest ffor	
francleyn	half a hundrith loodys off ffre att xij d	
payd	the loode	l s
More	Item to More ffor the sawyars by thomas barons	xx s
	Item to John Townesend for xx^ti loodes off ragg att iij d le loode	v s
	Item to John Bankys for a hundryth wayght ~~halff~~ and	
	iij quarterys off yron wer and on pownd halffe	xvj s iiij d
	Item to Sir wyllyams for hys costes to burford[219]	vj d
	Item to the caryar	ij d

Summa xvij li xviij s vij d

~~137li 17s 4d ob~~[220]   17li 18s 7d

[f. 45v; original f. 48v] [Blank][221]

	John Malowse	oooooo	iij s
	Richar [sic] Makegood	ooo	ij s
	Simon holman	o+oooø[222] oooooo	iij s ij d
	Nicholas herne	o+oooø oooooo	iiij s ~~iiij d~~
	Wyllyam brytten	o+oooø oooooo	iij s iiij d
	Wylliam kechynman	ø+oooø[223]	xvj d
	Xp'ofor sexten	ooc	x d
warde	Item to John warde the xxj day off august		xxxiijs iiij d
	Item to Archar for ij loodys caryage		iiij s
	Item to wyllyam broke for [blank]		ij s
	Item to Thomas phylyppys		ij s
	Item to wyllyam broke for a loode carriage		ij s
	Item to herry broke for a loode carriage		ij s
leyose	Item to Richard leyowse the xxj day off August		xl s

---

[219] Burford in Oxfordshire was close to Little Barrington, where the mason John Ward worked. Ward was responsible for making the windows of the college cloister.
[220] This sum was originally £13 but the 3 was crossed out and replaced with 7. It was then crossed out completely.
[221] No dates are given for this period, but it covers the working days Monday 9 to Saturday 21 August.
[222] The feast of St. Lawrence is celebrated on 10 August.
[223] Four of the labourers have a circle split by a vertical stroke against their names on some days, indicated here by ø. The value of this symbol is unclear, but it might represent a shortening of the working day, resulting in a reduction in wages.

AUGUST 1518

	~~Item to Richard parkar for settyng off the cloyster wyndoys~~	~~xvj s viij d~~
Richard parkar	Item to Rychard parkar for settyng off wyndoys off iij lyghtys and heowyn off squynchys[224]	iij s iiij d
Richard parkar	Item to the same for settyng and heowyng off squynchys ffor wyndoys off ij lyghtys	xiij s viij d
~~prest~~ \paid/	Item to the same in prest for hewyng off stoppys[225]	vj s viij d
	Item to Thomas stone for drawyng and leyng off xliij^C footes off bord att xij d le hundrith and for jesting ~~off~~ and levellyng off ix chamberys att xij d le chambre	lij s

[f. 46r; original f. 49r]

	Item to Jasper wase for xx loodys off ragg	x s
here	2 Item to walton for vij loodys off ragg ij fre	iiij s vj d
byggynyth	1 Item to haryson for xij loodys off ragg and on free on fr[...]vij s
his fre ston	5 Item to John wase for xiij loodes of ragg v fre	ix s
	Item to John francleyn for di' a hundrith loodes of ragg	vj s viij d
	~~7~~ Item for vij oode loodys	x d
	Item to bowdon for drawyng off a loode fre ston	iiij d
	Item to barns for a loode bord iiij^C xx^{ti} footes	ij s viij d
~~unpaid~~	Item to Mede for iiij^C footes carriage	ij s viij d
	Item to barns for a loode carriage conteynyng iiij^C	ij s viij d
Smyth	Item to John bankes for lockettys and stonderys waying a hundrith iij powdes di'	xvj s iiij d
	Item Sir wyllyams for horse hyer and rydyng to burford	xij d

Summa xij li ij s iiij d

12li 2s 4d

[f. 46v; original f. 49v]

This booke made ffrom the [...][226]

Richard makegood	x+oxoo[227]	oooooo	v s ij d
wyllyam Carter	o+xxoo	oooooo	iiij s iij d
wylliam Hamond	ooo		~~xij d~~ xvj d

---

[224] The *squynchys* in this entry probably refer to the chamfered corners of blocks of stone.

[225] The *stoppys* may refer to label stops.

[226] The date has been left blank, but the period covers the working days Monday 23 August to Saturday 4 September.

[227] The feast of St. Bartholomew is celebrated on 24 August.

	Simon holman	o+oooo	oooooo	iij s iiij d
	Wylliam Bryttayn	o+oooo	oooooo	iij s iiij d
	N herne	[blank]	[blank]	x d

Sawyars	~~I~~wylliam Castell and his fellow for viij days	viij s
Stone	Item to Thomas stone for laying and drawyng off xv hundrith at xij d le hundrith	xv s
bankys	Item to John bankys for xl lockys and xj stonderys waying iijC vj li att xvj s iiij d le hundryth	
	Item ffor a hundrith broddys	l s iiij d[228]
Richard leyowse	Item to Richard leyowse the v day of septembre John chare for the caryage off a loode off plankes w^t iij^C footes off bordys	xl s ij s viij d
	Item to wylliam broke for a loode caryage	ij s
	Item to harry broke for a loode caryge	ij s
baryngton	wylliam Archar for caryage off a loode off ffrestone from baryngton	ij s iiij d
Richard parkar	Item to Richard parkar settyng off wyndoys off ij lyghtys and oon lyght	xx s
	Item to Mr Vicepresydent ffor rydyng to walton in warwyke schyre \to vewe londys/[229]	xx d
	Item to Sir wyllyams for hys costes to Burford for the wyndoys off the cloyster	vij d

[f. 47r; original f. 50r]

	Jasper wase for ~~a~~ xxiiij loodys off ragg carriage	xij s
	John wase for vij loodys off ragg	iij s vj d
1	Item to Robert walton for xiiij loodes off ragg on fre	vij s vj d
32	Item to haryson for vj loodes off ragg and ~~iij~~ free	iiij s
	Item to John ffrancley for halffe a hundryth lood off ragg	vj s viij d

Summa ix li xvj s vj d

9li 16s ~~10d~~ 6d

---

[228] These two payments to John Bankys totalled together.
[229] This entry refers to a visit that the Vice-President, Robert Morwent, made to view land at Walton in Warwickshire, probably with a view to adding to the properties belonging to Corpus.

[*f. 47v; original f. 50v*]

This booke ffrom the [*blank*][230]
unto the xix^th day off Septembre

	Richard Makegood	oxoooc	ij s x d
	wyllyam carter	oooo	ij s
	wylliam hamond	ooooooo [*sic*]	iij s x d
	Simon holman	oc+ooo	oo+ooo[231]	iij s ij d
	Nicholas herne	oc+ooo	oo+ooo	iij s
	wylliam bryttayn	oc+ooo	oo+ooo	iij ij d[232]
	John Jonson for a iij quarterys off a day		iiij d
Carow	Item to Robert carow ffor the fframe off the cloyster	v li
lyme	Item to Elys larden ffor xxxiij quarterys off lyme	xxxiiij s viij d
prest	Item to the same in prest	~~iij s iiij d~~
More	Item to Nicholas More the v day off Septembre	xx s
Richard leyowse	Item to Richard leyowse the xviij day off Septembre	xl s
ston from baryngton	Item to wyllyam brooke ffor ij loodys caryage from baryngton	iiij s v d
	Item to the same for a loode caryage	ij s
Smyth	Item to garrate for viij kasementes for the lyberary att a ij footes long after xviij d the kasement	xij s
warde	Item to warde the xviij day off Septembre	xl s
	Item ffor corde	iiij d
caryar	Item to gamson the caryar for the caryage off ij pypys off books off Greke from london waying ix^C iij quarterys[233]	xj s vj d
	Item ffor too pypys to the same bookys	ij s x d
	Item ffor the caryage off the same bookes ffrom the marchant to the caryar ys ynne	xij d

---

[230] The first working day of this period was Monday 6 September.

[231] The feast of the Nativity of the Virgin Mary is celebrated on 8 September and the Octave of the Nativity of the Virgin Mary on 15 September. 15 September may have been kept as a day of rest in preference to Tuesday 14 (the feast of the Exaltation of the Holy Cross) as it was also the first of the autumn Ember Days, which were supposed to be kept as days of prayer and fasting.

[232] A number of these sums do not equate with the standard rates of pay.

[233] The *pypys* mentioned in this entry refer to a form of container in which goods could be kept or carried. This entry refers to two pipes containing Greek books for the library at Corpus.

80 BUILDING ACCOUNTS OF CORPUS CHRISTI COLLEGE

[f. 48r; original f. 51r]

	3 Item to Jasper wase ffor x loodys off ragg and iij free	vj s vj d
	3 Item to John wase for xvij loodes off ragg and iij free	x s
	Item payd to John ffrancleyn and for a quarter off a loode hundrith off ragg	iij s iiij d
parkar	Item to Rychard parkar ffor hewyng off stoppys	iij s iiij d
	Item to the same for the settyng off a doore	ij s
	Item to the same for hewyng off squynchys and quoyns	x
	Item to the same for settyng and parelyng off wynd\o/ys off ij lyghtys and off oon lyght	x s
	Item to bowdon for dyggyng off a loode off free stone	iiij d
bankes payd	Item to bankes in prest	xx s
	Item to Sir wyllyams for goyng to netylbed	iij s […] xj d
sond	Item to townesend ffor xx loodys off gravell	v s

Summa xvij li viij s vj d[234]

.6.   Summa Ciiij li xv s viij d[235].6.

xvij li viij s vj d
17li 8s 6d

[f. 48v; original f. 51v] [Blank][236]

	Richard makegood	x+xxoo	ooo+oo[237]	iiij s ij d
	Wylliam carter	x+xxoo	oo(+)oo	iij s vj d
	Item to the sawyars for sawyng			vij s iiij d
	Item to hamond for	ooo		xviij d
	Symon holman	o+oooo	oo+ooo	iij s iiij d
	N herne	o+oooo	oo+ooo	iij s iiij d
	w bryttayn	o+oooo	oo+ooo	iij s iiij d
nayles	Item for ij^M vj penny nayle			vj s viij d
	Item for a thowsond x penny nayle			vj s
R. leyowse	Item to Richard leyowse the second day off octobre			l s
	Item to the same Richard leyowse			x s

[234] The total of ff. 47v and 48r.
[235] The total of ff. 41v to 48r, Monday 28 June to Saturday 18 September.
[236] No dates are given for this period, but it covers the working days Monday 20 September to Saturday 2 October.
[237] The feast of St. Matthew the Evangelist is celebrated on 21 September and the feast of St. Michael the Archangel (Michaelmas) on 29 September.

september/october 1518

w est	Item to wyllyam Est the second day off octobre for makyng an settyng off cresse table and severall after iiij d the foote iij li vj s viij d	~~vj s viij d~~ iij li vj s viij d
Elys ~~larden~~	Item to Elys larden in prest for lyme	~~[.j] s iiij d~~
More	Item to Nicholas More the [blank] day off septembre	xxvj s viij d
	Item to wylliam broke for ij loodys	iiij s iiij d
	Item to Roger broke for a loode	ij s ij d
	Item to herry broke for a loode	ij s
	Item to M^r claxton[238] for hys costes rydyng to the chaunceller off lincon \for saynt Jonys hall/	xxj d ob
parkar	Item to Richard parkar for settyng ~~off~~ \and hewyng off squynchis to/ x wyndoys off ij lyghtys att iiij s the ~~lyght~~ \wyndoo/ and for every wyndo off on lyght xx d where off he hath receyvyd xliij s	viij s
	Item to the same for makyng off a launcelate	xij d
	Item to the same for makyng off a dore in to a chambre	ij s
	Item to same for settyng off a wyndoo off iij lyghtes	iij s iiij d

[f. 49r; original f. 52r]

	Item to Thomas Stone for drawyngd and leying off vij^C footes off bord att xij d le hundrith	vij s
	Item to the same for levellyng and geystys of a chambre	xij d
5	Item to Jasper wase for xij ragg v ffree	viij s vj d
2	Item to John wase fo ix ragg ij ffree	v s vj d
2	Item to Robert waalton for xij ragg ij ffree	vij s
3	Item to haryson for iij loodys off ffree	xviij d
	Item to ffrancleyn for a quarter off a hundryth ragg	iij s iiij d
	5 8 10	
	Item in prest to ffrancleyn for ~~rag~~ \freestone/	xiij s iiij d
Smyth	Item to John bankes the second day off octobre ffor lockettes and stonderys waying iij^C pownde wheroff he hath receyvyd xx s	xxix s
	Item for naylys	ij d
	Item to bryghtwell for my lordes letter[239]	vij d
warde	Item to John ward the ixth day off octobre	iij li

---

[238] There were several men named Claxton associated with Oxford University in the early sixteenth century.

[239] An entry recording payment for a letter, either addressed to or from Bishop Fox. The word is abbreviated to lett' and so it is possible that it refers to more than one letter.

82   BUILDING ACCOUNTS OF CORPUS CHRISTI COLLEGE

Est | Item to wylliam Est the same day | xxvjs viij d

Summa xix li viij d ob

19li 8d ob

[f. 49v; original f. 52v]

This Booke made from the second day
off octobre unto the xvj day off the same monyth

	Simon holman	oooooo	o(o)(+)oox[240]	iij s iiij d
	Nicholas herne	oooooo	x(x)(+)ooo[241]	iij s
	wylliam Bryttayn	oooooo	oo+ooo	iij s viij d

lyme	Item to Elys larden ffor xxvij quarterys off lyme att xiij d le quarter \and v boshelles/	xxviij s ix d
Richard leyowse	Item to Richard leyowse the xvj day off octobre	xl s
borde from netylbed	Item to John Chare for a loode off borde carriage	ij s viij d
	Item to Thomas wylschyre for iiij^C iiij footes bord	ij s viij d
stone ffrom baryngton	Item to John Marman for iiij^C footes iiij footes borde	ij s viij d
	Item to Brooke for the caryage off a loode off wrowght stoff	ij s viij d
	Item to herry Brooke for A loode	ij s
	Item to Archer ffor a loode	ij s
	Item ffor mendyng off an eowere[242]	xvj d
	Item for ij lateyse to the closett[243]	ij s
	Item for Androys exspence for rydyng to walton[244] in warwyke sheyre for v li londes	ij s
	Item for powlys expence from oxford to wynchester and from oxforth to Guyttyng[245]	iiij s ij d ob

[240] The feast of St. Edward the Confessor is celebrated on 13 October.
[241] On Tuesday 12 October the clerk mistakenly entered + (to indicate a feast day) against the names of Simon Holman and Nicholas Herne. He subsequently corrected these by overwriting the + against Holman's name with o to indicate a day worked, and the + against Herne's name with a black dot, to indicate a day not worked. He also initially marked them down on Wednesday 13 with black dots, as if they had not worked on a regular working day. He subsequently overwrote the dots with a cross to indicate that it was in fact a holy day.
[242] A ewer.
[243] A wooden fretwork panel or lattice for the closett or small room, that could be fixed into a window to allow fresh air but prevent birds from entering. For lattice, see Salzman, 186.
[244] The hamlet of Walton in the parish of Wellesbourne, Warwickshire, mentioned above in n.229.
[245] An entry recording the payments made to Andrew for travelling to Walton in Warwickshire

OCTOBER/NOVEMBER 1518

Item for ~~lathe~~ vj^c lathe nayle	vij d
Item ffor bastyng roopys	iij d
Item ffor a skynne off parchement to wryght M^r ffrost ys Indenture[246]	iiij d

[f. 50r; original f. 53r]

1	Item to Jasper for carriage off xiij loodes of ragg and on fre	vij s
1	Item to J wase for xvijj loodes of ragg and on fre	ix s vj d
3	Item to haryson for v ragg iij free	iiij s
	Item to walton for xij loodes of ragg	vj s
	Item to John Coke for xiiij loodes of ragg	vij s
	Item to John ffrancleyn for iij^xx and too loodes and for x loodes debet att the last \debet xxij/	vj s viij d
	Item to Thomas Stone […	

parkar	Item to Richard parkar for makyng of corbell table and settyng att iij d the foote	xiij s iiij d
	Item to John Townesend for xxxij loodes of gravell att iij d the loode	viij s
Glowester College	Item delyveryd to the prior off Studentes off Glolcyter [sic] College by my lordes co'mawndment[247]	x li

Summa xviij li vs vij d ob

18li \5s/ 7d ob

[f. 50v; original f. 53v]

This Boke made from the xvj day off octobre
unto the vj day off novembre

carpenter	Richard makgood	ooo			xviij d
Joyner	Robert Carvar	ooooooooooooooo [sic]			viij s
laborars	Simon holman	++oooo	ooo+oø	++oooo[248]	iij s x d
	Nicholas herne	++oxoo	ooo+oc	++oooo	iij s vj d
	william Brittayn	++oooo	ooo+oc	++oooo	iij s x d

and Paul who rode from Winchester to Oxford and then onto Temple Guiting in Gloucestershire where Bishop Fox had purchased property for the college.

[246] William Frost was Bishop Fox's steward.
[247] Gloucester College was a Benedictine establishment within Oxford University.
[248] These three weeks included the feasts of St. Luke (18 October), St. Frideswide, patroness of Oxford (19 October), Ss Simon and Jude (28 October), All Saints (1 November) and All Souls (2 November).

Richard leyowse	Item to Richard leyowse the vj day of novembre	xx s
Sawyars	Item to wylliam keft and his fellow for iiij days	iiij s
lyme	Item to Elys larden for xxvij quarters of lyme	xxviij s iiij d
warde	Item to warde the ~~vj~~ iij day of novembre \sue Indentura/[249]	xx s
parkar	Item to Richard parkar for makyng of corbell table and settyng \in part of payment by Indenture/	xiij s iiij d

13
3   Item to Jasper for xiij loodes of ragg and 3 free   viij s
13
3   Item to John Coke for xiij loodes of ragg and 3 free   viij s
17
1   Item to Robert walton for xvij loodes of ragg and on fre   ix s
8
    Item to haryson for viij loodes of ragg   iiij s
7
1   Item to John wase for vij loodes of ragg on free   iiij s
    Item to John francleyn for iij quarterys of a hundrith ragg   x s

Item to Thomas wylshyre for ij loodes of borde from netylbed   v s iiij d
Item to John Marman for ij loodes bordes planckes   v s iiij d
Item to John Chare for iij loodes of planckes bordes   viij s
Item to Richard Chare for a loode of bordes   ij s viij d
Item to Robert Colyar for a loode of tymber   ij s viij d
Item to the said Robert for halfe a loade caryage   ~~viij d~~ xij d
Item to John wylshyre for a loode of bordes   ij s viij d

[f. 51r; original f. 54r]

stone from baryngton	Item to wylliam Archar for ij loodes carriage ~~o~~ from baryngton	iiij s viij d
	Item to harry broke for a loode	ij s
	Item to John Bray for ij loode	iiij s
	Item to John Bray for a loode	ij s iiij d
	Item to John phylyppys for a loode	ij s iiij d

Summa ix li xij s iiij d

9li 12s 4d

---

[249] Written above the preceding words.

[*f. 51v; original f. 54v*]

~~Jhus mary lady helpe amen dico vobis~~[250]

<1518> This boke made from the vj day of novembre unto
the xx^(ti) day of the same monyth

	Thomas Stone	ooo		~~vj d~~ xiiij d
	Robert carvar	ooo		xx d
	Symon holman	ooxøooo	oooooo	ij s viij d
	Nicholas herne	ooooxøo	oooooo	ij s viij d
	wylliam Brittayne	ooxøoo	oooooo	ij s viij d

Richard leyowse	Item to Richard leyowse the xx day of novembre	xvj s
parkar	Item to Richard parkar in part of payment for makyng of the corbell table by the foote after iij d le foote	x s
	Item to the same for makyng of iiij lawnslott wyndoys	v s ~~iij s~~ iiij d
Joyner	Item to Robert carver for xx^(ti) yardes seallyng in the tower and the churche	xj s viij d
ffremasons	~~Item delyveryd to the fremasons in part of payment for the carvyng off the gargelles by the grett~~	~~x s~~
Smyth	Item to John Abankes for a hundrith wayght of yron for iiij lawslottes	xvj s iiij d
	Item for roodes of yron for the canapy	xviij d
	Item for iij hoopys and too erys ffor a buckett	x d
	Item for a fyle and a wrest to the stone sawe	xij d
rag from hedyngton	3 Item to Jasper for xj loodes off ragg and iiij free caryage	vij s
	Item to John wase for xij loodes of ragg	vj s
	Item to walton for viij loodes of ragg	iiij s
	Item to haryson for vj loodes of ragg	iij s
	Item to John Coke for xj loodes of ragg	v s vj d
	Item to John ffrancleyn for di' a hundrith save too loodes	vj s viij d
	Item for a loode~~s~~ of [......] \pold ragg/	vj d
	Item to the water ~~bay~~ baylyff	viij d
	Item for seallyng off the Indentures of osney[251]	ij s
	Summa 5li 8s 10d	

---

[250] This line of text has been crossed through with a single horizontal line, probably at a later date deliberately to remove an overtly Catholic invocation.

[251] An entry concerning an indenture with Osney Abbey, which was a house of Augustinian canons in Oxford.

7. Sum*ma* 52li 7s 6 d[252]   Sum*ma* Tot*alis* 697li 17s 8[253]

totius lib:

[*f. 52r; original f. 55r*]

Ite*m* for ij payre of hengys weyng iiij and xx li tenyd(?)	iiij s
Ite*m* for viij chord naylys tenyng(?)	~~xvj d~~ xij d
Ite*m* for a hovyke [*sic*] and stappyll[254] veyng iiij li ~~vij d~~	vij d
Ite*m* for mendyng of ij payre of hengys	viij d
Ite*m* for ij nowe howyks to the saym hengys	ij d
Ite*m* for ij now loykys	xvj d
Ite*m* for iiij kasementes	vj s viij d
Ite*m* for iij now loykys	iij s
Ite*m* for vij and xx li of warke(?) \stapulles for stons and tymb*er*/[255]	iiij s
Ite*m* for ij now kayes	vj d
Ite*m* for xij li of verke(?)	xx d j d [*sic*]
Ite*m* for x sodelet bares[256]	x d
Ite*m* for maykyng of a payre of hengys of yowd stoyffe and tenyng(?)	viij d
Ite*m* for iij payre of gemos[257] to the kychyne	~~iij s~~ vj
Ite*m* for iij gemos to master presedent stode[258]	xviij d
Ite*m* for bollttes and stappyllys veyng v li	viij d ob
Ite*m* for iij now loykkes	ij s
Ite*m* for viij sodelet bares	xvj d
Ite*m* for mendyng of a […] payre of hengys	viiij d
	lix s vj d ob[259]
Ite*m* for a xij bolltes and stappyllys veynd xij li	xxj d
Ite*m* for vij chore(?) sodelet barres	xx s iij s iiij d
Ite*m* for a payre of [..o..e gemo..]	viij d
Ite*m* for a now kaye to the chappell dore	iij d
Ite*m* for a payre of hengys maykyng and howykes[260]	iiij d
Ite*m* for xij howykes to the kychyne \to hang on flesch/[261]	vj d

[252] The total of ff. 48v to 51v, Monday 20 September to Saturday 20 November.
[253] The total expenditure on materials, wages, etc., contained within these accounts, excluding the bill of John Bankes, smith, on f. 43r.
[254] A hovyke and stappyll refers to a latch and a hook.
[255] Written above the preceding word, and in a hand different from the rest of this page. Possibly in the hand of the principal scribe.
[256] Probably saddlebars also called soudlets used to secure windows in place. For soudlets, see Salzman, 181, 292.
[257] Probably the same as the hinges called gymmys above.
[258] The President's study.
[259] Written in the right-hand margin next to the preceding entry.
[260] Hooks.
[261] A reference to meat hooks.

Item for ij bolltes and stappyllys to master pressedent vendos   iiij d

iij li ~~xxj d~~ vj d ob

Unde solut' xviij die [Ju]lij – xxx s

[*f. 52v*] [*a line of about 10 symbols that elude interpretation; otherwise blank*].

[*f. 53r; original f. 56r*]

fol. 1[262]

The Chapell

The Rooffe off off [*sic*] the chaple ys in lengyth xx[ti] yards and on foote the compas off the same is ix yardes ij footes and a halffe the summe off yardes ij[c] lackyng di' foote after xvj d the yard
Summa   xiij li vj s viij d
Item for the seallyng off the hye alter att vj d le yard the some off x yardes[263]   v s
Item xiiij foote off trayle and Creest for the same altar att xij d the foote[264]   xiiij s
Item for xxv[ti] waynscottes for the knottes in the chapell rooffe xvj s viij d
Item to Thomas Roossell off westmester for the kerfyng off iiij[xxti] xviij hoole knottes and iiij halff knottes the summe off v[xxti] v hoole knottes att xvj d the peese[265]   vij li

The lyberary

The lyberary is In lengyth xx yerdes ij footes and the rooff in compas ix yardes on foote the summe off yardes x[xxti](?) xij yardes ij foote att xvj d the yard ~~x~~[266]   xij li xvij s iiij d
The closett att the lyberary end conteynyth in measure xxx[ti] yardes iij footes att xiiij d the yard[267]   xxxv s

---

[262] In a small italic hand, also used on the two remaining folios.
[263] This entry refers to the high altar in the college chapel.
[264] The *trayle and crest* probably refers to a decorative strip as were later carved for Hampton Court; see Salzman, 218.
[265] An entry recording that Thomas Roossell or Russell of Westminster was paid £7 for carving the *knottes* or bosses for the chapel at Corpus Christi.
[266] This entry shows that the library when first built was just over 60 feet in length. It has since been lengthened.
[267] The *closet* of the library was at the west end of the library; see Burnett Hillman Streeter,

[*f. 53v; original f. 56v*]

Mast*er* Presydent is chambre

The rooffe off the same chambre co*n*teynyth in measure xxxvj⁽ᵗⁱ⁾ yardes att xiiij d the yarde   xlj s iiij d

It*em* viij yardes off sealyng in the too wyndoys off the same chamb*er* att vj d the yard   iiij s

Item the seallyng att the beddys hedd w⁽ᵗ⁾ the presse in the wall co*n*teynyth in measure xv yardes at vj d the yard   vij s vj d

It*em* the study conteynyth in measure xxx⁽ᵗⁱ⁾ yardes att vj d the yard   xv s

Item M⁽ʳ⁾ vipresident is study[268] is xxxj yardes att vj d the yard   xiij s iiij d

        S*um*ma xxxij li vs x d   xiij s iiij d

[*f. 54r; original f. 57r*]

2.

The walles wrowght by the p*er*ch abowght the college

The towne wall conteynyth in lengyth from the corner off the drawfte unto the dore thatt \goyth/ in frydeswyd is grove iij p*er*ch di' in lengyth and xix foote hye

      S*um*ma p*er*chys iij⁽ˣˣᵗⁱ⁾ vj p*er*chys di'

ffrom the dore in lengyth towardes frydeswydes v perch di' and vj foote heye

      S*um*ma xxxiij⁽ᵗⁱ⁾ perchys

It*em* in the same wall iij p*er*che xv foote hye

      S*um*ma ~~xxxvti perchys~~ xlv

The wydedrafte

Item att the backe off the said draft in measure xij p*er*chis and xiiij foote off table

      S*um*ma xij perchys

The Chained Library. A Survey of the Evolution of the Library in England (London, 1931), 154.

[268] The Vice-President's study. The first Vice-President of Corpus was Robert Morwent, a former Fellow of Magdalen College.

COLLEGE WALLS

Item the wall att the church end is in lengyht [sic] a perch and vj foote and xviij footes hye the some off perchis

> Summa xxiiij perchys

Item the wall att the vestery corner In lengyth a perch and a halff and a ~~xij~~ xj footes di' hye

> Summa xvij perch

Item the wall agayn the poltery howse vij footes hey and ij perch lackyng iij footes long

> Summa xvj perches

Item the wall betwixt Merton college and the chaple ij perch iij foote long ix foote hye

> Summa xix perch di'

[f. 54v; original f. 57v]

Item abowght the wyde drawte by the powltery howse and ~~the gabull end~~ xx^{ti} perch
Item the wall att the masterys garden v perch long and xiij footes hey   iij^{xxti} v perch
Item the wallys off the cloyster be under the grow\nd/ and the wall off the master ys garden yn all is ij^C iiij^{xxti} xiiij perchys   [...]
Item for ix foote off pase stone att iiij d the foote beyng att the gate   iij s
Item for the stepp att Mr Presydent is parlower dore   xij d
Item for xxiiij^{ti} foote off corbell table for the common wydedrawght ~~att~~ ij d le foote   iiij s
Item the walles abowth te [sic] cloyster be levell above the ~~grownd v foote~~ fyrst coorse v footes compas a bawght the utter wall[269] is ix perch di' long and the yner wall is xiij perchys long iij footes

> Summa off perchys is v^{xx} xvj
>
> Summa ~~xxxv li xvj s~~ xxxvij li iij s[270]

---

[269] 'About the outer wall'.
[270] Payments made for the construction of walls round and about the college.

[*f. 55r (ult); original f. 58r*]

3.

Md' co'menawntyd and agreid by me M' John Claymond presydentt of corpus xpi' college w^t Robert carow carpenter for to fynd tymber workemanshypp bord caryage w^t all other manner off necessary thynges belongyng to a carpenter w^t on flower bordid and a rooffe to bere lede[271] w^t lede bord belongyng thertot and geistyd[272] betwene the bemys to bere sealyng w^t dorys wyndoys partycions and stayars accordyng to a platt made by humfray cooke the which conteynyth a hundrid foote xij ijynt(?) w^{t}in the walles in lengyth and wyde betwyxt the wall above xix footes accordyng att [*sic*] hytt apperyth in the sayd platt.[273] The sayd Robert carow to receyve and have for the performacion off them xliiij li. att the seallyng hereoff to receive   x li

Md' co'nenawntyd [*sic*] and agreid w^t wylliam Colyn and Nicholas More for the ~~makyng off~~ sawyng framyng and settyng upp off the rooff off the said cloyster for the workes off Robert carowys att the Est end toward the chaple and a long ~~to~~ by ye chaple to the west end off the workes off the said Robert carow accordyng to a platt thereoff: w^t too clere storys att the reysyng and the fallyng off they rooffys: the yoll peese[274] to be in boyd and levell geistid underneyth att every foote space: Mr presedent to fynd tymber and all manner off caryage they to have for the same[275]   viij li

[*f. 55v; original f. 58v*]

Item debet to the smyth hys bylles allowyd   iij li iij s ij d

---

[271] A roof to bear lead.
[272] Joisted.
[273] This contract is given in Salzman, 573 and briefly discussed by Newman in McConica, 611.
[274] A joll piece was a cornice or frieze; see Salzman, 169.
[275] Salzman, 573.

APPENDIX 1

A CHRONOLOGY OF THE DEVELOPMENT OF BISHOP FOX'S PLANS FOR AN EDUCATIONAL ESTABLISHMENT IN OXFORD AND THE BUILDING OF THE ORIGINAL COLLEGE

December 1508
After twenty years as a bishop, and handling problems with monks and nuns, and also worried about the state of the nation Fox contemplates founding an educational establishment in Oxford for the education of monks.[1]

1510
Archbishop Warham sells land at Overton in Hampshire to Bishop Fox as part of an endowment for the college he plans to establish.[2]

November 1511
A site in Oxford has evidently been chosen by Fox for his foundation, because the Fellows of Merton College begin to discuss the question of letting property (on the present site of Corpus), to an unnamed individual.[3]

21 December 1511
The governing body of Oxford University writes to Bishop Fox and acknowledges his plans to establish a college.[4]

8 February 1512
Purchase of lands by Fox from master mason John Lebons and his wife.

June 1512
Fox waits for a decision from Merton College with regard to the sale of their lands to him.

July 4 1512
Carpenter Humphrey Coke, and masons William Vertue and William East are sent to survey the proposed site in Oxford. Preliminary work may have

---

[1] Allen, 55.
[2] CCCO C1/Cap.1/Ev.145; Smith, 1988, 320, 338 n. 15. Fox and Warham quarrelled over the prerogatives of Canterbury soon after this sale; see Fowler, p.14.
[3] J. G. Milne, *The Early History of Corpus Christi College, Oxford* (Oxford, 1946), 2.
[4] Allen, 55–6; J. McConica, 'The Rise of the Undergraduate College', in McConica, 18.

begun on an old kitchen site.[5]

August 1512
A violent attack is made on Coke, Vertue and East by some of those completing the building work at nearby Brasenose College.[6] An Oxford carpenter, Robert Carow, was not assaulted.

Late autumn/early winter 1512
According to a reference in the college register, the Fellows of Merton decide to convey their properties of Neville's Inn and Corner Hall to St. Swithun's priory for an annuity of £3. There is no evidence of this conveyance ever having been engrossed.[7]

31 October 1512.
The Fellows of Merton College authorized the withdrawal from the muniment room, of the deeds of Neville's Inn and Corner Hall, but not those of the Bachelors' Garden.

November 1512
The Fellows of Merton decide to convey Bachelors' Garden to Fox in addition to Neville's Inn and Corner Hall.

21 November 1512
The Fellows of Merton approved the withdrawal of the deeds of the Bachelors' Garden. They have now agreed to convey the property, including the Bachelors' Garden, to the Prior and Convent of St. Swithun's in Winchester, thus providing the greater part of the site for Fox's new college.

16 January 1513
In January 1513, Fox went ahead with his side of the arrangement. He gave the £120 in cash to John Claymond, President of Magdalen, who delegated its distribution to Walter Morwent, who on 16 January 1513 began disbursing it to Fellows of Merton at regular intervals, receiving carefully worded receipts for each payment.[8]

28 February 1513
More money is delivered for the Warden and Fellows of Merton College with further payments made in March, April and May.

12 March 1513
A royal licence in mortmain is granted allowing Bishop Fox to establish a

[5] RCHM, 48.
[6] Fowler, 64–5; E. A. Gee, 'Oxford Carpenters, 1370–1530', *Oxoniensia*, 17/18 (1952/3), 134.
[7] We are grateful to Julian Reid for this information.
[8] Bodleian MS Wood D2; notes made by Brian Twyne who arranged Corpus library in 1627.f. 610v; Fowler, 65–7.

monastic college.⁹

March/April 1513
With the site secured and official permissions granted, work probably began in earnest on the building of Fox's college at Oxford.

30 June 1513
An indenture is drawn up between Bishop Fox and the Prior and Convent of St. Swithun's in Winchester (Appendix 4). It mentions in passing that work on Fox's college has begun, and refers to an earlier contract, presumably drawn up in 1512 or early 1513, between the Bishop, Vertue and Coke for the college to be completed.[10] The principal item is that Prior and Convent agree to complete the work if Bishop Fox is unable to do so. The agreement further implies that Fox's college had been planned in tandem with his chantry chapel in Winchester Cathedral, upon which work had also begun. On the same day, Bishop Fox departs for France in order to accompany King Henry VIII on his military campaign.[11]

August 1514
Significant building work is undertaken on Fox's college, including the construction of the foundations of the Front Quad.[12] A second brawl occurred on site, involving Henry Wright and William Barnes (probably students at Brasenose but not listed in the college register), and John Formby the former Principal of Brasenose. A Fellow by the name of John Leigh encouraged the violence, showing that 'Trojan' academic hostility was one of the motives. The mason, William East, was badly beaten and was in a critical condition, likely to die, so Wright and Barnes were held in custody until East recovered.[13]

5 December 1514
The manor of Temple Guiting in Gloucestershire belonging to the Huddleston family was sold to Fox and he took delivery of the manorial title deeds.

6 December 1514
An indenture is drawn up between Fox and Christopher Urswick for the recitation of prayers for the previous owners of the manor of Temple Guiting, John and Jane Huddleston, at an altar in the chapel of Fox's college that is to be dedicated to St. Cuthbert.[14] Urswick, who drafted the indenture,

⁹ Ward, xxv.
[10] Fowler, 61.
[11] Allen, 69.
[12] RCHM, 48.
[13] They were heavily fined by the University, and Formby and Leigh were each bound in £20 recognizance towards paying for East's medical treatment, and compensation.
[14] CCCO F1/Cap.1/Fasc.1/Ev.25.

refers to the college as being built 'in honour of Corpus Christi', but named 'Winchester College', suggesting that it still had a monastic purpose.[15]

7 December 1514
Payment is made for the manor of Temple Guiting in the presence of Thomas More and other legal witnesses.

29 December 1514
John Huddleston the younger brings a case in Chancery against Fox, wishing to frustrate his purchase of the manor of Temple Guiting.

January and February 1515
The case in Chancery continues and the first depositions are made in January and February.

June 1515
Archbishop Warham finds in favour of Bishop Fox in the Temple Guiting case. The hearing is enrolled amongst Chancery documents in July 1515.

Throughout 1515, the Church–state crisis became increasingly intense, leading to the conferences at Blackfriars and Baynard's Castle later in the year. At some point between December 1514 and October 1515, Fox considers making Corpus a college for secular clergy and prospective professional men, rather than entirely for monks. He puts pressure on the Fellows of Merton College to convey their land to him as arranged, but his change of mind probably became definite later, at Christmas 1515, when the situation worsened.

20 October 1515
The Warden and Fellows of Merton College act upon their earlier decision of 21 November 1512, and enter into an agreement with Fox for him to acquire Corner Hall, Neville's Inn and the Bachelors' Garden in consideration of the £120 disbursed in 1513, and their reservation of an annual rent-chage of £4 6s 8d, for the 'ground where the said meases now stand and gardens the said Bishop intendeth and purposeth by the grace of God to build and edify a college that shall be called Corpus Christi College'.[16] The earlier draft conveyance with the Prior and Convent of St. Swithun's was put aside and not engrossed. The decision and the wording of Merton College's action of 20 October 1515 narrows down Fox's change of mind about monks to somewhere within the period between October 1515, when the Church–state conflict intensified, and May 1516, when Cardinal Schiner arrived in London.

---

[15] Pers. comm. Julian Reid.
[16] Fowler, 67; Fulman drew a plan locating these properties which is reproduced in Fowler, 69.

When Fox alters his plan for the college at Oxford to educate not monks, but mainly non-monastic students, Corpus Christi College is already under construction, and requires enlargement. Instead of a Prior, eight monks and a few servants, the college would now have one President, 20 Fellows, 20 students, three lecturers and the chapel staff, so that accommodation needs to be increased fourfold. Coke and Vertue advised Fox on building plans. They decide to adapt the old plans ['double platte'] mentioned in the indenture of 1513, two-storeyed modules, each of four rooms, two upstairs, two downstairs, and a central staircase. Instead of two modules housing eight monks (one to a room), they decide to place five modules, along the north and west sides of the Front Quad, providing twenty rooms. Occupancy was to be doubled by each Fellow sharing his chamber with his pupil, thus accommodating forty. The college hall is structurally complete, but it was built for a small contingent of monks, as shown by the carved and painted details, including the date 1516 (Appendix 6). It is now enlarged, but the monastic imagery carved in several places in the hall is not removed.

May 1516
Bishop Fox and Archbishop Warham protest against war by leaving a meeting with Cardinal Schiner. Fox resigns Keepership of the Privy Seal.

26 November 1516
Bishop Fox is granted a royal licence in order that he might establish a secular (non-monastic) college with a President and 30 scholars.[17] The earlier royal licence in mortmain of 12 March 1513, which allowed him to establish a monastic college, is cancelled.

17 January 1517
Isabella Brainton, Abbess of Godstow, firmly agrees to sell Fox Nun Hall, the Abbey's small town house adjacent to the building site of his college.[18]

22 January 1517
Fox's translation of the Rule of St. Benedict for the nuns in his diocese is published.

9 February 1517
After a fortnight of anxious uncertainty for Fox, two properties on site called Urban Hall and Beke's Inn are obtained from the Prior and Convent of St. Frideswide.[19]

[17] Ibid., 57.
[18] Ibid., 68.
[19] Ibid.

21 February 1517
Fox writes to Claymond telling him that a barge has recently left Westminster carrying kitchen utensils and other items for Corpus. Robert Bailey of the Savoy is carrying an inventory listing the cargo. He is to survey the building work.

Late February 1517
At his episcopal manor in Esher, Bishop Fox receives the revised foundation charter for Corpus from Claymond listing the Fellows' full and correct names, titles, dioceses and county of birth.

1 March 1517
Bishop Fox signs the foundation charter for Corpus.[20]

2 March 1517
Humphrey Coke visits Fox at Esher, and is given the foundation charter to carry to Oxford.

3 March 1517
Coke delivers the foundation charter and additional monies for Corpus to Claymond.[21]

5 March 1517
Six Fellows are instituted to Corpus by Claymond, who now officially becomes the first President of Corpus. The new college buildings are formally handed over to Claymond.

May 1517
Work begins on digging the foundations for the cloister at Corpus.[22]

7 June 1517
The President, Fellows and other members of Corpus Christi College are formally discharged from canonical obligation to the see of Lincoln. Jurisdiction is transferred to the Bishop of Winchester.[23]

20 June 1517
Fox reads the statutes of his Oxford college in the chapel at St. Cross near Winchester. There are no monks in attendance. He also signs the licence permitting divine offices to be performed in the chapel at Corpus.[24]

---

[20] Ibid., 57.
[21] The foundation charter is CCCO A/2/1.
[22] CCCO H1/4/1, f. 18v; Fowler, 71.
[23] Fowler, 67.
[24] Ibid.

25–30 June 1517
Both William Vertue and Humphrey Coke are in Oxford and on site, no doubt checking on the progress of building work.

July, August and October 1517
The first students are admitted to Corpus, which suggests that the rooms were finished.[25] At the same time, an epidemic of the sweating sickness breaks out in Oxford resulting in the death and burial of several Fellows and students.

19 October 1517
The chapel at Corpus is dedicated.[26]

November 1517
Carved bosses are made for the college chapel by Thomas Roossell in London and are painted and gilded by Humphrey Coke.

Late 1518
It is likely that the rooms known as the cloister chambers are built at this time.

While construction of Corpus College comes to an end so this year sees the completion of Bishop Fox's chantry chapel in Winchester Cathedral.[27]

1519
Humanist scholar, Erasmus praises Fox's college at Oxford, this 'biblioteca trilinguis' (trilingual library: Latin, Greek and Hebrew), as 'inter praecipua decora Britanniae' ('among the greatest glories of Britain').[28]

---

[25] Ibid., 71.
[26] Ibid., 67, n.1.
[27] A. Smith, 'The Chantry Chapel of Bishop Fox', *Winchester Cathedral Record*, 57 (1988), 27–32.
[28] Allen, P. S., *Erasmi Epistolae*, III (Oxford, 1913), Ep. 990.

APPENDIX 2

A SET OF MISSING BUILDING ACCOUNTS

The building accounts for Corpus Christi College that cover 1517–18 are transcribed and discussed in this volume. They are the only accounts for the college known to exist today. However, another book of building accounts, relating to building works at Corpus in 1514, is known to have existed in the years immediately before and after the Second World War. The accounts were referred to in a short article published in 1937 by J. G. Milne, who was then librarian at Corpus, and were amongst college muniments that he listed in a hand-written document three years later.[1] In that list, the accounts were assigned the reference Arch.D.1 consistent with the 1517–18 accounts referenced Arch.D.2 and an early-eighteenth-century book of accounts listed as Arch.D.3.[2]

The introduction of Milne's article of 1937 referred to 'the original building accounts of the College' that were found in a large chest half filled with crumpled papers, that had probably been used 'for packing away the College plate during the troubles of the Civil Wars'.[3] Six years later, Milne co-wrote an article with the architectural historian, John H. Harvey, in which the authors explained that the President of Corpus, P. S. Allen, had drawn their attention to the chest in 1928. It is not clear who examined the chest and its contents, though it may have been Milne, for soon after, he and his wife Mary were invited to sort and organize the college archive.

The task of sorting the archive took Joseph and Mary Milne four years, for the college muniments were in a parlous state, as Milne commented in correspondence and reports to the President of Corpus. Milne published a brief article on the muniments towards the end of 1932, in which he confirmed that the organization of the archive was complete.[4] His article included a general outline of the types of document contained in the archive, though he did not mention any of the building accounts specifi-

---

[1] J. G. Milne, 'The Muniments of Corpus Christi College, Oxford', *Oxoniensia*, 2 (1937), 129–33.
[2] These three items also had the alternative references D.5.5–7.
[3] J. G. Milne and J. H. Harvey, 'The Building of Cardinal College, Oxford', *Oxoniensia*, 8/9 (1943–4), 129. The chest originally stood in the old bursary at Corpus above the gatehouse.
[4] J. G. Milne, 'The Muniments of Corpus Christi College, Oxford', *Bulletin of the Institute of Historical Research*, 10, no. 29 (1932), 105–8.

cally. The following year Milne accepted the role of librarian at Corpus.[5] The first published reference to the 1514 accounts emerges in an article on the Corpus muniments that Milne wrote in 1937. Towards the end of that article, Milne mentioned the 'numerous' minor accounts and amongst these, 'special records relating to various building schemes'. Milne added that the 'most valuable documents are the original building accounts of the erection of the College in 1514, which have lately been copied by Mrs Lobel for the use of the Commission on Historical Monuments, and a further account for 1517'.[6] There can be no doubt that Milne, a most assiduous historian, saw two sets of early-sixteenth-century building accounts for Corpus: accounts covering 1514 and the accounts discussed in this volume (CCCO H/1/4/1).

Milne's reference was to Mary Lobel (*née* Rogers), who worked on the City of Oxford volume for the Royal Commission on Historical Monuments (RCHM) with the Reverend Herbert Edward Salter in the late 1930s. A typewritten inventory exists of the Corpus manuscripts that were consulted by Mrs Lobel in connection with that project.[7] The inventory begins with the following statement: 'There are two Mss books of accounts relating to the original buildings in the College library. One is a collection of accounts for the year 1514 (mainly) and was discovered after Fowler wrote his history of the college'. The name B. M. Hamilton Thompson appears at the end of the typewritten inventory and must refer to Beatrice Hamilton Thompson, who was a librarian and archivist at St. Hugh's College in Oxford until 1939.[8] Hamilton Thompson may have been assisting Mary Lobel who was herself a former student of St. Hugh's. A register of loans of Corpus material covering the years 1876–1949 confirms that between 1935 and 1936, both Mary Lobel and Beatrice Hamilton Thompson borrowed the 1514 and the 1517 building accounts of Corpus.[9] Mrs Lobel made use of both account books between November 1935 and the following June and for an additional month in September 1936; Miss Hamilton Thompson borrowed the accounts for just three days in July 1935. The register of loans confirms that the account books were returned to the college after being seen by the women.

---

[5] He was also a Reader in Numismatics within Oxford University (until 1938) and a Deputy Keeper of Coins at the Ashmolean, a post he kept until his death in 1951.
[6] Milne, 'The Muniments' (1937), 131.
[7] The inventory is to be found *sub* Oxford in the RCHM archive at Heritage England in Swindon.
[8] She was the daughter of the eminent medievalist, Alexander Hamilton Thompson and was married to the Reverend Trevor Jalland.
[9] The register is held at Corpus and records loans made to individuals for research purposes as well as loans made to various institutions for purposes of exhibition.

The RCHM volume on the City of Oxford that Mrs Lobel worked upon was published in 1939.[10] It includes an inventory of architectural features drawn from observation and it is for this reason that no sources are given. The text does not include any details taken from the 1517 building accounts though it might be noted that one sentence seems to have been prompted by the information offered by the earlier building accounts covering 1514. That sentence states that considerable building was in progress in 1514. As likely as not that building included structural work on large sections of the college including the gatehouse, chapel and hall. However, since the 1514 accounts are lost, we can only speculate on their contents and assume that as was done in the surviving accounts for 1517–18, the clerk of the works recorded the sources, quantities and costs of materials required and the names of suppliers and those men employed on site.

The register of loans records a subsequent loan of the 1514 building accounts (Arch.D.1) to Christ Church between 19 February and 8 March 1944. Soon after their return, Milne borrowed the accounts for his own use on three separate occasions. The loans were presumably made in connection with Milne's research that culminated in an article co-written with John H. Harvey. That article concerned an important set of early building accounts for Wolsey's foundation of Cardinal College, which had been discovered in the Corpus chest in the late 1920s. Milne himself published a book entitled *The Early History of Corpus Christi College, Oxford*, soon after he retired as college librarian in 1946.[11] In the *Early History*, Milne briefly discussed aspects of the early building of the college but did not mention the 1514 accounts (Arch.D.1). There are no records in the register of loans for Arch.D.1 between mid-1944 and 1949, when it ends. There is no known record of loans of college material between 1949 and May 1952, when the next register opens. It seems likely that it was during this period that the building accounts for 1514 (Arch.D.1) went missing. Whilst the historians Louis Salzman and John Harvey both used details culled from the 1517 accounts for their ground-breaking books published in the early 1950s, neither refers to the earlier Corpus accounts for 1514.[12] This is particularly intriguing given the fact that Harvey had co-written an article with Milne just a few years earlier and might have been expected to have known about

[10] RCHM, England, *An Inventory of the Historical Monuments in the City of Oxford*, HMSO, xxxiii (London, 1939).
[11] The accounts for Cardinal College were seen by Brian Twyne in the early 1600s and he mistook them as accounts relating to Corpus Christi College; see Milne and Harvey, 'The Building of Cardinal College', 137.
[12] Salzman's *Documentary History of Building* was originally published in 1952 and Harvey's *Dictionary of Medieval Architects* two years later. Salzman evidently consulted CCCO H1/4/1, so if the earlier accounts had been available he would surely have cited those too. Harvey made use of Salzman's work prior to publication.

the earlier accounts. A hand-written list of the Corpus archives was produced in 1971 in preparation for the new *History of the University of Oxford*. This makes reference to the 1517–18 building accounts for Corpus but not the 1514 accounts, suggesting that their existence or whereabouts was no longer known.

The authors of this volume searched for the missing building accounts of 1514 at Corpus and the Bodleian Library amongst other repositories. A number of scholars who might have been able to shed light on the whereabouts of the book were also contacted but all was to no avail.[13] The situation created a dilemma for the authors: whether to proceed with publication, or to refrain in the hope that the missing manuscript, if it has survived, might be discovered. The matter, however, was resolved by the voice from the past of the above-mentioned distinguished Oxford historian who was at the heart of the Oxford research. In 1922 the Reverend Herbert Edward Salter wrote 'delay is unwise. Those who are long past middle age should print their material, if it can be of use to others, and not wait to make it more perfect. In a work of this kind there is special temptation to delay, for there is a risk that some important manuscript is being overlooked, but risks must be taken if there is to be progress.'[14] On this occasion, Salter's advice has been taken.

---

[13] Accordingly, we are most thankful for assistance given by Martin Biddle of Hertford College, Richard Hoyle of VCH and the archivists at the Oxfordshire History Centre and Historic England.

[14] H. E. Salter, *Chapters of the Augustinian Canons, Oxford*, OHS 74 (Oxford, 1922), preface.

APPENDIX 3

PURCHASE OF LAND FROM MASTER MASON, JOHN LEBONS

In the archive of Corpus Christi College, Oxford, are numerous documents pertaining to the lands and properties that Bishop Fox purchased as an endowment for his foundation. Amongst the documents are title deeds for lands in Hampshire. The title deeds include a contract drawn up on 8 February 1512, transcribed below, that reveals that Fox purchased property in north-east Hampshire from a freemason called John Lovibone (Plate 11).[1] The contract is significant, for it provides hitherto unknown details about Lovibone who is more widely known as John Lebons, and was an important mason in royal pay as well as one of the craftsmen who regularly worked for Cardinal Wolsey.[2]

Several facts of particular interest emerge from the contract. The document reveals that John Lebons was based in Wandsworth. Moreover, the contract reveals that Lebons was married to Alice Polleyn. Her late father John, who, according to the contract, was sometimes known as John Waterygge, is also named in the document and also lived in Wandsworth.[3] The properties that John and Alice Lebons sold to Bishop Fox were located in Odiham, Dogmersfield and Crondall in north Hampshire and Sutton near Wandsworth in Surrey. Some of these properties may have been part of Alice's inheritance as her father made a large bequest to her and her first husband, a mason called John Gryth.[4] Fox paid Lebons the considerable sum of £43 for the properties, which suggests that John and Alice Lebons were relatively wealthy.

There is no documentary evidence to link Lebons with building Corpus Christi College, Oxford or any of Bishop Fox's other building works. Lebons may have previously worked in Oxford and he was involved in the

[1] CCCO C5/Cap.11/Ev.109. The document is signed by Bishop Fox; Lebons has used his mason's mark as a signature.
[2] Variants of his name include Lobins, Lovebone, Lobbens and Lubyns.
[3] Polleyn's profession is not specified in the contract, though a carpenter of this name is recorded as having entered into a bond with the warden of Winchester College in the 1430s; see Harvey, 233.
[4] John Polleyn died in 1506. For his will, see PROB, 11/15/5. Alice's husband John Gryth, died the following year; he named Alice as one of his executors. For Gryth's will, see PROB, 11/15/426.

preparatory work associated with the making of Henry VII's tomb in that king's chantry chapel at Westminster Abbey, a project with which Bishop Fox was involved in his capacity as executor to the late king.[5] The two men are likely to have known each other, since Bishop Fox's duties as executor were carried out contemporaneously with his planning of Corpus.[6] Their acquaintance, however, is confirmed by a noteworthy coincidence. Bishop Fox was generally too busy with political affairs to have personal involvement in buying lands with which to endow his college, and so was usually represented by a land agent, but when this purchase agreement was drawn up, Fox himself was present.

In the years when the Corpus was being built, Lebons is recorded as master mason for Wolsey at Hampton Court.[7] By the mid-1520s, Lebons was resident in Oxford, working as a master mason at Cardinal College, Wolsey's own foundation adjacent to Corpus where he was responsible with Henry Redmayn for the design of sections of Tom Quad.[8]

THE INDENTURE: CCCO C5/CAP.11/EV.109.

This indenture made beytwext ye riyght Rev[er]end Father in God Richard Bishop of Wynchester, on the o[o]ne p[ar]tie and John Lovibone of Wansworth in the County of Surrey Freemason and Alice his weyfe, daughter and heyre of John Waterygge, otherwise called John Poleyn late of Wansworth aforeseyd, now decessed on the other party. Weytnesseth that the seyd John Levibone and Alice have bargayned, Covenented, and solde, and by these p[re]sents bargayned and sell, to the foresayd Bishopp and to his heyres all those londs and ten[emene]ts, Rents, reversions, and Services with ye appurtenances that ye seyd John in his owne ryght or in ye right of ye seyd Alice hath, or any other p[er]son or p[er]sons to those of them, or any of them, hath or have in the townes, Ham[e]letts and parishes of Odiham, Dogmersfield, Sutton and Crondale in ye County of Suthhamton, And allsoe all suche londs and ten[emen]ts, rents, and S[er]vices with ye appurtenances, which were ye seyd John Wateriggs at ye time of his death in ye townes Hamletts and parishes of Odiham, Dogmersfield, Sutton, Crondale aforeseyd. And ye seyd John Levibone covenanteth, bargeyneth and by these p[re]sents granteth to ye seyd Bishopp, that hee the seyd John, and Alice, on this side [of] ye fest of Penteycost next comyng, after ye date hereof,

---

[5] Harvey suggests that Lebons may have been the John Lubyns who built a chimney at the Christopher Inn in Oxford for Lincoln College between 1509 and 1510.
[6] Harvey, 172.
[7] Ibid.
[8] Ibid.; Milne and Harvey, 'The Building of Cardinal College', 139.

att the coste and charge in ye Law of ye seyd Bishopp shall make or cause to bee made, to ye seyd Bishopp and his heyres, or to such other person or persons or their heires, as by ye seyd Bishopp shall bee named a sufficient, sure, and Lawfull estatt in ye Law, of all ye seyd Londs, ten[emen]ts, Rents, rev[er]sions [and] services, bee it by deed enrolled grant [and] relees, with warrantye, fine, Recov[e]ry, or otherwise in such fourme as shall bee devysed by ye Lernerd Counsell of ye seyd Bishop, And over that shall afore ye seyd fest of Pentecost, deliv[e]r or cause to bee delivered to ye seyd Bishopp or to his assignes all maner Evidences, fines, Recoveries Courtrolles, escripts, and other in muniments that hee ye seyd John or Alice or any other person or persons, by them or to thuse of them or any of them, or by their delivery hath concerning ye foreseyd Londs, ten[emen]ts, rents, rev[er]sions [and] services or any part thereof. Allsoe ye seyd John covenanteth by these p[re]sents to ye seyd Bishopp [that] hee the seyd John afore ye fest of Easter next comming after ye date of these p[re]sents shall clearely discharge ye seyd Londs, ten[emen]ts, Rents and services of all former sales barganes uses statutes, recognisances, Annuities, execucions, judgments, And of all other charges going out or to bee levied, or lawfully to bee demanded out of ye p[re]sentes or any part thereof except ye quit rent due to ye Lords of fee out of ye p[re]mises after ye date of these p[re]sents. And ye seyd John farther covenanteth, and granteth to ye seyd Bishopp that hee ye seyd John [and] Alice or either of them, at all times heareafter when they by ye seyd Bishopp, or his assignes lawfully shall bee required shall doe and after to bee done, all [and] every things of ye for making sure [that] ye seyd londs Ten[emen]ts, Rents, Rev[er]sions [and] services with the appurtenances to ye seyd Bishopp [and] his heires, or to other person, or persons by him to bee named, that the lerned Councell of ye same Bishopp shall bee devised, at ye costs, and charges of ye same Bishopp. For all which ye premisses afore bargeyned and sold by ye seyd John [and] Alice to the Bishopp. The seyd Bishopp shall pey or doe to bee payed to ye seyd John Levibone [and] Alice or to any of them XLIII li. of good and lawfull money of England in forme following that is to sey XX li. parcell thereof at ye sealing of these p[re]sent Indentures Whereof ye seyd John knowledgeth himselfe by these p[re]sents to bee truly content and payed. And XXIII li. residue of ye seyd XLIII li. to bee payd by ye seyd Bishopp immediately after ye estate made, and fyne levied by ye seyd John and Alice of ye seyd Londs, ten[emen]ts rents, rev[er]sions [and] services to ye seyd Bishopp [and] his heires, or to such persons or their heires, as by ye seyd bishopp shall bee named to th[e] use of ye seyd Bishopp, his heyres [and] assignes. In witnesse whereof the parties aforesayd to these p[re]sent Indentures have severally put to their seals.

Yeven ye VIIIth day of ye Moneth of February ye the third years of ye reigne of o[u]r Soveryn Lord Harry ye VIIIth.

APPENDIX 4

INDENTURE OF 1513 BETWEEN BISHOP FOX AND THE PRIOR AND CONVENT OF ST. SWITHUN'S PRIORY, WINCHESTER

In mid-1513, Henry VIII joined forces with the Holy Roman Emperor, the Spanish and the Swiss in a military offensive against the French king, Louis XII. Over the course of the summer months, several French towns were besieged and battles fought, amongst them a pseudo-battle known sardonically as the 'Battle of the Spurs' – named for the spurs seen glinting as the French cavalry galloped past. Bishop Fox had been amongst the final contingent to leave England for France which he did on 30 June in the company of King Henry and many thousands of troops.[1] Fox was an unwilling observer of the conflict: he was in his sixties and keen to promote peace rather than war. Indeed, he was beginning to prepare to step down from active political life, for his plans for a college at Oxford were under way and preparations had been made to construct his chantry chapel in Winchester Cathedral, where two priests would soon begin to recite daily prayers for Fox's soul. The bishop was concerned that his plans would be jeopardized by the Anglo-French conflict because it was possible that he would be killed, wounded or taken hostage during the campaign and would be unable to complete his building projects. To this end, he drew up an agreement before his departure with Thomas Silkstede, the Prior of St. Swithun's in Winchester, in which he outlined how Winchester's Benedictine monks would be enabled to finish his chantry chapel and also the college at Oxford, which at that stage was intended to educate monks.[2]

The indenture between Fox and Silkstede is dated 30 June 1513 but was probably signed a few days earlier, and Richard Gardiner, Fox's diocesan

---

[1] In a letter to Wolsey dated 21 May 1513, Fox wrote that he would probably follow King Henry to France (see Allen, 69) A contemporary draft of the campaign reveals that the bishop travelled in the King's entourage; see BL Lansdowne MS 818, f. 2v.

[2] CCCO A1 Cap.1 Fasc.1 Ev.1; the indenture is referred to in Fowler, 60–7. Silkstede was elected Prior of St. Swithun's shortly before Fox had been translated to Winchester. Although he was Prior for a quarter of a century, Silkstede remains a shadowy figure. It is, however, clear that he shared Fox's interest in building for he was responsible for completing the reconstruction of the Lady Chapel at Winchester Cathedral and established his own chantry chapel in the south transept.

Treasurer, delivered the signed document to the Prior and Convent on 27 August. It begins by referring to some of Fox's belongings, including tapestries, plate and books, that had been delivered to the Prior and Convent of St. Swithun's. Some items were evidently to be used by the Prior and Convent of St. Swithun's; others were to act as security for the Bishop's foundation. The indenture states that further items from Fox's episcopal manor at Esher were in the care of Richard Nix, Bishop of Norwich, and goods from Fox's lodgings at St. Mary Overy in Southwark were in the care of Thomas Laund at the Hospital of St. Cross near Winchester. The Prior agreed to purchase lands from Merton College, Godstow Abbey, and St. Frideswide's Priory in Oxford and also to continue work on the college and furnish it upon completion. Furthermore, if the college is incomplete at Bishop Fox's death, the Prior is to call upon the assistance of three men: the Abbots of Glastonbury and Reading and the Prior of Lewes, whose task will be to appraise the items listed in the indenture. The goods are to be sold within twelve months with the exception of certain items that Fox has set aside for use within his chantry chapel. All the profits from the sale of the goods were to be spent on finishing Fox's college.

The indenture includes directives for the functioning of Bishop Fox's college at Oxford. Fox specified that ten monks were to be nominated within twenty days of its completion; four to be called Prior's scholars, three Convent scholars, two chantry priests and one to act as warden. Fox designated that Prior Silkstede and the monastic community at Winchester were to be responsible for the wages of the college staff (porter, launderer and so on), all of whom were to be 'learned in Grammar' – a strong indicator of his commitment to meritocracy. The Prior and Convent were also declared responsible for maintenance of the college. The agreement continues with Bishop Fox's directives concerning the functioning of his chantry chapel, its furnishings and specifications regarding the chantry priests. The indenture makes plain the fact that Bishop Fox's foundation at Oxford was planned and designed in tandem with his chantry chapel in Winchester Cathedral.

The final section of the indenture concerns what should be done with the goods in bond, should the college at Oxford be finished in Bishop Fox's lifetime. The agreement states that if Bishop Fox requires money, for instance if he were held to ransom, the goods in bond are to be sold, or, on the occasion of a royal visit, the goods are to be released for eleven days for the Bishop's use. However, if Fox has no need of the goods, then they were to be sold and the monies spent on providing a new vault over the shrine of St. Swithun (located in the retrochoir at Winchester Cathedral) and new stone vaults erected above the presbytery aisles and transepts. A copy of the indenture survives in the archive at Corpus Christi College. It includes references to the college and chantry chapel and is given in full below.

Fox remained with King Henry and his troops in France throughout the summer and autumn.[3] He was present when the town of Thérouanne fell to the English in August. An able negotiator, Bishop Fox was called upon by King Henry to assist in negotiations with the French after the capture of the town of Tournai in September. Bishop Fox had been heavily involved in organizing the military preparations prior to the French campaign, particularly in the victualling of the army and navy.[4] However, it would be his protégé Wolsey who was rewarded by King Henry. Once he had returned to England, Fox's influence was vital in procuring the Bishopric of Tournai for Wolsey.

✤

This indenture made ye last day of June the V yere of the reigne of Kinge Henry ye Eighth between ye right reverend father in god Richard Bisshop of Winchester on the one p[art]ie and Thomas Prior of the Cathedrall Church of St. Swithuns in Winchester in the County of South[ampton] and the Convent of ye same place on ye other party. Witnesseth [tha]t ye said Bisshop hath of his benevolent and free will geven [and] graunted [and] by these present[s] geveth and graunteth unto ye sayd Prior and Convent of St. Swithun [and] to their successours to have and to enjoy to them and theyr prop[er] use all such parcels [and] peeces of silke, clothese of silk, clothes of gold, parcells of plate some of them of gold, some of them of silver and all wholey gilt, some of the of silver p[ar]cell gilt [and] some of them of cleane wh[i]te silver, certaine aultar clothes, copes, vestments books for ye quire, crosses, images, chalices, candlesticks for aultars [and] other ornaments [and] jewells of silver, diap[er], Clothese jewells, and diverse other things; stuff [and] other goods. The certainty of all, which with ye weight of ye sayd plate to the sayd Prior [and] Convent of St. Swithun is before sayd by ye sayd Bisshop, given [and] to ye sayd Prior to ye use of him [and] ye sayd Convent of St. Swithun, delivered, plainely [and] p[ar]ticarly doth appeare by certaine writings indented between ye sayd Bisshop on the one party [and] the sayd Prior on the other party bearing date the last day of Aprill[5] the fifthe yere of ye reigne of o[u]r soveraig[n]e Lor[d] Kinge Henry the eighth. And over this the sayd Bisshop hath given [and] graunted [and] by these pre[se]nts giveth [and] graunteth unto the sayd Prior [and] Convent of St. Swithun to have [and] enjoy them [and] to theyr prop[er] use certaine hangings, Tapetts, celars,[6] Testers, Beds [and] counterpoints of

---

[3] BL Stowe MS 146, f. 106.
[4] Smith, 1988, 80–1.
[5] The earlier agreement of 30 April 1513 mentioned here is not known to have survived.
[6] These were celures or selers, a form of canopy above a bed (*OED*).

Tapestre Arras [and] verdos,[7] spevers,[8] [and] celars, testers, Beds, counter-points [and] cushions, some of silke [and] some of cloth of gold: Carpets, Featherbeds, Bolsters, Pillos, Fustians,[9] sheets, Pillowcases, Rochitts,[10] Curtains of silke, mantles of wooles, clothrobes, some furred [and] some lined hoods, Tippets, certaine pieces of linen cloth, quilts, trussing beds, Books of divers sciences and faculties [and] diverse other things, stuffe [and] goods, of ye certainty of all, w[hi]ch p[ar]cells to ye sayd Prior [and] Convent of St. Swithun by the sayd Bisshop, given [and] to same Prior of St. Swithun to the use of him [and] the sayd Convent of St. Swithun delivered, appeareth by other indentures thereof made betwene ye sayd Bisshop [and] the sayd Prior of St. Swithun, the date of w[hi]ch indentures is in likewise the sayd last day of Aprill. And over this, ye sayd Bisshop hath given [and] graunted [and] by these p[re]sents giveth [and] graunteth unto the sayd Prior and Convent, as with all other such other his plate goods [and] Chattles that he hath in the Mannor of Essher in the County of Surr[ey],[11] the certainty of ye p[ar]celles thereof appeareth in certaine bills indented, made between ye sayd Bisshop [and] S[ir] Thomas Nix,[12] Parish Priest of the Parish Church of Essher aforesayd, in whose keepinge the sayd goods [and] Chattles remaine [and] all other his plate jewells [and] goods which he hath in ye Priory of St. Mary Overe,[13] in ye sayd County [and] in the keepinge of ye Prior of the same place[14] the certainty whereof allsoe appeareth, in certaine other bills indented, between ye sayd Bisshop [and] the foresaid Prior of St. Mary Overe; as all other goods and Chattles whatsoever they bee in what places of or places they be in, except [and] allway reserved to the sayd Bisshop [and] to his assignes all such goods [and] Chattles as be of the stocke of the Bishoprick of Winchester [and] have used to continue [and] remaine unto ye Bisshops of Winchester [and] to theyr successors [and] all such goods, plate, jewells, ornaments [and] other stuff of the sayd Bishops which S[i]r Thomas Laund hath in his keepinge at St. Crosse[15] in the County of Suth[ampton] of ye delivery of ye Bishop: the

[7] Probably verdures, a type of decorative hanging depicting flowers and birds (see OED).
[8] A sparver was a canopy for a bed.
[9] Fustian was a thick cloth made from flax and cotton, often used for blankets.
[10] A rochit was a linen vestment similar to a surplice.
[11] An episcopal manor house was at Esher in Surrey. Cardinal Wolsey was later given permission to stay at Esher when Hampton Court was being built.
[12] Thomas Nix was probably related to the bishop of Norwich, Richard Nykke or Nix who had served first as an archdeacon when Fox was Bishop of Exeter and then Bath and Wells and later as vicar general when Fox became Bishop of Durham. In 1502, a cleric called Thomas Nix was one of two chantry priests chosen by Fox to serve in the Curteys chantry chapel at Grantham (see *Lincolnshire Notes and Queries*, 12 (1912–13), 221).
[13] Bishop Fox had episcopal lodgings in the Priory attached to St. Mary Overy in Southwark.
[14] Bartholomew Linstead was Prior at St. Mary Overy from 1512 until the Dissolution.
[15] Thomas Laund or Lawne was the custodian of the Hospital of St. Cross near Winchester.

INDENTURE OF 1513

certainty of the p[ar]cells thereof, appeareth in other Bills indented made between the sayd Bishop [and] the foresaid S[i]r Thomas Laund. In consideration of which gifts of all the forsayd cloths of silke, clothes of gold, p[ar]cells of plate, aultar cloths, vestments, books, crosses, images, chalices, candlesticks, ornaments, jewells, stuffe [and] goods [and] other ye peases specified in ye sayd two indentures whereof either of them beare date of sayd Bisshop unto ye sayd Prior [and] Convent [and] his Church of St. Swithun had [and] done [and] allsoe for ye good [and] gracious minde, purpose, [and] intent [tha]t ye sayd Bisshop hath to these Monkes of ye sayd Church of St. Swithun [and] of other places [and] monasteries of ye same religion[16] of those Monasteries in especiall hereafter named, the heads [and] p[art]ties whereof have beene, are, the most special kind [and] loving brethren [and] greate friends of ye sayd Bisshop, to increase in virtue, learnings of ye laws of Christe Church by reason wherof almighty god shall by them, be the more honourably [and] better served, [and] good religion [and] the true observance of ye same be the better kept [and] observed. The foresayd prior and Convent of St. Swithun covenant p[er]mitt [and] graunt unto ye sayd Bisshop, by these p[re]sents, [tha]t ye sayd Prior and Convent of St. Swithun [and] their successors, shall obtaine [and] p[ur]chase to the[m] [and] to theyr successors for ever, of the M[aste]r [and] ffellows of Merton College in Oxon[ia] in the County of Oxon[ia], certaine places [and] p[ar]cells of ground, lying in Oxford, aforesayd, [and] of the Abbess [and] Convent of Godstow[17] in ye County of Oxford aforesayd, another p[ar]cell of ground lyinge in Oxford aforesayd [and] of the Prior and Convent of St. Frideswith in Oxford aforesayd another p[ar]cell of ground in Oxford aforesayd, upon w[hi]ch p[ar]cells of ground the sayd Bisshop, by the assent of ye sayd M[aste]r [and] Prior of St. Frideswith,[18] hath begunne to build [and] lease one howse for a College, [and] as hereafter more largely doth appeare. And further more, the sayd Prior [and] convent of St. Swithun for them [and] theyr successors the sayd Bysshop [and] his assignes faithfully, p[er]mit [and] graunt, [and] by these presents covenant, [and] bind therafter [and] theyr successors to the sayd Bishop [and] his assignes that whereof the sayd Bisshop hath begunne to build of upon the said places [and] grounds [and] by the sufferance [and] grace of God almighty, intendeth not onely to p[er]forme [and] finish upon the sayd places [and] grounds a place [and] a house ((places [and] howses)) for a

---

Fox collated Laund to the living of Mottisfont in 1508 and to Asshe in Surrey two years later (see HRO 21M65/A1/18, ff. 15, 21). He was present at St. Cross when Fox read the statutes of Corpus (Ward, 233). Laund died in 1518 and was interred in the chapel at St. Cross.

[16] Benedictine.
[17] The Abbess at Godstow was Isabella Brainton.
[18] John Burton was elected Prior of St. Frideswide in 1513.

college of a Warden [and] certaine number of Monks [and] Secular schollers, to be there ordained [and] stablished [and] erected upon ye sayd places [and] grounds after ye mannor of a double platt[19] made for ye over ye nether lodging of the same buildings [and] howses w[h]ich plats subscribed as well w[ith] ye hands of the sayd Bysshop, as with ye hand of ye sayd Prior of St. Swithun, remaineth in ye keeping of William Vertue freemason [and] Humfry Cooke Carpenter of ye sayd works, but allso, to garnish ye Chappell [and] aultars [and] every of them that shall be in the sayd howse or College w[i]th Chalices cruets, candlesticks, vestments, aultarclothes, books and all other ornaments necessary [and] convenient for ye same. And in likewise to furnish all ye howses of offices w[i]thin ye sayd College, with all manner of utensils [and] employments necessary [and] convenient for them accordingly. And over this, the sayd Bisshop, by ye sufferance of Almighty God is in full purpose [and] minde [and] intendeth to purchase [and] give in his life or cause to be appropred [and] given lands, tenements, rents [and] pensions spirituall [and] temporall of both to the yearly value of CLX livres to the sayd Prior [and] Convent of St. Swithun [and] theyr successors, to behoofe [and] use of ye same Prior [and] Convent of the same St. Swithun [and] theyr successors for the sayd College, and for ye making of such payments sustaining of such charges [and] p[er]formance of such things not exceeding the clere value of ye sayd rents and revenues [and] the price of ye sayd stuff goods [and] other things conteyned in the sayd Indentures every of them of ye sayd date of the sayd last day of Aprill, as ye sayd Prior and Convent of St. Swithun [and] theyr successors shall, by the ordynance [and] devise of ye sayd Bysshop of his Executors of Assignes be ordained [and] assigned [and] appointed to doo by these Indentures or by any otherwise ... any time hereafter, And in parte of the accomplishing of ye sayd purchase of lands and tenements temporall, the sayd Bysshop hath purchased certaine lands, Mannors, lands [and] ten[emen]ts beinge of the clere value yearly of xxviii li. And therin off virtue of the king's licence by his letters patents[20] under his great Seale for the amortisment of lands [and] other ten[emen]ts temporall to the yerely value of Cli., benefices Spirituall to the yerely value of a Cli. above all charges [and] reprises by ye sayd Bysshop. This p[ro]per cost [and] charges obtained and by him, to the sayd Prior of St. Swithun delivered, hath amortised, given [and] appropreth to the sayd Prior [and] Convent of St. Swithun [and] theyr successors as by certaine deeds [and] estates thereof to them made, delivered more plainely doth appeare, That if the sayd Bysshop doe not wholely finish [and] p[er]forme the sayd buildings [and] howses in his life according to the sayd

---

[19] Unfortunately, the platt or plan is not known to have survived.
[20] The king had granted letters patent six months earlier.

plats, [and] also garnish not the Chappell [and] aultars of ye same College [and] e[v]ery of them with Chalices, cruets, candlesticks, vestments, aultar Clothes books and all other ornaments necessary [and] convenient for the same, allsoe all other howses of offices of ye sayd College w[i]th all mannor utensils [and] implements necessary [and] convenient for them accordingly, nor in his life purchase nor aproper [and] give not cause to be purchased ap[ro]pered, nor geven to ye sayd Prior [and] Convent of St Swithun to the use above sayd land tenements rents [and] pensions spirituall or temporall with ye mannor lands and tenements to the[m] as is afore sayd by the sayd Bisshop [and] other p[er]sons his feofes, [and] to his use before the date of those presents for ye same cause [and] intent given [and] graunted, to the yerely value of abovesayd that the Prior of St. Swithun Convent and theyr successors for ye full performance and finishing of ye sayd buildings, howses according to ye plats above rehersed, and allsoe for ye garnishing of the aultars of ye sayd College [and] other stuff [and] implements necessary [and] convenient to be occupied in the howses thereto belonging. And for the purchasing [and] amortisinge of the sayd lands, tenements, rents or [and] pensions sp[irit]uall or temp[or]all (with the Mannor, lands [and] tenements) to the yearly value above specified or as much of lands [and] tenements as shall thereof want, a lacke unpurchased by the sayd Bysshop in his life for the sayd sustentation of ye charges of the sayd College, shall within foure months after the death of ye sayd Bysshop calling to him or them the Abbots of Glasto[n]bury,[21] in ye Countyof Somers[et], Redinge in ye County of Berks[hire], [and] Prior of Lewes in the County of Sussex for the time beinge, cause to be praysed [and] esteemed, the sayd plate, stuffe, goods [and] all other the p[re]mises in ye sayd Indenture, [and] every one of them bearinge date ye sayd last day of Aprill specified, [and] eve[ry] parcel thereof at reasonable price in the p[re]sence [and] by the ov[er]sight, [and] also use of the sayd Abbots of Glastonbury [and] Redinge [and] Prior of Lewes for ye time beinge, or of theyr deputies in theyr absences, by three discrete p[er]sons, expert [and] well skilled in prezinge[22] of such plate, goods [and] other stuff, to be chosen [and] thereto appointed by the sayd Prior of St. Swithun, Abbotts of Glastonbury [and] Redinge [and] Prior of Lewes (theyr sayd deputies and the sayd Prior of St. Swithun or his successors, President of Magdalen College, Chancellor Treasurer [and] Ralph Lepton or any of ye sayd) three praysers (for the sayd pries or any other, or by any otherwise or mannor). Except allways [and] (reserved out of ye sayd stuffe [and] goods

---

[21] Richard Bere was preferred to the abbacy of Glastonbury in 1493. It was through Fox's influence that Bere appointed Claymond to the living of West Monkton in 1500. Bere later granted a licence to Fox in order that Fox could purchase lands for his college.
[22] The wording here refers to the appraisal or valuing of Fox's belongings.

[and] the prizing [and] sale of the same all such ornaments [and] other stuff [and] goods) for the time beinge or the sayd deputies in theyr absences advising to the sayd preysers Mr. John Claymond, President of Magdalen College[23] in Oxon[ford] Mr John Dowman[24] Chancellor to the sayd Bysshop Mr. Richard Gardiner, Treasurer of Wolvesey,[25] Mr Ralph Lepton,[26] w[hi]ch will acquaint [them] ye value [and] price of ye sayd plate and stuffe as theyr were bought for, by the Bysshop before … [and] the sayd Abbots of Glastonbury and Reding[27] [and] the sayd Prior of St. Swithun and Lewes for the time beinge if they be pre[se]nt or in ye absence of the same Abbotts of Glastonbury, Redinge [and] Prior of Lewes, before theyr sayd deputies [and] the sayd Priors of St. Swithun or his successors, President of Magdalen College, Chancellour, Treasurer [and] Ralph Lepton or before five of them, the sayd Prior of St. Swithun or his Successors, the sayd Treasurer [and] Ralph Lepton beinge Always three of them, if ye sayd Treasurer or Ralph Lepton be then alife, [and] if either of them disease them before the Prior or his Successors, [and] the ovirliver of [these] two, [and] if ye sayd Treasurer [and] Ralph be bothe diseased then before the sayd Prior or his successor [and] such two Presidents as ye sayd Abbots of Glastonbury or his successors shall now appoint, the sayd three praysers shall before they take upon them the sayd praysinge, make an oath upon the holy Evangelist, truly, evenly [and] … to prayse the sayd plates, goods [and] stuffe [and] every part thereof w[i]thin fifteen days immediately after theyr oath is made next ensuing. And allsoe the sayd Prior of St. Swithun, for ye time beinge shall cause to be sold at the same price as can be goodly may be done, [and] at the farthest w[i]thin xii months next, after the sayd estimation [and] praysinge made [and] done, all the sayd plate and stuffe [and] every p[ar]cell thereof, w[i]thout retaining, keeping or byinge any p[ar]t thereof, to ye behoofe or use of any of ye sayd Abbots of Glastonbury [and] Redinge or Prior of St. Swithun or [and] Lewes,[28] the sayd Deputies, Chancellor, President,

---

[23] John Claymond.
[24] John Dowman was Bishop Fox's chancellor, commissary and also a vicar general.
[25] Gardiner was Treasurer of Wolvesey Castle in Winchester.
[26] Ralph Lepton served Fox for many years. Lepton, a cleric, was educated at Cambridge. He received the living of Ermington in Devon from Fox in 1489 and followed Fox north in 1494. Lepton was rewarded by the prelate with a number of livings including the deanery at Darlington. He was later chaplain to Fox at Winchester, a post he held into the 1520s. Lepton added a rectory to the parish church in Guildford in which he was later buried (BL Additional MS 39959, f. 39r).
[27] The Abbot of Reading was John Thorne who regularly attended Parliament with Bishop Fox. In 1510, Fox assisted Thorne in founding a chantry at Reading; see *Calendar of Patent Rolls, 1485–1509*, II (London, 1916), 452.
[28] The Prior of the Cluniac house at Lewes was John Ashdown. The Prior and Convent at Lewes were patrons of several livings within the Winchester diocese and owned a house in Southwark that was under Fox's jurisdiction.

Treasurer or Ralph Lepton or any of the sayd three praysers for ye sayd price or any other, or by any wise or manner, except allways [and] reserved out of the sayd stuffe [and] goods [and] the praysinge [and] sale of the same; all such ornaments [and] other stuffe [and] goods as shall hereafter by these p[re]sent be appointed [and] assigned for the use [and] garnishing of the Chappell [and] aultar where ye sayd Bysshop hath chosen his sepulture[29] within the sayd Church of St. Swithun. And all such sums of money as shall grow upon the sayd plate, goods [and] other stuffe, except before excepted or as much thereof, as by ye sayd Abbots of Glastonbury [and] Redinge [and] Prior of Lewes for the time beinge shall be thought necessary, the sayd Prior of St. Swithun for ye time beinge, shall w[i]thin all goodspeed and at the farthest within III yeres next ensuing the death of ye sayd Bysshop, truly, wholy [and] p[ro]fittably imploy [and] borrow about the accomplishment of all [and] every the p[re]mises, And over this it is covenanted [and] agreed betwixt ye sayd parties [and] the same Prior [and] Convent of St. Swithun answereth, covenanteth [and] promised to the sayd Bysshop his executors [and] assignes [tha]t the same Prior [and] Convent of St. Swithun shall w[i]thin xx dayes next after the sayd howse [and] College be builded [and] endowed, as before ye sayd have hold [and] keepe [and] from thenceforth continually have hold [and] keep w[i]thin ye sayd College foure Monks w[hich] shall be called Bysshops Schollers, every of them professed w[i]thin the sayd Monastery of St. Swthun every of the[m] beinge convenient age to learne [and] study in the Sciences, [and] faculties, ensuing [tha]t is to say of the age of eighteen yeres at the least, of good [and] vertuose disposition, well [and] substantially learned in gram[m]er [and] having good natural capacity of witt to learne, study [and] p[ro]fit, w[i]thin ye sayd howse [and] college successively in Sophistry, Logicke, Philosophy [and] Divinity whereof one shall be warden of the sayd College, [and] ye sayd Prior and Convent of St Swithun shall of the rents [and] revenues of ye sayd lands to them by the sayd Bysshop given [and] to be given yerely [and] perpetually while ye world shall endure, give, pay [and] deliver w[i]thin the sayd College to the sayd Warden (of ye sayd College [and] the sayd Prior [and] Convent of St. Swithun) for ye time beinge at two times of ye yere by even porcions, that ys to say the day of theyr first entry into the sayd howse or college, or at the first day of ye next six months then next ensuing accounting the moneth allway [and] after the months of calendar X li. [and] to every of the other III moneths of ye sayd rents [and] revenues yerely [and] p[er]petually, while this world shall endure, X markes within the sayd College by the sayd porcions [and] at ye sayd termes for, [and] in

---

[29] This refers to the site on the south side of the presbytery in Winchester Cathedral, where his chantry chapel would be located and where he wished to be buried.

ye lawe [and] steade of their whole exhibition [and] in full contentestation of the same [and] sure use, nor, moreover [and] above the charges of ii Chauntrie Monkes dayly in such maner as herafter is specified to say ii masses in ye Chappell where the sayd Bysshop hath ordained his sepulture to be made within the Cathedrall Church of St. Swithun; [and] the same ii monkes shall have by ye hands of ye sayd Prior of St Swithun [and] his Successors, either of them dayly three pence of ye p[ar]cells [and] revenues of ye sayd lands, tenements, rents [and] pensions spi[rit]uall or temp[or]all by the sayd Bysshop [and] at his cost [and] charge now purchased [and] obtained, the which shall be payde [and] contented first [and] before the charges of ye sayd howse [and] College or any other whatsoever it be. And over this ye sayd Prior and Convent of St. Swithun [and] theyr successors have covenanted [and] agreed, by these pre[se]nts covenant, agree [and] promise to ye sayd Bisshop [and] his assignes [tha]t they shall within ye sayd XX dayes have hold [and] keepe [and] from thenceforth continually [and] p[er]petually have hold [and] keepe in ye sayd College iiii other semblable monks, brothers of ye same monastery one of them w[hi]ch shalbe called ye Prior Scholler, to have yerely p[er]petually payed w[i]thin ye sayd College by ye sayd porcions [and] at ye sayd termes for his whole exhibition of ye Prior of St Swithun, for ye time beinge of ye Rents [and] revenues [and] other possessions of ye Priory of St. Swithun aforesayd [and] appertaininge [and] allotted to ye Prior of St. Swithun for ye time beinge [and] to his porcion X Mark. And the other iii which shall be called the Convent Schollers every of [the]m for theyr whole exhibition [and] in full contentation of ye same of ye sayd Prior and Convent of ye same Monastery of St. Swithun yerely p[er]petually payed w[i]thin ye sayd College by ye sayd Prior [and] Convent of ye revenues of [and] rents appertaininge [and] allotted to ye porcion of ye sayd Convent, at ye sayd times [and] by ye sayd porcions X marks [and] noe more nor noe lesse. All which monks [and] every of them shall have w[i]thin ye sayd place, [and] College, at costs [and] charges of ye sayd prior [and] Convent of St. Swithun [and] theyr [and] theyr successors of ye sayd rents [and] revenues over [and] above ye sayd pensions to ye sayd monks for theyr exhibitions as before is sayd appointed [and] assigned, theyr chambers free w[i]thout paying anything for them. And allsoe all the cost [and] charges theyr barber [and] lawnder [and] lecturers in sophistry, logicke [and] Philosophy. Moreover, the foresaid Prior of St. Swithun [and] Convent of the same place, graunt for the[m] [and] theyr successors, by these pre[se]nts, unto ye foresaid Byshhop [and] his assignes, that they shall of ye sayd rents [and] revenues, yerely pay or cause to be payed, ye wages [and] stipend of ye officers [and] servants of ye College, after ye rate ensuing, that is to say off the manciple of ye same College for ye time beinge yerely at Easter [and] Michaelmas by even porcions 40s. to ye chiefe cooke in likewise [and] manner 26s.8d. to ye under cook in likewise [and] manner 20s. to ye buttler likewise [and] manner 20s. to ye pauter likewise, [and] manner 20s. to the lawnder in likewise [and] manner 26s. 8d. to the barber in likewise [and] manner 26s. 8d. to a servant to serv the[m] at ye table in likewise and manner 13s. 4d. to the warden's servant of the College, w[h]ich shall allsoe serve at ye table in likewise [and] manner 13s.4d. to ye reader of Sophistry [and] logicke in likewise [and] manner 40s. sterling [to] the reader of Philosophy in likewise [and] manner, 5 marks sterling to ye Bible Clerke which after his lecture be finished shall also serve at ye table in likewise [and] manner 26s.8d. [and] to ye Clarke of ye Chappell w[hi]ch shallbe also sacristane [and] likewise serve at table 26s.8d. And over this the sayd Prior of St. Swithun [and] his successors shall weekly, [tha]t is to say, at ye latter end of ye weeke, pay to ye Steward of ye sayd College, for ye time beinge, the Cominiss of ye sayd manciple, cook, underclerke, Buttler lower servants at ye table, Warden's servant, Bible Clark [and] Sacristane [tha]t is to say, for every of the[m] 8d.for every weeke [and] yerely [and] the feast of Easter ... every of ye foresaid Manciple, Chiefe Cook, buttler, Pawter, ye servant at ye table; ye Warden's servant, ye Bible Clark [and] sacristane, one gowne cloth all one couleur, for every gowne 4 broade yards every yard price 3s.4d. Provided allways [tha]t ye sayd buttler, pawtor, servant at ye table, Warden's servant, Bible Clarke [and] Sacristane [and] every of the[m] be before any of the[m] (and every of t[hem]) be admitted to ye sayd rooms [and] offices or any of the[m] substantially learned in Gram[m]er [and] after theyr admission, keepe theyr study [and] learning in Sophistry [and] logick [and] Philosophy [and] be at ye lectures, rehersals [and] disputations in ye same after ye manner [and] in ye same wise as any of ye sayd monks shall doo [and] as shall be now plainely ordained by such statutes as shallbe made by ye sayd Bisshop in his life or assignes after his death for ye sayd observance [and] keeping, whereof they shall be bound as they touch them. And furthermore ye sayd Prior [and] Convent of St. Swithun [and] theyr successors to ye intent [tha]t ye, foresaid Monkes be not chargeable nor charged w[i]th any other costs, expenses nor charges w[i]thin ye sayd College but onely for theyr com[m]yns [and] table for meals [and] drinks shall yerely [and] forever pay all rents forms [and] goings out of ye sayd College or garde[n] thereunto annexed, [and] of ev[er]y parcel of ye same, [and] also beare ye charge of ye reparations of ye sayd College [and] of all howses, wells [and] closures p[er]taining to ye same [and] in likewise of all hangings [and] of all other apparels, utensils for the howses of offices [and] all ornaments of ye chappell w[i]thin ye sayd College, [and] when neede so requireth ye sayd Prior [and] Convent [and] theyr Successors shall build [and] make of new the sayd howses walls, hangings, apparels [and] ornaments [and] all other ye premises or any of the[m], as good as they were at ye first making, [and] deliv[er]ing [and]. And over this ye same Prior [and] Convent of St. Swithun [and] theyr successors, shall at theyr costs [and] charges find all such was [and] bread that as shall be requisite to be spent within the sayd Chappell, or ye aultars in ye sayd College, [and] in likewise all wood, coles [and] fuell for ye p[re]paring of meate, bread [and] drinks for ye sayd monks, shall be w[i]thin ye kitchinge, bakehowse or bruinge-howse of ye sayd College, necessary, expedient or requisite. And allsoe, where ye sayd Bysshop, to ye laud of ye holy Trinity intendeth in ye honour of ye same to dedicate ye aultar of ye sayd Chappel wherein he hath chose[n] his sepulture, it is accorded [and] agreed by ye sayd Bishop [and] the sayd Prior [and] Convent of St. Swithun that ye sayd President, chancellor, Treasurer, [and] Ralph Lepton or any 3 of them or any 2 of them overlivinge ye other or if they all fortune to discease them, ye forthsayd Prior or his successour at any time or times that it shall please the[m] for th[e] adorning [and] garnishing of ye sayd Chappell and aultar after theyr discretions chooses [and] take out of ye sayd plate, goods [and] stuffe for ye use of ye sayd Chappell [and] of ye Monkes that shall dayly say masse within ye same ye ornaments following, [tha]t is to say ii chalices, ii patens [and] iiii cruets, whereof ye one chalice w[i]th ye paten [and] ii cruets thereto belonging be of gold [and] ye other chalice [and] ye paten [and] ii cruets shall be every of the[m] of silver wholy gilt at ye sayd choise [and] election, iiii candelsticks all of silver [and] wholy gilt whereof ii shall be greater [and] the other ii lesse as ye sayd choise [and] election, ii paire of basons wh[i]ch ye sayd Bisshop did com[m]only use in his closet,[30] either of them being greater than the other, And the sayd Prior of St. Swithun shall cause ye greater paire of them to be wholy gilted, one faire massebooke, handwritten in parchment after Salisbury use, the which ye sayd Bysshop had of the gift of his cousin Lathell,[31] one faire large portuose[32] otherwise called a lydger handwritten in parchment, the w[h]ich ye sayd Bysshop had of the gift of M[agiste]r William Sylke;[33] foure double aultar clothes of linnen diaper cloth, every of them in length of the aultar w[i]thin ye sayd

---

[30] This closet was almost certainly a small oratory probably in Wolvesey Palace dedicated to Bishop Fox's private devotions.

[31] Fox's cousin Lathell has not been identified though the appellation cousin did not necessarily mean a blood relative. A Nicholas Lathell had been a clerk of the pipe in the Exchequer in the late fifteenth century. Lathell died in 1501 and although Fox was not named in his will (PROB, 11/13/75), they acted together in 1499 in connection with the delivery of lands; see Smith, 1988, 397.

[32] A large breviary.

[33] On Sylke, see Emden, BRUO, 1701–2. Sylke was vicar general to Fox at Exeter and was installed to the prebendary of Combe pursuant to a mandate issued by Fox in 1493. He was Precentor at Exeter from 1499 until his death in 1508. Sylke bequeathed a large manuscript book to Fox, who supervised his will (see PROB, 11/15/730), perhaps the fair large portuose noted in this indenture. Sylke is buried in a chantry chapel in Exeter Cathedral.

Chappell requireth; the same iiii aultar clothes to be taken [and] cut out of such diaper table clothes as remaine amonge the sayd stuffe [and] goods [and] the sayd choisirs election; two coverings for same aultar either of them of new same length of course cloth imperiall of the new making, remaining among ye sayd stuffe [and] goods at the sayd choise [and] election vi aultar clothes for the nether front of the sayd aultar (of ye sayd aultar) whereof one shall be of needleworke of ye Lord bearing ye Crosse, remaining amonge ye stuffe [and] goods; the second shall be the shortest aultar cloth of velvet, w[i]th lossanges of cloth of gold, remaining likewise amongst the sayd goods and stuff [and] for third of like length, they shall take as much of the best cloth of gold that they shall finde amonge ye sayd stuff as shall suffice for ye sayd aultar clothe [and] for ye fourth they shall choose as much of the best cloth of Bawdikyn that they shall find amonge the sayd stuff [and] the fifth shallbe white damaske of like length, powdered w[i]th drops of blood, w[i]th a crosse floury in the mids of ye Redd Sattene for Lent season, [and] the sixth shall be blak velvet for days of obits w[i]th a white crosse of damaske in ye mids thereof six preest's vestments w[i]th theyr amyses, albes, parures, stoles [and] phanons for ye Monkes that shall say masse at the saide aultar w[i]thin ye sayd Chappell, whereof one shall be of black velvet velvet w[i]th a white crosse of damaske for days of Obits, [and] another of white damaske w[i]th a ross flourry in ye mids of yt, red sattyn for Lent season [and] other iiii shall be such as the sayd President, Chancellor, Treasurer [and] Ralph Lepton or three of two of them or if it fortune the[m] all to desease then by ye sayd Prior of St. Swithun [and] his Successors, with such other two persons as the sayd Abbott of Glastonbury [and] his successors as is before sayd shall name and appoint; they after theyr discretion shall choose [and] take out of the same stuff [and] goods. And in this election [and] choise of the forsayd aultar clothes [and] vestments, the sayd electors [and] chosers shall have one special discreet regard to the diversities of ye solemne feasts, Sundays [and] hollydayes kept in ye church in ye honour of o[u]r Lord [and] Lady or any other saints, Martyrs, Confessours [and] Virgins [and] in likewise to ferial days the time of Lent [and] days of obits so that for the same [and] ev[er]y of them there be chosen [and] ordained such aultarcloths [and] vestments, as may for the service of God, conveniently changeable [and] accordingly be used, worn [and] occupied at ye sayd aultar [and] at ye sayd feasts days times [and] obits [and] none otherwise. And in case [tha]t there be noo such aultar clothes nor vestments amonge the sayd stuffe [and] goods ready made, the sayd Prior of St. Swithun for ye time beinge shall cause such aultar clothes [and] vestments to be made of such cloth as before is for the same intent specified, [and] for lacke of cloth meete and convenient for ye sayd aultar clothes [and] vestments he shall buye such cloth as ye sayd aultar cloths [and] vestments may be made of by wh[i]ch

... ye sayd President, Treasurer, Chancellor [and] Ralph Lepton or any three or two of them or if them all fortune to disease then by the oversight of such other two persons as ye Abbot of Glastonbury or his successo[rs] shall have [and] appoint [and] for the price [and] making of the same to take money of ye price [tha]t shall grow of the same stuffe of goods; three good carpets either of them of eight foote longe to be taken out of the sayd stuffe [and] goods as the sayd choise [and] election whereof one of them shall continually lye before the sayd aultar [and] another of them shall in likewise continually lye upon the deske w[i]thin ye sayd Chappell (And the third of them) foure good [and] fine corporals of fine brussell cloth, w[i]th foure of ye finest [and] most goodly corporals cases that they shall find amonge ye sayd stuffe, two carpets, cushions to lye under foote in ye deske w[i]thin ye sayd chappell, at ye sayd choise [and] election foure other cushions to lye upo[n] ye sayd deske whereof oon shall be of velvet [and] the other two of cloth of gold at ye sayd choises [and] election. All which chalices, patens, cruets, candlesticks, basons, massebookes, portuose aultarcloths, vestments [and] other ornaments ye sayd Byshhop giveth [and] graunteth to ye sayd Prior [and] Convent to have [and] to hold to them [and] theyr successors, for ev[er]more to [and] for ye sayd use onely, [and] for none other [and] the sayd Prior and Convent of St. Swithun graunteth [and] by these pre[se]nts p[er]mitt that they shall cause two Monkes of sad, virtuous [and] religious life beinge Bachellours or Doctors of Divinity, if any such them be w[i]thin the Monastery of St. Swithun [and] that observe ye rule of St. Bennet [and] such as be not bounden to say ye day masse or masses satisfactory for any saule to say dayly whiles ye world shall endure at the sayd aultar within ye sayd Chappell though ye sayd Bysshop be not buried w[i]thin ye same; two masses the one dayly of ye day [and] the other every Sunday of ye Trinity, ye Monday of th[e] angels, the Tuesday of ye holy Ghost the Wednesday of Salus Populi, the Thursday of Corpus Christi, ye Friday of Jesu [and] ye Saturday of Requiem, having ye day of ye obit of ye sayd Bysshop upon which day either of ye sayd Monks shall say Masse of Requiem [and] w[h]ich ye sayd Prior [and] Convent of St. Swithun [and] theyr successors shall dayly give to either of ye sayd monks iii pence for ye sayd Masses saying, and also finde dayly [and] continually to ye sayd two monks one massebooke of theyr own use to say ye sayd masses over [and] bread [and] wine [and] two tapers of wax in proportion to stand upon ye sayd Candlesticks to burn continually duringe either of ye sayd Masses [and] the sayd Prior [and] Convent of St. Swithun [and] theyr successors at theyr proper charges fro[m] time to time [and] as often as necessity honest[l]y or conveniently it shall be requisite, shall repair [and] of new make as good as they were at the first deliverance of them all the sayd chalices, cruets, patens, candlesticks, basons, massebookes, aultarcloths, carpets [and] any

INDENTURE OF 1513

part of them to be stolen, brent or by any other chance lost destroyed or consumed [and] the sayd ornaments [and] every part of them shall be continually kept at the peril of ye sayd Prior [and] Convent [and] of theyr successors in a sure chest under locke [and] key in ye little howse standing beside ye sayd aultar in ye sayd Chappell ready therefore. The sayd Monks that shall occupie [them] about the saying of ye saide masses except such aultarcloths as for time remane upon ye saide aultar for ye garnishing of ye same; And except also it be thought expedient to the sayd Prior [and] his successors for ye more surely of ye sayd Chalices, pattens, cruets, candlesticks, [and] basons to be kept in revestry or any other place within ye sayd monastery. And ye sayd Prior [and] Convent of St. Swithun [and] theyr successors, ye rents, profits [and] revenues of the lands te[neme]nts [and] other ye premises by ye sayd Busshop now bought [and] purchased or hereafter for ye same intent to be purchased and of ye w[hi]ch certaine parcells is to them given [and] graunted to ye use [and] for ye behoofe of the sayd College and Chauntrie as is aforesayd at all times hereafter to them and to theyr successors to the use above rehearsed shall take [and] receave. And if ye sayd Bysshop in his life ende finish [and] performe the sayd building [and] howse [and] garnish ye Chappell or ye sayd Colleges [and] howses of officers w[i]thin ye same w[i]th ornaments, jewels, stuff, utensils [and] employments as is aforesayd [and] allsoe doe purchase [and] give lands, tenements, rents [and] pensions sp[irit]uell or temporall with ye mannors lands [and] tenements to them as it be foresaid now given to the yerely value of CLX li above all charge to ye sayd Prior [and] convent of St. Swithun [and] to theyr successors in manner [and] forme [and] to ye use [and] intent before rehearsed, the sayd Prior [and] Convent of St. Swithun [and] theyr successors by those p[rese]nts covenant [and] graunt to ye sayd Bysshop [and] to his assignes that they [and] theyr successors all the sayd plate, stuffe [and] jewells afore specified [and] rehearsed [and] every parcel thereof except such parcells onely as ye sayd Bysshop hath as above ordained [and] disposed for the sayd Chappell wherein he hath chosen his sepulture shall at the pleasure [and] request of ye sayd Bysshop redelivered to him [and] his assignes to have [and] retaine it to his proper use and behoofe [and] to dispose it [and] every part [and] parcel thereof as it shall please him. And if ye sayd Bysshop in his life have not nor require to have noo deliverance thereof, [that] then the sayd Prior of St. Swithun [and] Convent [and] theyr successors shall in ye manner [and] forme [and] w[i]thin the time limited [and] before the persons before rehearsed, prayse [and] esteeme or cause to be esteemed [and] praysed, all the sayd plate, stuffe, goods [and] jewells [and] every [parcel thereof [and] the money cominge [and] growinge of the price of ye same bestow [and] employ of [and] upon such things as hereafter be expressed or that the sayd Bysshop at anytime hereafter by any of his writings or otherwise shall expresse, ordaine [and] devise; And if the same plate, stuff [and] jewells before not except nor reserved be not delivered by ye sayd Prior of St. Swithun nor his successors so ye sayd Bysshop nor to his assignes in his life, not yf the sayd Bysshop make nor determine noe will in writing how the sayd Plate, jewells [and] stuff or such part of them as shall remaine nor destroyed by the sayd Prior [and] Convent of St. Swithun or by theyr successors over [and] above the p[er]formance of the premises, that then ye sayd Prior [and] Convent of St. Swithun for them [and] theyr successors, graunt by theyr p[rese]nts to ye sayd Bysshop [and] his assignes, that they the value of ye sayd plate, jewells [and] stuff aforespecified [and] not excepted [and] as before sayd praysed [and] esteemed or as much thereof as shall remaine with them [and] not employed as is before sayd, shall by ye oversight of the sayd Abbots of Glastonbury Redinge [and] Prior of Lewes or ye successors or successors of them or any of them for the time beinge, employ [and] bestow ye same plate, jewells [and] stuff or such p[ar]t as shall remaine thereof upon the making of a new vawte of stone over St swithun his shrine[34] [and] of the new making [and] vaulting with stone of two Isles upon the side of ye same Church [and] the vaulting of the Cross-Isle[35] in ye sayd Cathedrall Church of Winchest[er] with stone after the manner [and] forme of the vaulting of ye sayd Cathedrall Church. And allsoe ye foresaid Prior [and] Convent of St. Swthun covenant, p[er]mitt [and] graunte unto ye sayd Bysshop [and] his assignes, that they be theyr sufficient writing ensealed w[i]th theyr seale, shallmake, depute [and] assigne Will[ia]m Fletcher of Ichenstoke[36] in the County of Sout[hampton] to be receiver of the sayd lands, ten[emen]ts [and] other ye premises by the sayd Bysshop or other his feoffees, now to the sayd Prior given or hereafter to be given during his life, to levie [to]geder, take [and] receave the whole rente, issues, revenues [and] p[ro]fitts of all the sayd manners, lands [and] tenements to the use of the sayd Prior [and] Convent of St. Swithun [and] of theyr successors. The same rents, issues, profits [and] revenues to be employed by them to the use, purchase [and] intent aforesayd [and] yf the sayd Will[ia]m Fletcher of his recept of the sayd maners, lands, ten[emen]ts, rents [and] revenues doe pay all manner of chiefe [and] quite rents due [and] growing out of ye premises or of any parcel of them. And over that the sayd William doe pay yerely to ye sayd maistor [and] fellows of Martyn College [and] to the sayd Abbasse [and] Convent of Godstow [and] to the sayd Prior [and] Convent of

---

[34] The shrine of St Swithun was in the retrochoir of Winchester Cathedral. It was destroyed during the dissolution of the monasteries in the late 1530s.
[35] This refers to the transepts of Winchester Cathedral.
[36] William Fletcher of Itchenstoke was made Bailiff of the Manor of Highclere by Fox in 1512 (see WCL, Ledger Book, II, f. 90v). Fletcher is described as Fox's servant in a letter from Bishop Fitzjames dated 1519 (see Allen, 90).

Godstow [and] to the sayd Prior [and] Convent of St. Frideswith theyr severall forms [and] rents for ye places [and] grownd that they have severally graunted, [and] shall graunt hereafter to the sayd Prior [and] Convent of St. Swithun [and] to theyr successors for the building [and] making up of ye sayd College howses [and] gardens, unto such time as they [and] ev[er]y of them be otherwise recompensed for ye sayd rents [and] forms. And over it is covenaunted, graunted [and] accorded, between the sayd Bysshop, Prior [and] Convent of St. Swithun that if at any time hereafter it shall fortune the sayd Bysshop by and chance to fall within or without the realme of England, in such debt or danger by reason whereof he shall for his releve [and] redemption have need of the sayd plate [and] stuffe or any p[ar]t or parcel of ye same before excepted, nor reserved, that then in that case of casis the sayd Prior [and] Convent covenant, p[er]mitt and graunt unto ye sayd Bysshop [and] his assignes, that they at any time when they shall be thereto required by the sayd Bysshop, by his sufficient writings deputy or assignes shall give [and] deliver to him or to his assignes [and] to his proper use [and] behoofe, all the sayd plate [and] other ye p[re]misses before not excepted, or all such parcells or parcells thereof as shall remaine w[i]th ye sayd Prior [and] Convent [and] by them not bestowed nor employed to the use [and] intent in mannor [and] forme as is before specified. It is farther covenanted agreed [and] accorded betweene ye foresaid Bysshop [and] the sayd Prior of St. Swithun [and] Convent of the same that if ye sayd Bysshop at any time hereafter, shall have neede to have any of ye sayd plate, stuff or other the p[re]misses before not excepted, or of any p[ar]te or p[ar]cell of them to be occupied by him against or for any sollemne feast of ye yere or at ye comeinge to him of the Kinge or ye Queene or any other estate or honourable p[er]son or p[er]sons that he desire [and] require the sayd Prior [and] Convent of or any theyr successors to both of them the sayd plate, jewells or stuff or any p[ar]cell or p[ar]cells thereof before not excepted remaining in theyr keeping [and] not employed nor bestowed to any use of purpose as is before specified [and] declared, that then ye sayd Prior [and] Convent or theyr successors shall w[i]thout any contradiction or delay by writings indented thereof to be made betwixt them [and] the sayd Byshhop, leve [and] by way of love deliver for the space of XL dayes to ye Bysshop or his assignes the sayd p[re]misses [and] every p[ar]t of them such p[ar]t [and] p[ar]cells thereof as shall to by ye sayd Bysshop of them be required so to doe. Farthermore ye foresaid Prior of St. Swithun [and] Convent of ye same promitt [and] graunt for them [and] theyr successors by these p[re]sents to ye sayd Bysshop [and] his assignes, that they shall truly wholy [and] indifferently observe [and] keepe or doe as much as in these is possible to cease to be observed, [and] kept as well all such statutes, p[ro]visions, rules [and] ordinances which the foresaid Bysshop or th[e] Abbots of

Glastonbury, Redinge [and] Winchcombe[37] [and] Prior of Lewes for ye time beinge, by the request [and] desire of ye sayd bysshop to the honour of almighty god increase of vertue learning of ye laws of Christ's Church [and] th[e] observance of good religion shall make, ordaine [and] stablish or cause to be made, ordained or stablished to be continually observed [and] kept w[i]thin ye sayd College as allsoe keepe all [and] singular obbitts according as ye sayd Bysshop or Abbotts of Glastonbury, Redinge [and] Winchcombe [and] Prior of Lewes shall ordane, assigne [and] appoint to be done, kept [and] observed as in ye same College. And in likewise provide [and] pay for all such pittances as by the sayd Bysshop, Abbotts [and] Prior of Lewes shall be ordained [and] appointed to be had within the sayd College in all things according to the statutes [and] ordinances for the sayd p[re]misses [and] every of the[m] in ye behalf to be made [and] ordained. And in case the sayd statutes, rules [and] ordinances be not made by ye sayd Bysshop in his lifetime then [and] in that case the sayd Abbotts of Glastonbury, Redinge [and] Winchcombe [and] Prior of Lewes [and] theyr successors shall after theyr wisdoms, virtuous discretion [and] good conscience make [and] reestablish or cause to be made the sayd statutes, rules [and] ordinances. And the same statutes, rules [and] ordinances made by ye sayd Bysshop in his life or by ye sayd Abbotts of Glastonbury, Redinge, Winchcombe [and] Prior of Lewes after his discease the sayd Prior of St. Swithun and his successors shall to the best of theyr powers not onely keepe [and] observe in for [and] by them self as farr as they shall touch them, but also endeavor them [and] cause the same to be well, truely, entirely [and] p[er]fectly kept [and] observed by all other whome the sayd statutes shall doe touch. For the true performance of all which covenants, p[ro]misses, graunts [and] every one of them one of the p[ar]tes behalf of ye sayd Prior [and] Convent of St. Swithun aforespecified to be well [and] truely by them [and] theyr successors performed, fulfilled [and] kept the sayd Prior [and] Convent of St. Swithun by these p[re]sents, p[er]mitt, covenant [and] graunt to the sayd Bisshop his executors [and] assignes that w[i]thin two monethes next [and] i[m]mediately ensuing the sealing [and] deliverance of theyr parte of this present indenture to the sayd Bysshop [and] his assignes by theyr writings [and] obligatory sufficient [and] in law to be made [and] with theyr convent seale ensealed binde them self [and] theyr successors to the sayd abbotts of Glassonbury [and] his successors in ye sum[m]e of CCCCC li of lawful money of England[38] w[i]th a condition in the back of ye same obligation for ye true

---

[37] Richard Kidderminster was Abbot of Winchcombe in Gloucestershire, and like Fox, an enthusiast for the New Learning; see James G. Clark, *The Benedictines in the Middle Ages* (Woodbridge, 2011), 312.

[38] £500, a considerable sum of money in early Tudor England.

performance of all [and] singular covenants, agreements, p[re]misses [and] graunts on the behalf of ye sayd Prior and Convent of St. Swithun [and] theyr successors comprised in this present Indenture. And in like forme within the sayd time [and] upon like condition the same Prior [and] Convent of St. Swithun p[er]mitt [and] graunt to ye sayd Bysshop to be bounded to ye sayd Abbott of Redinge [and]his successors in another obligation containing the sume of CCCCC li of lawful money of England. And in like manner within the sayd time [and] upon like condicion the sayd prior [and] convent of St. Swithun p[er]mitt [and] graunt to the sayd Bysshop [and] his assignes to be bounde to the sayd Prior and Convent of Lewes [and] theyr successors in five hundred pownds. And if it shall soo fortune that any of ye sayd Abbotts of Glassonbury [and] Redinge or Prior of Lewes or any of theyr successors at any time hereafter against the sayd now Prior of St. Swithun or againe any of his successors the sum or sums of money [tha]t he [and] his Convent for the cause before specified is severally bounden to the[m] in [tha]t then they [and] every of them [that] soo shall recover against the sayd Prior of St. Swithun or against any of his successors doe in convenient time [and] space after such recovery [and] execution against the sayd now Prior of St. Swithun or any of his successors soe had employ [and] bestow all such money as by any of them shall be soe be recovered to such use [and] p[ro]fit or the College as ye Prior [and] Convent of St. Swithun [and] his successors shall appointe, limit, name [and] assigne; And over this the same Prior [and] convent of St. Swithun for ye true p[er]formance of all [and] ev[er]y article, covenant, agreement, graunt [and] p[re]misse on theyr behalf as is afore rehearsed [and] specified to be by them truly p[er]formed observed, executed [and] done [and] bind them self [and] theyr successors by these p[re]sents in the sum of three thousand pounds to ye sayd Richard Bisshop of Winchest[er] [and] to his assignes. Provided allways that the foresaid Prior of St. Swithun be not at any time hereafter charged nor chargeable by reason of any gift, covenant, agreement, p[ro]mise or graunt by these p[re]sents made by him unto the foresaid Bysshop like as is before particularly specified [and] expressed for the purchasing of any lands or ten[emen]ts building of ye sayd College furnishing of ye same w[i]th chalices, crosses, candlesticks, cruets, vestments [and] other ornaments, hangings, beds, napery [and] all other utensils [and] stuff in mannor [and] forme as is before expressed nor to noo other charge w[hi]ch he by the p[re]sents hath covenanted p[er]mitted [and] graunted to doe p[er]forme observe [and] keep further then such lands [and] ten[emen]ts as now be given or hereafter shall be given to the sayd Prior [and] his successors [and] such sum[m]e [and] sum[m]s of money as the sayd Prior [and] his successors shall have [and] receave of the sayd lands [and] ten[emen]ts [and] of [and] for such plate, jewells [and] other goods [and] c[h]attells comprised [and] specified in ye foresyad indentures or in any of them w[hi]ch be appointed to be sold [and] that in the money comminge [and] growing of the sale of the sayd premises [and] unto y[ou]r sayd Prior of St. Swithun or of to his successors will amount [and] extend unto. In witness of all which p[ro]misses the sayd partyes have to these indentures enterchangeably set theyr seales that is to say the sayd Bysshop to the one p[ar]te of this Indenture remaining w[i]th ye sayd Prior hath set his seale. And ye Prior [and] ye Convent of St. Swithun for them [and] theyr successors to the other p[ar]t of this Indenture remaining w[i]th the sayd Bysshop have set theyr com[m]on seale yeven the same the day [and] yere abovesayd.

[in dorso]
M[emoran]d[um], that ye xxvii day of august the fifth yere of the reigne of the kinge w[i]thin specified M[agister] Richard Gardiner Treasurer of Wolv[e]sey in ye name of the w[i]thin specified Bisshop of Winchester hath delivered this Indenture to the w[i]thin named Prior [and] Convent.

APPENDIX 5

JOHN AND JANE HUDDLESTON AND THE MANOR OF TEMPLE GUITING

The archive at Corpus contains a significant collection of title deeds and other documents relating to the properties that Bishop Fox and benefactors gave to the college. The collection includes a series of documents pertaining to the manor of Temple Guiting in Gloucestershire, that Fox purchased in December 1514, from Jane Huddleston. The property was left to Jane two years earlier by her husband, Sir John Huddleston, but the bequest was subject to dispute by one of Huddleston's executors as well as his son, also called John.[1] As a result, a case was heard in Chancery in 1515 to determine the matter.[2] Detailed depositions were made during the hearing and three refer to the building of Fox's college and the agreement made to commemorate John Huddleston and his wife in the foundation.

John Huddleston's last will and testament had been drawn up on 5 November 1511.[3] He left instructions regarding his burial, listed bequests and specified what should be done with the lands that he owned.[4] These lands included the manor of Temple Guiting that Huddleston had purchased a few years earlier, a substantial property of several thousand acres. Huddleston directed that his wife Jane keep Temple Guiting and that at her death (or remarriage) the property should be sold and the proceeds distributed by his executors 'for the welth of both theire soules'. Huddleston's executors were his son John, Robert Southwell, John Dalston, who was a neighbour in Gloucestershire, and priest Christopher Urswick, a good friend of Fox.[5] Thomas Stanley, the Abbot of Hailes Abbey, witnessed the will and was designated to supervise its execution. The Abbot was present at Huddles-

---

[1] Jane (*née* Stapulton) was Huddleston's second wife. He had previously been married to Joan Fitzhugh. Jane was previously married to Sir Christopher Harcourt.
[2] Amongst the deponents was Thomas More, of the parish of St. Stephen Walbrook in London, who, given that he was aged about 37, may be the future Chancellor; see A. J. Kendell, 'Thomas More, Richard Fox and the Manor of Temple Guyting in 1515', *Moreana*, 23, no. 91–2 (1986), 5–10.
[3] The will is in the archive at Corpus. Huddleston was born c.1450, the second son of a staunch Yorkist, Sir John Huddleston of Millom in Cumbria. He received several royal appointments in the south-west, was pardoned in 1486, knighted soon after and settled in Gloucestershire where he held the stewardship of Sudeley Castle.
[4] Huddleston (and later his wife) were interred in Hailes Abbey.
[5] Dalston owned property at Dumbleton. Southwell died soon after Huddleston.

ton's deathbed and he later recalled that he had heard the dying man insist that his son John should not inherit Temple Guiting.

John Huddleston died on 2 January 1512. Within weeks, Jane Huddleston's ownership of Temple Guiting was challenged by two executors, one being her late husband's son (and her stepson) John, and the other John Dalston.[6] According to Abbot Stanley, neither would sign the will of the deceased John Huddleston, insisting that Temple Guiting become the property of the younger John Huddleston. Another executor, Robert Southwell, died in 1514, which left Christopher Urswick, as the only executor, to uphold the terms of Huddleston's will. The depositions made in Chancery in 1515 reveal that the problems continued, so much so that Jane decided to sell Temple Guiting. Urswick organized the sale of the manor to Bishop Fox. The two men had been very well acquainted for thirty years and so Urswick was fully aware of the bishop's need for lands with which to endow his Oxford foundation, as well as being aware of the legal problems any sale would arouse.[7] Documents in the archive at Corpus include an indenture of 5 December 1513 concerning the sale of Temple Guiting by which Fox agreed to pay £750 for the manor. A second indenture was drawn up the following day that fulfilled the terms of John Huddleston's will; Bishop Fox agreed to ensure that the Prior and Convent of St. Swithun's would take responsibility for the performance of a daily mass for John and Jane Huddleston and would keep an obit on behalf of the couple each year on 2 January.

The terms of the second indenture were later rehearsed in three of the depositions made in Chancery, namely those made by Urswick, Fox and his chaplain, Ralph Lepton. According to Urswick, Bishop Fox agreed that he

> should cause the Pryor and Convente of the Monasterie of St. Swithin's in Winchester by theire deedys indented under theire Comen Seal to grant to the Wardens and fellowship of All Sowles College in Oxford that the sayde Pryor and his successours in perpetuite shall cause oon Masse to bee oferide dayly by a monke in an chappell w[i]thin the college in Oxenford now beeyng in buyldinge by the saide Bishopp w[h]ych shall bee called Winchester College at an altar there to be called St. Cuthberty's altar for the soule of the saide S[i]r John Huddle[ston] as more largly apeereth by another Indenture there upon made dated the VI day of December the VI year of the Reigne of King Henry the VIII .[8]

---

[6] According to the younger Huddleston's deposition, his father made a later will in which he bequeathed Temple Guiting to his heirs rather than his wife. Dalston tried to recover the manor for the younger John, causing Jane Huddleston to resort to law.

[7] In 1487, Fox appointed his 'beloved' Urswick to a prebend; see E. Chisholm-Batten, *The Register of Richard Fox while Bishop of Bath and Wells* (London, 1889), 12. Urswick continued to receive livings from Fox; he also leased land himself to Fox in the early sixteenth century.

[8] CCCO Rej. Glos. 5 (4 February [1515]).

It is plain that the mainly monastic college Bishop Fox planned to establish in Oxford was under construction by December 1513. Moreover, as a result of his purchase of Temple Guiting, Fox had committed Prior Silkstede and the Convent of St. Swithun's in Winchester, to pray on a daily basis for John Huddleston and his wife Jane. Fox had already determined that the altar at which these prayers were to be recited was to be dedicated to St. Cuthbert, the patron saint of Durham, where he served as bishop in the late 1490s. The mention of All Souls College is noteworthy. The details in the Chancery hearing reveal that the altar dedicated to St. Cuthbert was not ready for use in December 1514. In his deposition, Bishop Fox stated that he had agreed with Urswick that the Prior and Convent of St. Swithun's at Winchester, would make a financial grant to the Warden of All Souls College with regard to prayers for the Huddlestons. It may be presumed that the grant would cover the costs incurred in the recitation of such prayers at All Souls College, until such time that the monks in Fox's college chapel could take on the responsibility. In the archive at Corpus is a letter from Thomas Ryckes to Urswick, dated 4 February (no year but certainly 1515), recording the writing of a *remembrance* for the souls of John and Jane Huddleston to be placed upon the organ in the chapel at All Souls.

Following the agreement drawn up on 6 December 1514, payment was made for the manor of Temple Guiting. According to the accounts made by deponents in the Chancery hearing of 1515, monies brought by Ralph Lepton to Bishop Fox's episcopal lodging at St. Mary Overy in Southwark were counted out into four bags and stored overnight in a locked chest. The bags were carried by boat the following morning to Urswick's lodgings near Blackfriars.[9] Once the money had been handed over, a third indenture was drawn up between Fox and Urswick. By this agreement Bishop Fox agreed to ensure that Prior Silkstede and the Convent of St. Swithun's make a grant to the Warden and Fellowship of All Souls College soon after the following Easter. The grant was made as payment to the Warden of All Souls for prayers to be recited at an altar in that college until such time as St. Cuthbert's altar in Fox's foundation was consecrated and could be used.

In Chancery, Archbishop Warham, the Chancellor, made a final decision in Fox's favour in July 1515. The purchase of Temple Guiting could be finalized, and soon after, the legal documents were drawn up for Bishop Fox to receive seisin (possession) of the manor. Although the accounts for the early phases of building are lost, we can be fairly certain that the hall at Corpus was completed sometime in 1516 for this is the date that is carved in the wooden frieze beneath the great hammerbeam roof. The wooden frieze also bears the heraldic arms of John Huddleston. Some time between December

---

[9] Barry Collett, *The Fox and the Tudor Lions* (forthcoming), chapter 9.

1514 and the middle of October 1515, Fox's plans for his foundation altered and so when the endowment of Temple Guiting was finally made on 29 July 1517, it was named as the property not of 'Winchester College' but, instead, of the non-monastic Corpus Christi College. The altered plans did not, however, impact the agreement Fox had made with Urswick; the college statutes enshrined the memory of the Huddlestons for whom prayers were to be regularly offered and their armorials remained as testimony to their role in providing a valuable endowment for Corpus.

APPENDIX 6

CARVED DETAILS IN THE HALL AT CORPUS CHRISTI COLLEGE

It was Bishop Fox's original intention to establish a college in Oxford to benefit the Benedictine monks of St. Swithun's Priory in Winchester. Preparatory work began in 1512 and building started the following year, continuing when the bishop's plans for the college altered late in 1515 and during 1516. With Fox's decision to take secular students, the hall was extended to accommodate greater numbers, and was completed late in 1516. It is dominated by a great hammerbeam roof, the design of which is generally attributed to Humphrey Coke who some years later designed a larger and more elaborate version for Cardinal College. Coke was a very busy craftsmen and he probably sub contracted the Corpus roof to others. It is thought to have been made in the workshop of Oxford-based carpenter, Robert Carow. His team completed the installation of the roof in 1516 and this date features as a carved detail (Plate 12). Other carved imagery refers to the Prior and Convent of St. Swithun's, and reflects Fox's original intention to establish a monastic college. The carved details were left unaltered after Fox's plans changed.

CORBELS

The lower vertical members or wall posts of the hammerbeam roof terminate in stone corbels. These corbels have been carved and the detail picked out in paint. The colour is not original but gives a good idea of the bright hues that were widely used on wood and stone in Tudor decoration. The detail on the corbels includes scrollwork inscribed in blackletter, with Bishop Fox's motto, *Est Deo Gracia* (Plate 13). One corbel features a scroll inscribed with an abbreviated dedication, *Scti Swi.thi.ni.* (Plate 14), a dedication to St. Swithun, the patron saint who was venerated until the Reformation, by the monks of Winchester Cathedral.[1] The link to Winchester is confirmed on the corbel by the addition of the heraldic arms of that See which bear the

---

[1] Interestingly, the letter *n* is reversed, probably suggesting that the carver responsible for this corbel was illiterate and was copying from a model.

keys of St. Peter crossed with the sword of St. Paul.[2] It should be noted that those who carved the corbel reversed the position of the sword and keys and the modern colours of the paint with which the charges have been picked out, show the lower of the two keys gold (*or*) instead of the usual silver (*argent*) colour. Interestingly, the heraldic shield carved on the corbel also bears the initials, *TSP* for Thomas Silkstede, who was Prior of the Convent of St. Swithun's in the early sixteenth century. Silkstede's initials can also be seen on three heraldic shields bearing the arms of the See of Winchester below the oriel window above the college gatehouse.[3] Clearly the decoration of this corbel, and the gatehouse, was determined before Bishop Fox decided to alter his plans for the college from a monastic to secular institution.

CARVED DETAILS ON THE FRIEZE IN THE HALL[4]

A horizontal wooden frieze can be seen immediately below the hammer-beam roof on the east and western sides of the hall. The frieze is divided into six sections on either side of the hall. Each section on the east side and the three northernmost sections on the west side of the hall, contain five square panels. Each panel contains a roundel within which is a quatrefoil containing further carved detail. The three southernmost sections on the west side of the hall comprise three panels separated by thinner arched panels containing a trefoil. Each trefoil frames an heraldic shield; the quatrefoils in the square panels feature a variety of carved detail. Horizontal cracks in the wood are apparent in sections of the frieze owing to shrinkage of the oak over time and in places the carved detail has been lost. Some of the damage may have been deliberate though it is unclear why or when this would have occurred. It is possible that some details were lost when the frieze and the hammerbeam roof immediately above were treated with a thick coat of black paint in the early 1700s. Although the paint has fallen away in some places, it continues to obscure the carved detail and any polychromy that may have been used to pick out specific features.

The frieze on the east side of the hall comprises thirty square panels with twenty-four on the west side. Within the quatrefoil of each panel, further carved detail may be seen. Eleven of the quatrefoils seem to be purely decorative, simply featuring stylized foliate forms. Two quatrefoils

---

[2] The arms for the see are: gules, two keys endorsed in bend, the uppermost *or*, the lower, *argent*, a sword, the point in chief interposed between them in bend sinister of the second pommel and hilt *or*.

[3] The sword and keys are positioned correctly in two of the three shields on the gatehouse.

[4] Aside from a brief description on the college website the carved detail has previously been very briefly mentioned in RCHM, *An Inventory of the Historical Monuments in the City of Oxford*, HMSO, xxxiii (London, 1939), 51.

on the east side of the hall have all but lost their carved detail though an unidentified fragment survives in one of the panels towards the northern end.[5] The remaining quatrefoils contain a mix of royal and personal devices, religious and heraldic imagery and three monograms. There is no evidence that a systematic programme was followed.

Bishop Fox is commemorated by his personal device of a pelican pecking its breast (vulning), which is carved in three quatrefoils (Plates 16a and 16b). There is a distinct difference in style in the approach taken to depicting the subject, for one pelican is shown covered with feathers and the other two examples are not. This suggests that there were at least two craftsmen at work on these carvings. The vulning pelican was widely recognized in the late-medieval era as a symbol for Christ's sacrifice and was invariably used as a decorative detail in all of the works with which Fox was associated. Indeed, the pelican is evident in the glass of the hall window where it is depicted in yellow stain in each of the individual quarries (Plate 15), which though nineteenth-century in date may echo the device that was almost certainly a feature of the early-sixteenth-century glass with which many of the college windows were glazed.

Fox's status as a bishop is reflected in the image of an episcopal mitre carved in a quatrefoil on the east side of the hall (Plate 16c). Tudor badges reflecting Fox's loyalty to the dynasty make up more than a third of the quatrefoils on the frieze in the hall at Corpus and are reminiscent of identical imagery carved on the bosses over the quire in Winchester Cathedral which were commissioned by Fox in the latter years of Henry VII's reign.[6] Most numerous at Corpus are the eleven examples of the Tudor rose; in addition there are five examples of fleur-de-lys, four examples of the portcullis alluding to the Beaufort family and a single pomegranate for Granada which was the badge signifying Henry VIII's queen, Katherine of Aragon used in early Tudor times (Plate 16d). A similar array of Tudor badges including the pomegranate, feature in the chapel at Corpus on the bosses that were carved by Thomas Roossell of Westminster and gilded by Humphrey Coke.[7]

Aside from Fox's pelican device, there are relatively few examples of overtly religious imagery on the frieze in the hall, which is perhaps surprising given the fact that Corpus was originally designed as a monastic college.

---

[5] The surviving fragment looks like an ear and could have originally symbolized the ear of Malchus which features on several bosses commissioned by Bishop Fox for the east end of Winchester Cathedral. If this is the case, then the lost section of the carving in the hall at Corpus might have been the sword which was used to cut off Malchus's ear.
[6] See Angela Smith, *Roof Bosses of Winchester Cathedral* (Friends of Winchester Cathedral, 1996).
[7] For the chapel bosses, see Reid, J., 'The Bosses of Corpus Christi Chapel', *The Pelican Record*, 49 (2013), 15–24.

However, one panel on the north end of the west side of the hall is carved with a bird holding a scroll in its beak. At first glance the bird might seem to be another example of Fox's pelican device, but the scroll in the bird's beak suggests that the bird is an eagle and symbolizes St. John the Evangelist.[8] Another image in the carved detail on the frieze and with religious significance is a heart set within a crown of thorns. The heart surrounded by a crown of thorns represents the wounded heart of Christ, which, though rarely seen with the Arma Christi, was used in fifteenth-century poems associated with the cult of the wounds and appears in other examples of late-medieval carved wood.[9]

As an individual who had a long history of close involvement in both his own architectural projects and the royal works, Fox would have indicated the subjects he wanted to see carved in the hall at Corpus. It is uncertain whether Thomas Silkstede, Prior of St. Swithun's, offered any ideas on subject matter. The only obvious visual reference to the Prior and Convent of St. Swithun's in the frieze carvings are two examples of the heraldic arms of the See of Winchester, featuring the keys of St. Peter and sword of St. Paul – though one of the carvings depicts the keys in the wrong position. One other image carved upon the frieze may have a connection with Winchester. This carving shows a bear standing alongside a ragged staff, a motif that was used as an heraldic device in the Middle Ages by the Beauchamp family of Warwick.[10] A mythical member of that family and hero of popular medieval romance was Guy of Warwick, whose exploits were described by Thomas Rudbourne, a monk at St. Swithun's in the mid-fifteenth century. According to legend, Guy saved Winchester for the Saxon King Athelstan by killing his enemy's champion, a giant called Colbrond, in a duel. Guy was highly esteemed at Winchester and venerated by the monastic community of St. Swithun's in the later Middle Ages. Indeed, a relic believed to be Colbrond's battle-axe was kept in the Treasury of St. Swithun's where it served as a reminder of the momentous event.[11] The axe was one of many

[8] A bird holding a scroll in its beak is carved on a misericord in the chapel of New College, Oxford; see RCHM, pl. 156 (1).
[9] For example "Oh Man Unkynde"; see Shannon Gayk, 'Early Modern Afterlives of the Arma Christi', in *The Arma Christi in Medieval and Early Modern Culture*, ed. Lisa H. Cooper and Andrea Denny-Brown (Ashgate Publishing, 2014), 287 et seq. A heart within a crown of thorns can be seen carved on a former bench-end in the church of St. Peter and Paul in Churchstanton, Somerset.
[10] The bear and ragged staff is, for example, in evidence as a decorative element in the Beauchamp Chapel at St. Mary's Church in Warwick, which was built in the mid-fifteenth century.
[11] Thomas Warton, *The History of English Poetry* (London, 1775), 89. The sword disappeared at the Dissolution. Warton also records seeing the fragmentary remains of a wall painting in the north transept of the cathedral, which depicted the combat of Guy and Colbrond, though subsequent scholars disputed his identification of the subject.

Saxon relics treasured and promoted at Winchester. It might be remembered that the early-sixteenth-century programmatic organization of the east end of the cathedral devised by Bishop Fox, used these Saxon relics to promote and endorse the Tudor dynasty.[12]

Amongst the images carved on the frieze on the east side of the hall is a heraldic shield within a garter, which has not previously been identified (Plate 17a). The shield is carved with a lattice-like pattern of diagonally laced bendlets. The lack of colour (tincture) hinders identification of the owner of the shield. The heraldic arms do not belong to any of the benefactors of the college. However, they can be shown to be the family arms of the Huddleston family who sold Fox their property at Temple Guiting in Gloucestershire that formed a considerable part of the endowment Bishop Fox made to Corpus.[13] The sale of the manor was agreed between Fox and Christopher Urswick in 1514. Neither John Huddleston nor his son were members of the Order of the Garter, so the carvers at Corpus clearly made a mistake in placing the shield within a Garter badge. Notwithstanding this error, the arms were undoubtedly carved upon the frieze to commemorate the acquisition of lands from the Huddleston family and acted as a perpetual reminder to those who saw them to pray for those who had contributed to establishing the college. It might be noted that the Huddlestons had been fervent supporters of the Yorkists in the fifteenth century and had made several advantageous marriages with the Neville family, who through marriage with the Beauchamps used the bear and ragged staff as a badge. Indeed, John Huddleston himself had taken Joan Fitzhugh, the niece of Warwick the Kingmaker, as his first wife.[14] Jane Huddleston, who agreed to sell the manor of Temple Guiting to Fox, was John's second wife and not a Neville by birth but it is possible that the bear and ragged staff we see carved on the frieze in the hall at Corpus and discussed above commemorates the royal connections that the Huddleston family had earlier enjoyed in the 1480s.

The frieze on the west side of the hall at Corpus features three quatrefoils containing monograms in black letter. Such monograms were not uncommon in early-sixteenth-century imagery, where they generally carried religious significance, or were formed by the letters of a patron's name. The monograms at Corpus are not easy to interpret and the conclusions discussed

[12] The relics included the bones of Saxon kings reinterred in specially commissioned wooden mortuary chests that were displayed upon the presbytery screens. The array of carved wooden bosses upon the vault of the quire included the heraldic armorials of these kings.
[13] The Huddleston arms (gules fretty argent) can be seen on the tombs in the family chapel at Holy Trinity Church at Millom in Cumberland near the family seat.
[14] John Huddleston's older brother Richard married Margaret Neville, an illegitimate daughter of the Kingmaker and his younger brother William, married Isabel Neville, the Kingmaker's niece. These marriages placed the Huddlestons close to the crown since Richard, Duke of York, who became king in 1483, was himself married to Warwick's daughter.

below remain inconclusive. One monogram appears to be formed using the letters, R V and an inverted V, and two others are carved with the letters M and W (Plates 17b, c and d). The monograms at Corpus do not to refer to Bishop Fox, whose RF is carved on bosses he commissioned for Winchester Cathedral, a scheme that also includes royal monograms for Henry VII, the future king Henry VIII and Katherine of Aragon. Nor do the monograms in the hall at Corpus represent the status or initials of Prior Silkstede, for whom a T (for Thomas) and S can be seen in the carved ornament on the screen of his chantry chapel at Winchester.[15] Silkstede's monogram features with the letters MA, which was widely used as an abbreviated form of Mary, signifying a devotion to the cult of the Virgin.[16] A number of letters were used in late-medieval art and architecture to signify the Virgin Mary, including R (for Regina), V and M, all of which can be seen in the carved imagery in the hall at Corpus. The letter M is one of the most commonly used monograms for Mary, though the example at Corpus is elaborated by the addition of a carved arrow and nails. These are emblems associated with the Passion, which often featured in works commissioned by Bishop Fox, including the bosses carved for the chapel at Corpus. The carved letter interpreted as a W is in fact composed of two Vs and is set against a stylized flowering plant. The letter M or MA was often depicted in late-medieval art with one of the flowers that symbolized the Virgin. What we see in the hall at Corpus is another monogram associated with Mary: a V and a V signifying the Virgin of Virgins. These carved letters seem to be an abbreviated visual form referring to the Seven Sorrows and Seven Joys of the Virgin, a popular subject in late-medieval art and one that inspired a set of stained glass windows that Bishop Fox commissioned for Winchester Cathedral.[17] A third monogram in the hall at Corpus is carved with a letter R for Regina, encompassing a V and an inverted V, a variant form referencing Mary as Queen as Virgin of Virgins.

EAST SIDE OF THE HALL, NORTH–SOUTH

Tudor rose
shield
unidentified – possibly the ear of Malchus

---

[15] Silkstede's monogram TS, ornaments the entrance to his chantry chapel in Winchester Cathedral.
[16] The Lady Chapel in Winchester Cathedral, that was completed after Silkstede became prior and was his responsibility, was decorated with an extensive set of wall paintings illustrating miracles associated with the Virgin Mary.
[17] See Angela Smith, 'Bishop Fox and Stained Glass in Early Tudor England', *Journal of Stained Glass*, 31 (2007), 35–52

Tudor rose
fleur-de-lys

fleur-de-lys
Tudor rose
Tudor rose
pomegranate (Plate 16d)
shield

Tudor rose
Beaufort portcullis
heart within a crown of thorns (Plate 16c)
episcopal mitre
pelican vulning (Plate 16a)

flowers
flowers
flowers
Arms of See of Winchester
Tudor rose

heart within a crown of thorns
heraldic arms for the Huddleston family (Plate 17a)
fleur-de-lys
pelican vulning (Plate 16b)
Beaufort portcullis

Tudor rose
flowers
flowers
flowers
'empty' quatrefoil

WEST SIDE OF THE HALL, NORTH–SOUTH

Tudor rose
monogram (V and V) (Plate 17b)
eagle symbol for St. John the Evangelist
heraldic arms of See of Winchester (reversed)
Beaufort portcullis

bear and ragged staff
plain shield
Tudor rose

Beaufort portcullis
fleur-de-lys

plain shield
pelican vulning
monogram (inverted V and V) (Plate 17c)
plain shield
monogram (R, V and inverted V) (Plate 17d)

Tudor rose
fleur-de-lys
Tudor rose

flowers
shield carved with year date 1516
flowers

stylized foliage
form with four triangular arms
stylized foliage

APPENDIX 7

BISHOP FOX'S BERKSHIRE ENDOWMENT OF THE COLLEGE

The letter below shows Fox's typical style and methods when buying property to endow the College. His agent in this particular matter was Thomas Barker, a farmer at Arborfield in Berkshire, five miles south-east of Reading, about thirty miles from Oxford. The background to the purchase is uncertain, but given what is already known about Fox, his political situation late in 1516 and his other purchases, reasonable conjectures are possible.[1]

By the end of 1516 the construction of Corpus was well under way and Fox was looking for sound investments with which to endow the College. He maintained a wide network scouting for properties available for purchase, and had known Barker for some time and trusted his judgment and honesty. Fox had earlier written asking Barker to evaluate Thomas Dorsett's land ('hyt hath pleased youre gode lordeshyp to wryte on to me to a vewe a howse with certen lond lyying in the parisshe of Erberfeld, of Thomas Dorsett'), and any other that was available. Perhaps the education of his son Anthony arose in the course of discussion about Dorsett's land. Barker visited Dorsett's land and another property, noted their quality and features and sounded out the owners on purchase prices, but had not yet replied to Fox by 22 December 1516. Fox, however, urgently needed Barker's assessment of the properties, and sent a reminder, perhaps by a courier riding between Winchester and Oxford ('yowre own to [t]hys powyr [poor] Thomas Barker'). This explains why the farmer hastily wrote the letter while the courier and his horse waited and rested. In the letter, Barker noted that the house under consideration was undergoing repairs but the farm comprised nine acres of good-quality land, hedged or fenced ('gode land lyyng there to and inclosyd'). Thomas Bullock, whose family owned Arborfield manor, held an acre and a half of meadow adjacent to Dorsett's meadow, and this also would be available for sale. Dorsett's asking price for the house and land was 20 marks (£13 6s 8d), which he told Barker several of his neighbours would be willing to pay ('he wulnat selle hyt vnder

---

[1] J. G. Milne, 'The Muniments of Corpus Christi College, Oxford', *Bulletin of the Institute of Historical Research*, 10, no. 29 (1932), 105–8; 'The Muniments of Corpus Christi College, Oxford' *Oxoniensia*, 2 (1937), 129–33; 'The Berkshire Muniments of Corpus Christi College, Oxford', *Berkshire Archaeological Journal*, 46 (1942), 32–44, 78–87.

Xxti marke, for he syeth he maye haue so of dyuers of hys neybors'). Barker himself thought that Dorsett's asking price of 14s 4d rental per annum for the land was reasonable.

Barker had also viewed property belonging to Richard Newland in the same parish. Three crofts of arable land were adjacent to Dorsett's house, which meant that the two properties could perhaps be amalgamated ('Newlond ... hath iij croftis of arrabull lond lyyng in the same parishhe, nye on to the howse of the seid Thomas Dorsett'). Newland wanted 8 marks (£5 6s 8d) after sixteen years purchase, that is, him continuing to farm the land for the sixteen years at a rent of 6s 8d per annum, bearing all charges and serving the lord and the king. Barker did not make any adverse comments about the properties, and Fox bought them both in the first few days of January 1517, soon after this letter, confirming that Fox trusted Barker's judgment and honesty.

Thomas Barker's acknowledgement that Fox has been a good lord to him with 'your grete beyuolens and kyndnes schewyd onto me at all tymys' was significant. Fox, himself a farmer's son who has risen by ability and education, had presumably encouraged young Anthony Barker to study at Oxford. Thomas Barker expected that Anthony would show lifelong gratitude for Fox's encouragement: 'my powyr ladde: of whom I truste in God ye schall have a trewe bedman duryng his lyfe', while Barker himself would show gratitude with 'my seruys and prayour' for Fox. The reference to Anthony Barker in this letter is an example of how the opportunities for education and social mobility that the founder offered to the sons of craftsmen (Appendix 8) were also offered to other bright boys, making Corpus a significant instrument of Tudor social mobility.

With Fox's encouragement, Anthony Barker (c. 1500–51), the son of a farmer, entered Corpus Christi College as a *discipulus* on 21 October 1517. He survived the outbreak of sweating sickness that swept through Oxford that term and became a Fellow in 1519 and MA on 10 February 1523. Anthony Barker then carried out unspecified tasks in France for Henry Stafford, Earl of Wiltshire (d. 1523), and was in Paris when the younger Huddleston, following his unsuccessful Chancery hearing of 1515, petitioned Parliament for possession of Temple Guiting. The Earl of Wiltshire was a highly placed nobleman, related to the Woodvilles, who also knew Fox, and his confidence in Barker must have been strengthened by Fox's own assessment of the young farmer's son. Wiltshire asked young Barker to advise him on the matter and Barker robustly commended the College's continued possession of the manor, describing Corpus as the place 'where I was browght upp', and the College's case 'as the cause of a lx or lxxx fatherlys childerne that be there contynually browght upp and noryshed'. Barker's employment and his confident response to the Earl provide striking evidence of the processes of social mobility during the early sixteenth century. Barker entered Holy Orders, and became vicar of Wroughton (1530), West Ham, Essex (1538) Burford (1542) and Burghfield (Berkshire) in 1547. He also became Prebendary of Winchester, then Lincoln in 1540, a canon of St. George's Chapel, Windsor from November 1541, and a Fellow of Eton. He later helped with the sale of ornaments from St. George's Chapel, from which Ollard deduces that he was a reformer in theology. Anthony Barker died in November 1551.[2]

THOMAS BARKER'S LETTER TO FOX, 22 DECEMBER 1516.[3]

Ryght reuuerend and my syngular gode lord,

In the moste humbe wyse that I can, I recommend me on to youre gode lordshyp of your grete beyuolens and kyndnes schewyd onto me at all tymys, and specyalle that ye be so goode lorde on to my powyr ladde: of whom I truste in God ye schall have a trewe bedman[4] duryng his lyfe, and my seruys and prayour.

And where as hyt hath pleased youre gode lordeshyp to wryte on to me to a vewe a howse with certen lond lyyng in the parisshe of Erberfeld, of Thomas Dorsett, I haue seyn hyt, and hyt ys worth XIIIJs IIIJd by the yere. The howse ys sumwhat at reparacion, and IX acre of gode land lyyng there to and inclosyd. And he schwyth me that he hath spokyn on to Thomas Bullokk for an acre of mede and di.[5], the wyche he sculd haue in hys me;[6] and he made answer, yf he kowde schewe a de[7] ther of, that he schuld haue hyt.

Also I haue spokyn on to a nothyr man callyd Richard Newlond; the wyche hath iiJ croftis of arrabull lond lyyng in the same parishhe, nye on to the howse of the seid Thomas Dorsett. The wyche he wull selle after XVJ yere purches, and that he schall haue hyt to ferme for VIs, VIIJd by the yere; and he to bere all maner chargis, and to serue the Kyng and lord.[8]

Also I haue comynyd with the same Thomas Dorsette, to vnderstond what he wuld haue for hys howse and lond. An he seyth that he wulnat

---

[2] CCCO Rej. Glos.2 (December, n.y. one paper.); 'My poor lad' was Anthony Barker, of Berkshire. *The Inventories of St. George's Chapel, 1384–1667*, ed. M. F. Bond (Windsor, 1947), 197; Ollard, S. L. and M. F. Bond, *Fasti Wyndesorienses: The Deans and Canons of Windsor* (Windsor, 1950), 156. J. Foster, *Alumni Oxonienses, 1500–1714* (Oxford, 1891), 70.
[3] CCCO A1/1/7; see Allen, 84–5.
[4] A 'trew bedman' or true bedesman is one who prays (recites bede) sincerely.
[5] Dimidium is a half. Thus 'an acre and a half of meadow'.
[6] Sic; 'mede' is mead.
[7] Sic; 'dede' is deed.
[8] The 'purches' was the annual rent or return from land, in this case 6s 8d. 'After sixteen years purchase' the sale price was therefore £5 6s 8d. The vendor would have it to farm, and would bear the manor charges and also serve the lord and the king.

selle hyt vnder Xxti marke, for he syeth he maye haue so of dyuers of hys neybors.[9] And his neybor Richard Newlond wulnot selle hys vnder VIIJ marke; the wyche ys after XVJ yere purchys.

Also where as Thomas Fest and Thomas Creswell where infeffyd in the seid howse and lond to the vse of hym and hys wyfe, the same feffeys hath delyueryd the same dede to the same Thomas Dorsette. And yf I can haue knowledge of anye othyer land that wull be shold in our cuntre, your lordshyp schall haue knowledge there of schortlye: with the grace of Jhesu, who preserue [you] to his plesure.

Wretyn in haste the XXIJti daye of Decembre.
By yowre own to hys powyr
Thomas Barker.
To the reuerend fathyr in Godd and moste syngler gode lord, my lord of Wynchester, thys bylle be delyeryd in haste.

---

[9] Thomas Dorsette asked 20 marks for his house and land.

APPENDIX 8

EDUCATIONAL OPPORTUNITIES FOR CRAFTSMEN'S SONS

In establishing Corpus Christi College, Bishop Fox made provision for the education of young men from those parts of England with which he had a particular connection.[1] Some of the first students at Corpus were from families who had close personal ties with the bishop. Another group, a handful of students who came up to Corpus in its first decades, was the sons of craftsmen who are known to have worked for Fox. In this respect, Fox was continuing a tradition that earlier bishops of Winchester had pursued.[2] More generally, Fox clearly believed in a policy of meritocracy, by which opportunity was available to talent as much as it was to status, such as it had been for him during the 1460s.

In June 1522, nineteen-year-old John Helyar from Hampshire was admitted into Corpus. Whilst there is no documentary proof that his father or any other member of his family worked for Bishop Fox, the circumstantial evidence is strong. The Helyars were a well-established family in the south and at least two individuals surnamed Helyar were recorded in Winchester in the early sixteenth century. Indeed, scrutiny of the manorial records recorded in the Pipe Rolls for Bishop Fox's episcopate in the Hampshire Record Office, reveal that several members of the Helyar family worked for the bishop as tilers on episcopal properties. John, who studied at Corpus, was evidently a competent student, for Anthony Wood relates that he was given an MA two years after entering Corpus and proceeded into the patronage of Cardinal Wolsey who admired the young man's proficiency in Greek, Latin and Hebrew.[3]

Richard Bartew was admitted to Corpus Christi College in February 1533. He was seventeen and the son of Thomas Bartew or Bertie, a mason who was employed by the Prior and Convent of St. Swithun's in Winchester and may also have worked for Bishop Fox. On graduation, young Richard

---

[1] McConica discusses the background and career paths of students entering Corpus in the sixteenth century; see J. McConica, 'Elizabethan Oxford: The Collegiate Society', in McConica, especially 666–93.
[2] John Wynford was admitted to New College Oxford, which had been designed in the 1370s by his father, master mason William Wynford, for Bishop Wykeham; see Harvey, 354.
[3] Anthony Wood, *Athenae Oxoniensis*, I (London, 1813), 107.

Bertie did not choose a scholastic career nor did he enter the church. By the late 1540s, Bertie was serving in the household of Katherine, Baroness Willoughby de Eresby, the young widow of the Duke of Suffolk. Bertie subsequently married Katherine and they had a family but were forced into exile due to their Protestant convictions during the reign of Queen Mary. Their descendants were the earls of Lindsey, dukes of Ancaster, barons Willoughby de Eresby and Rockingham and the earls of Abingdon.

Eighteen-year-old John Lybyn was admitted to Corpus on 29 March 1541. The late John Harvey suggested in his *Dictionary of English Medieval Architects* that Lybyn could have been the son of the master mason John Lebons and his conjecture is strengthened by the fact that Lebons had sold lands to Bishop Fox (of which Harvey was unaware).[4] Moreover, the last will and testament of John Lebons, drawn up in 1533, refers to his son and heir who is named John.[5] The mason may, in fact, have been employed by Fox on some of his episcopal building projects though no documentary evidence has come to light that might confirm this. However it would appear that young Lybyn, like a number of other scholars, was one of many who benefited from the late Bishop's generosity long after his death. In so doing, some, like Richard Bertie, were able to move into a higher social level.

Opportunities for education and social mobility offered to the sons of Fox's craftsmen were also offered to other bright boys, making Corpus a significant instrument of social mobility. Appendix 6 includes the case of Anthony Barker (c. 1500–51), whose father, a farmer, appraised farming land for Fox to buy as part of the endowment for the college. With Fox's encouragement Anthony entered Corpus Christi College as a *discipulus* on 21 October 1517 and eventually became a highly placed cleric.[6]

---

[4] Harvey, 173.
[5] PROB 11/24/102. William Holgill, Master of the Savoy and formerly a land agent for Bishop Fox was a feoffee named in Lebons's last will and testament.
[6] Anthony Barker, 'my poor lad', of Berkshire, CCCO Rej. Glos.2; M. F. Bond, ed., *Inventories of St. George's Chapel, 1384–1667* (Windsor, 1947), 197; S. L. Ollard and M. F. Bond, *Fasti Alumni Oxonienses Wyndesorienses: The Deans and Canons of Windsor* (Windsor, 1950), 156; J. Foster, *Alumni Oxonienses, 1500–1714* (Oxford, 1891), 70.

APPENDIX 9

BUILDING INDUSTRY LEGISLATION, 1514

During the fifteenth century, the feudal system of a lord claiming service from his tenants changed as craftsmen and labourers increasingly did not give service, but were hired and paid wages according to their abilities and time worked. These changes partly reflected technical developments in established trades, such as glazing, and changes in sealing with caulk and improvements in shipbuilding. In general, wages rose, although the old practice of providing workers with food ('mete and drinke') remained and was taken into account in setting wages. The national situation was complicated, with varied working conditions and levels of pay for hired skilled craftsmen and labourers occurring in different counties, towns and boroughs. From time to time Parliament tried to regulate working conditions and levels of pay for hired skilled craftsmen and labourers, hoping that a measure of uniformity would prevent the destabilizing movement of skilled labour from one region to another and indeed, from one job to another.

In 1514, a parliamentary 'Acte concernyng artificers and labourers' listed problems in the building industry.[1] It referred to earlier legislation in the thirty-fourth year of the reign of Henry VI (1455), the provisions of which were now, nearly sixty years later, inadequate or often neglected. In southern England, skilled workers on one project often moved to other building sites or migrated from one region to another at a time of high demand for skilled labour. The Act intended to stop such movement by restraining wages through fixing maximum levels of pay, with punishments (unspecified but applied locally) for employers who offered higher rates and workers who accepted them.

The Act of 1514 also tried to regulate working conditions on building sites by defining seasonal variations in hours and wages. It capped the wages of artificers (craftsmen) and labourers within certain categories of work, and also their hours of work, but did not specify different rates for the various levels of skill within each category, thus allowing employers some scope for offering higher pay for exceptional skills. This loophole was congruent with the pragmatic Fox's views on the importance of skills at all levels, and was

---

[1] 6 Henry VIII, c.13. HLRO HL/PO/PU/1/1514/6H8n3. Scanned images of the document and transcriptions are both available on-line.

often implemented, as in the case of John Smyth, a joiner working at Corpus on door and window frames, earning 8d per day (technically without food).[2]

The working hours and meal breaks were specific and varied according to the season. During the warmer months, from mid-March until mid-September ('ev[er]y Artificer & laborer must be at work before v. of the Cloke in the mornyng') and not finish work until between seven or eight o'clock ('till betwene vij & viij of the Cloke in the evenyng'). Workers broke for half an hour for breakfast and an hour in the middle of the day for dinner, though during the hottest three months, from the middle of May to the middle of August, the dinner break was extended by thirty minutes, making a total break of one hour and a half to allow workers to sleep after eating.

From mid-September to mid-March, during the colder months of autumn, winter and early spring, 'ev[er]y Artificer & laborer be at theire worke in the springyng of the day & dep[ar]te not till nyght of the same day'. In these cooler months there was no need for a siesta and they were to 'slepe not by day', and shorter meal breaks applied, that is, half an hour for breakfast, half an hour for an additional light meal (*nonemete*) about noon, and in mid-afternoon an hour for dinner. Thus, every day, summer and winter, workers spent two hours eating and resting.

Having defined the hours of work, the Act of 1514 set wages primarily in terms of cash rates based on skills, and secondarily on deductions for meals ('mete and drink'). Foremen, overseers, master masons and master carpenters in charge of at least six men, whose physical work was relatively light, were to receive 7d per day without food and drink and 5d with food and drink, all the year around, so that deductions for meat and drink constituted nearly thirty percent of their wages. Skilled craftsmen, freemasons, carpenters, rough masons (layers of stone), bricklayers, master tilers, plumbers, glaziers or joiners, from Easter to Michaelmas received 6d a day without sustenance, but 4d with food and drink, but from Michaelmas to Easter, when the days were shorter, they were paid 5d a day without food, and 3d with food (i.e. 2d deducted from 5d which equals forty percent deduction).

Labourers and other artificers were paid 2d a day less than skilled craftsmen but deductions for food were higher, at 50 per cent of wages. During the summer months from Easter to Michaelmas labourers received 4d per day without food and drink, 2d with food and drink. From Michaelmas to Easter, they were paid 3d per day without food and drink; and one penny and a half per day with food and drink. Thus, throughout the year male labourers had half their wages deducted for food and drink, reflecting their need for large meals, protein-rich food, probably roast meat, cheese and beer. Women and 'other' labourers (perhaps youths and girls) were paid a

[2] CCCO H/1/4/1, Payment 15–25 April 1517.

halfpenny less for their labour but had only one penny deducted for food (perhaps they ate less, or more probably were being encouraged), so that the net wage for a female labourer taking meals was 2½d per day, which gave her more than the male rate (with food deducted) of 2d per day.

The Act included several disciplinary measures. If workers arrived late or left early, 'theire defaults to be marked by hym or his deputie that shall pay theire wages & at the weeks end to be abated of suche rate of tyme as they have offended'. Workers were held to their initial agreement to stay until the job was finished provided that the employer needed and wanted their services. Were a worker to leave his job then he would suffer imprisonment and a fine of 20 shillings. Some of the disciplinary measures refer to offences which are difficult to pin down, 'dayly by theire subtell ymaginacion in defraude of the said estatutes'. Some workmen took advantage of the shortage of labour; they worked for only part of the day or half-day for which they were paid, they arrived late, left early, lingered over meals, slept too long during their meal break: they 'wast[e] most part of the day and do not des[er]ve theire wages some tyme in late comyng to theire werke erly dep[ar]tyng therfro[m] long syttyng att theire brekefast at theire dyn[er] & at theire nonemete & long tyme at slepyng at aftir none'. The new Act defined punishments such as deductions of pay or imprisonment for assaults upon superiors, giving clear recognition those who had charge of workers, and a new emphasis to skills in the exercise of authority. Attempts by foremen to impose discipline sometimes resulted in abuse or physical assaults though violence on the building site was forbidden and severely punished:

> if any artificer or laborer reteyned in s[er]vice with any p[er]son for bilding or Rep[ar]acon do assaute or make or cause to be made any assemble to assaute herme or hurte any p[er]son assigned to countroll and ov[er]see theym in thair working that he or they so defending have imprisonement for a yere withoute letting to baill or maynprise And forthermore to make fyne at the Kings will The same assemble or assaute to be tried by examynacion before the Justices of peace as is aforesaid.

The Act of 1514 had a particular significance for Corpus Christi College. It clearly implied that food was to be provided on site, and, as suggested above, this probably consisted of three daily meals, of meat, beer, bread and cheese. According to the building accounts, however, most workers on the Corpus site were paid full rates for their labour, without deductions for food, but this is rather puzzling. Possibly they were local men who could easily bring their own food to work. But in that case, why would Fox much earlier rebuild Urban Hall's old kitchen to make the new Corpus kitchen, and build the hall nearly a year before the first student intake, and in March 1517, fully six months before the first students arrived, bring new 'ketchyn stoof' from

London, kneading troughs, pastry boards, and tables? One obvious answer is that the kitchen, hall and equipment were intended to feed the workers, who were offered food, without charge, while the hall, built in 1516, was being used, not only for storage and meetings, but as a shelter for workmen to eat during bad weather in the autumn and winter of 1516 and 1517.

Fox's stratagem, if it existed, probably reflected the government's expectation that the Act would be enforced firmly in the north but in the south more discretion would be allowed by local officials – which doubtless meant that the Corpus building site, being the personal project of Bishop Fox, was given considerable discretion.[3] Moreover, such discretion would have reflected Fox's ability to formulate honest but devious solutions to problems, in this case by paying non-food wages but making food openly available during the stipulated rest breaks – offering it free for the taking, if desired – effectively raising daily wages by up to 2d (50 per cent for labourers), circumventing though not, strictly speaking, contravening the Act of 1514, in order to retain reliable and highly skilled workers. The provision of free food may also explain why food money was deducted mainly from the wages of short-term workers on the Corpus site, and why disciplinary problems were apparently absent. It would also explain why there were few short-term workers – only a few, who appeared briefly on the payroll and were then replaced by men who remained.[4]

AN ACTE CONCERNYNG ARTIFICERS AND LABOURERS (1514)[5]

HENRY R. Soit baill[e] Aux Com[mun]
Where dyv[er]se estatutes bifore this tyme have ben made & ordeyned for s[er]vaunts of Husbandry and also laborers and Artificers by dyv[er]s and roiall and noble p[ro]genitours unto o[ure] Sov[er]aigne Lord the Kyng nowe beyng, ... whiche notw[ith]stondyng grete and many defaults dayly encrease rest and contynue amonge laborers and artificers some by cause of the said estatutes be not executed and some by cause the remedie of the seid estatutes is not very p[er]fite nor gevith certeyne ne hasty remedie so that dayly by theire subtell ymaginacion in defraude of the said estatutes many of the Kyng o[ure] Sov[er]aigne Lordes Subiettis be hurt deceived lette and damaged in thaire buyldyng & husbandry. Be it therfore establisshed enacted and ordeyned by auctorite of this p[re]sent p[ar]leament First that noo bal-

---

[3] P. A. Fideler, 'Poverty, Policy and Providence: The Tudors and the Poor', in Fideler and T. Mayer, eds, *Political Thought and the Tudor Commonwealth* (London, 2014), 199–228, esp. 215.
[4] For example, two of the eight carpenters employed for the week 16–21 March 1517 were replaced on 23 March by two new carpenters, who remained.
[5] Regulations for shipbuilding and other maritime work, not relevant to the building site at Corpus Christi have been removed.

liff of husbandry shall take for his wages by yere above xxvj s. viij d. for his clothing v s. w[ith] mete and drinke, noo cheif hyne [henceforth] as a Carter or cheif Shepard above xx s. by the yere & for his clothing v s. w[ith] mete & drink, noo comyn s[er]vant of husbandry above xvj s. viij d. by yere and his clothing iiij s. w[ith] mete & drinke noo woman s[er]v[au]nt above x s. by yere and for hir clothing iiij s. w[ith] mete & drink noo child w[ith]in age of xiiij yeres above vj s. viij d. by yere and for his clothing iiij s. w[ith] mete and drink And that noo artificer ne laborer herafter named take no more ne gretter wages than in this Statute is limetted upon the payn seassed aswell to the taker as to the gever that is to say A fremason m[astir] carpent[er] rough mason brekelayer m[astir] tyler plommer glaseo[ur] kerver ne joiner fro Estre to Michelmas ev[er]y of theise Artificers aforesaid vj d. by the day w[ith]out mete & drink and w[ith] mete & drink iiij d And fro Michelmas to Estre v d. w[ith]out mete & drinke & w[ith] mete & drink iij d .... Be it also enacted that in suche Shires & Cuntres that where it hathe be & is nowe used to giff lesse wages that in those Shires & Cuntres they shal giff And the taker of the wages be compelled according as they have lesse used to take this acte not w[ith]stondyng And the M[astir] Mason & M[astir] Carpenter whiche shall take the charge of the werke havyng undir hym of theym vj men shall have vij d. w[ith]out mete and drinke & v d. by day w[ith] mete & drinke And that ev[er]y p[er]son & Artificer specified in this Statute beyng not reteyned in any s[er]vice for any werke be compelled to s[er]ve ev[er]y other p[er]son for such wages as in this this Statute bifore is limytted And that no Artificer reteyned in any s[er]vice to warke w[ith] the Kynges Highnes or any oy[ther] p[er]son dep[ar]te not from his seid Hieghnes or from the seid oy[ther] p[er]son till suche tyme as the warke be fynysshed if the p[er]son so reteynyng thartificer so long will have hym & pay his wages upon payne of imprisonment of any p[er]sone so dep[or]tyng by the space of a moneth & to make fyne of xx s Always p[ro]vided and forsene that if the same Artificer be desyred to the Kynges s[er]vice and warke that then he may lawfully dep[ar]te so that he entre & be in the Kynges s[er]vyce and warke. And it is further ordyned by the seid auctorite that ev[er]y oy[ther] laborer & Articificer not affore named shall take from Estre to Michelmas for ev[er]y day that he so laboreth except the season of Hervest iiij d. w[ith]out mete & drinke & ij d. w[ith] mete & drinke and from Michelmas till Estir iij d. w[ith]out mete & drinke & i d. ob. w[ith] mete & drinke; and in the said tyme of Hervest ev[er]y mower shall take by the day iiij d. w[ith] mete & drink and w[ith]out mete & drink vj d a repar and Cartar ev[er]y of theym iij d. by the day w[ith] mete & drynke & w[ith]out mete & drynke v d A woman laborer & oy[ther] laborers ev[er]y of theym ij d. ob. by the day w[ith] mete and drink & w[ith]out mete & drinke iij d. ob and that noo artificer nor laborer warkyng but the half day take no wages but for the half day & noo thinge for the holy day. And if any baillif of Husbandry Hyne [henceforth] Carter Shepard comen s[er]vant Woman s[er]vnt or child s[er]vnt above specified not reteyned in any s[er]vice or werke refuse to s[er]ve or werke according to the orden[a]nce above specified Then the same p[er]sone to be comytted to ward by the Constable or oy[ther] hedde officer w[ith]in the Citie Towne or Village where the partie so refusyng is at complaynt of hym that will receive suche s[er]v[au]nte there to remayne till he have founde surtie to s[er]ve accordyng to the seid Ordynnce Ferthermore if any Artificer or laborer being not reteyned in any s[er]vice or werke refuse to s[er]ve after the rate of [his] astate or to take gretter or more wages than therein is lymytted for the same Artificers & laborers or if any artificer or laborer take wages for the holy day where he werketh but the half day, that then ev[er]y Artificer & laborer offendyng in any of the forsaid articles forfeite for ev[er]y defaulte as oft as they offend xx s and they to be comytted for ev[er]y suche defaulte by p[re]sentment affore the Justices of peace in the Sessions accordyng to the comen lawe or by examynacion of the Justice in the same Sessions or by examynacion of too Justices of peace out of the Sessions in any place w[ith]in the Shire wherin they ben Justices & where suche default shalbe made & that the said forfeture of xx s. to be lyvied of their lands goods & catellis so offendyng. And ferthermore where dyv[er]se artificers and laborers reteyned to warke & s[er]ve wast most part of the day and do not des[er]ve theire wages some tyme in late comyng to theire werke erly dep[ar]tyng therfro long syttyng att theire brekefast at theire dyn[er] & at theire nonemete & long tyme at slepyng at aftir none to the losse & hurte of such p[er]sons as the seid Artificers & laborers ben reteyned w[ith]in s[er]vyce It is therefore establisshed enacted & ordeyned by acutorite aforeseid that ev[er]y Artificer & laborer be at wereke betwen the Mydd[es] of the moneth of marche & the mydd[es] of the moneth of September before v. of the Cloke in the mornyng, & that he have but half an houre for his brekefast & an houre & an half for his dyn[er] at such tyme as he hath season for slepe to hym appoynted by the seid estatute, & at suche tyme as it is herin appoynted that he shall not slepe then he to have but an houre for his dyn[er] & half an houre for his nonemete and that he dep[ar]t not from his werke betwene the middes of the seid monethes of marche & Septembr till betwene vij & viij of the Cloke in the evenyng And if they or any of theym offende in any of theise Articles that then theire defaults to be marked by hym or his deputie that shall pay theire wages & at the weeks end to be abated of suche rate of tyme as they have offended And that from the midd[es] of Septembr to the Middes of marche ev[er]y Artificer & laborer be at theire worke in the springyng of the day & dep[ar]te not till nyght of the same day and that the seid Artificers and laborers slepe not by day but only from the middes of the moneth of May unto the middill of the moneth of August Also it is establisshed and enacted that by the said auctorite that if any artificer or laborer reteyned in s[er]vice with any p[er]son for bilding or Rep[ar]acon do assaute or make or cause to be made any assemble to assaute herme or hurte any p[er]son assigned to countroll and ov[er]see theym in thair working that he or they so defending have imprisonement for a yere withoute letting to baill or maynprise And forthermore to make fyne at the Kings will The same assemble or assaute to be tried by examynacion before the Justices of peace as is aforesaid This acte to begyn and take effecte at the fest of Whitsontide next comyng and in the meane tyme the same to be p[ro]claymed in ev[er]y goode Citie borow and Towne of this Realme.

APPENDIX 10

CRAFTSMEN, SUPPLIERS AND CARRIERS

The individuals listed below are named in the Corpus Christi College building accounts.

CRAFTSMEN

Alye, George Plasterer
Antony Carpenter
Avenell, John[1] Carpenter
Bankes/Abankes, John Smith
Barkar, John Carpenter
Benett, John Sawyer
Bodkyn, Gerrard Plasterer, perhaps related to Richard Bodwyn (or Bedewyn), who worked as a carpenter in Oxford in the 1450s.[2]
Bond, John Layer
Browne, John Work on Corpus is not specified but he is possibly the carpenter called John Browne who worked at Magdalen College 1520–7.[3]
Brytton, Wylliam Labourer who worked with William Hobbys on Cardinal College in the 1520s.[4]
Bull, John Labourer
Bustared, Garrett ? Carpenter
Carow, Robert A prominent mason who supplied materials, offered advice and was engaged to produce the structural carpentry for Corpus.[5] Carow was warden of the carpenters who were involved in building Wolsey's Cardinal College.[6]
Carter, Wylliam Unspecified
Carver, Robert Carpenter
Castell, Wylliam Sawyer

---

[1] Perhaps the same as carpenter, John Awell, who worked at Merton College in 1520; see E. A. Gee, 'Oxford Carpenters, 1370–1530', *Oxoniensia*, 17/18 (1952–3), 163.
[2] For Richard Bodwyn, see Gee, 'Oxford Carpenters', 147.
[3] See Gee, 'Oxford Carpenters', 158.
[4] See Milne and Harvey, 'The Building of Cardinal College', 139, 140.
[5] For biographical details, see Gee, 'Oxford Carpenters', 129–33, and Harvey, 48–9.
[6] Milne and Harvey, 'The Building of Cardinal College', 142, 146.

Chayney/ Cheyney, John Freemason
Chest, John Made 'staples'
Clerk, Robert Carpenter and carver, who according to Gee may have been related to Cornell Clerke.[7]
Clerke, Cornell Carpenter and carver, who contracted to make the desks for the library at Corpus.[8]
Coke, Humphrey A craftsman in royal pay who had been Master Carpenter at the Savoy in London and who was appointed King's Carpenter in 1519.[9] He was involved in the design of Corpus Christi College and was paid for his advice on site and, according to the building accounts, for gilding the bosses for the chapel. Coke undoubtedly carried out other specific tasks which are unrecorded. In the 1520s he one of the master craftsmen involved in the design of Cardinal College for Wolsey.[10]
Colyn, John Carpenter, possibly related to Wylliam Collyn listed below
Collyn/Colyns, Wylliam A carpenter paid for his expenses for travelling from London. He also worked at Magdalen College.[11] Colyns trained with and later worked alongside Humphrey Coke.
Desford, Thomas Labourer with mate
Eger, David Layer
East/Est, Wylliam A mason, East was seriously injured by members of Brasenose College in 1512. In 1517–18 he was paid for, amongst other things, the supply of 'table' made of Taynton stone. East had previously worked for Oriel College and also received contracts in connection with Queen's College.[12] In the 1520s he was living in Burford.
Forster, Thomas Labourer
Gamson [see Samson]
Glasyer, Robert Glazier
Gossop, John Rough layer
Gryffith, Roger[13] Joiner
Grove, Richard Labourer
Grove, Robert Labourer
Grymshave, John Carpenter

---

[7] Robert Clerk was also responsible for making the library presses for Queen's College, Oxford; see Gee, 'Oxford Carpenters', 142.
[8] For biographical details, see Gee, 'Oxford Carpenters', 138–40.
[9] Harvey, 64.
[10] Ibid., 65.
[11] Gee, 'Oxford Carpenters', 158.
[12] Harvey, 90.
[13] A carpenter called Gryffyth squared wood at Magdalen College in the mid-1520s; see Gee, 'Oxford Carpenters', 158.

Gyttens, Thomas   Carpenter
Hamond, John   roughmason
Hamond, Wylliam   Layer (of stone) who worked on building Cardinal College in the 1520s as a roughmason.[14]
Herne, Nicholas   Labourer
Heys/Heyse, Richard   Layer
Hobbys, John   ? Labourer
Hobbys/ Hoogys, William   Labourer who was employed, with Wylliam Brytton to saw stone and other tasks during the building of Cardinal College in the 1520s.[15] He may have been related to John Hobbys listed above.
Holman, Simon   Plasterer
Horneclyff, Harry   ? Rough mason
Hynton, John   Unspecified
Johan   Labourer
Jonson, Robert   Rough mason who was later engaged in the building of Cardinal College.[16]
Joyner, John   Plasterer
Kechynrooffe/Kechynman, Wylliam   Unspecified
Kelly/Keft, William   Carpenter
Lenche, James   Carpenter, associated with carpenter Robert Carow from the early 1500s; named as one of Carow's taxable servants in 1524.[17]
Lewose/Leyose, Richard   Mason and supplier of lime, employed as a roughmason in the building of Cardinal College.[18]
Looder, Wylliam   Slate layer
Lytall, Thomas (sawyer)   Sawyer of wainscot
Makegood, Richard   Carpenter
Makyns, John   Labourer and plasterer; possibly the John Mekyns who sawed wood and took down a house for Lincoln College in 1524–5.[19]
Malowse/ Malow, John   Freemason; possibly the mason named John Mawe who was engaged in building Cardinal College in the 1520s.[20]
Maryn, John   Labourer

---

[14]   See Milne and Harvey, 'The Building of Cardinal College', 140.
[15]   Ibid. 139.
[16]   Ibid. 140. He may have been related to William Jonson, another mason, who co-designed Cardinal College; ibid. 139, 145.
[17]   Ibid. 149 where his surname is spelt Lynche; for biographical details, see Gee, 'Oxford Carpenters', 136.
[18]   Ibid. 140. In the Cardinal College accounts he surname is spelt Luys.
[19]   For Mekyns, see Gee, 'Oxford Carpenters', 151.
[20]   See Milne and Harvey, 'The Building of Cardinal College', 139.

More, Edmund A specialist carver who made the heraldic arms of Hugh Oldham, Bishop of Exeter, to ornament Corpus and commemorate the prelate's benificence. More was based in Kingston upon Thames.[21]
More, Nicholas Carpenter
More, Richard Sawyer
More, Richard Joiner
Morwent, Roger Carpenter
Morys, Wylliam Carrier of timber who may be the man of that name who supplied and carried quarried stone for Cardinal College.[22]
Myller, John Supplier of timber and occasional labourer
Myllett, Wylliam Labourer
Myllwell, Wylliam Unspecified
Mylton, Thomas Carpenter
Owen, Matthew Labourer
Parker, Richard Freemason
Perpoynt, Harry Layer
Poys, Wylliam Sawyer
Roossell/Russell, Thomas A carpenter and specialist carver, based at Westminster, paid for making the bosses (*knottes*) for the college chapel. Russell was a member of an important dynasty of carpenters associated with royal works. Little is known about his career except that he worked for Cardinal Wolsey at Hampton Court in the 1520s.[23]
Ryley, Rychard Slate layer
Schelman, John Rough layer
Sexton, Christopher ? Labourer
Slater, Lawncelate ? Slater, supplier of laths.
Smyth, Garratt Ironmonger and blacksmith
Smyth, John A freemason and supplier of penny nails and masonry work.
Smyth, John Plasterer
Spyllisby, John Layer; probably related to Wylliam Spyllisbye listed below. A carpenter named Spyllysey was paid for his work in underpinning a building in Oxford in 1508–9.[24]
Spyllisbye, Wylliam Rough mason
Stanley, John Layer
Stanley, Wylliam Rough layer

[21] For biographical details of More, see Harvey, 207.
[22] See Milne and Harvey, 'The Building of Cardinal College', 140.
[23] Harvey, 260. He may also be the Thomas Russell who worked at Westminster Abbey and St. Margaret's Church nearby in the early 1500s.
[24] See Gee, 'Oxford Carpenters', 148.

Stevens, Richard Labourer
Steyle, John Carpenter
Stone/Stome, Thomas Carpenter who is named in the building accounts for Cardinal College for six days work 'about the building of Saint Frideswydes'.[25]
Symons, John Labourer
Tayler, Thomas Plasterer
Thomas, Wylliam Plumber
Threder, Richard Carpenter
Threder, Thomas Unspecified
Townesend, John A pavyar who sourced sand and also supplied and carried timber, gravel and loam (clay).
Vanderbye, Pet[er] Joiner
Vertue, Wylliam An important early Tudor mason who was granted the office of King's Master Mason in July, 1510.[26]
War[?], Richard Slate layer
Ward, John A freemason based at Little Barrington in Gloucestershire, contracted to make the windows for the cloister. Ward supplied one hundred tons of stone for the construction of Cardinal College in the mid-1520s.[27]
Whorlton, John Plasterer
Whorlton/Warleton, Wylliam Plasterer also involved in carrying out masonry work.
Whyght, John Sawyer.
[Whyght] Whytte, Roger Plasterer who may be the carpenter Roger Wrght listed below.
[Whyght] Whytte, Wylliam Labourer who may be the William White named in connection with the collection of quarried stone for the building of Cardinal College.[28]
Wyllyngton, George Plasterer
Whytakers Thomas Sawyer working with his fellow
Wryght, Roger Carpenter, who between 1511 and 1519 worked on various tasks at Magdalen College.[29]
Wrykshman, John Labourer
Wyld, Robert Labourer

[25] See Milne and Harvey, 'The Building of Cardinal College', 142.
[26] Harvey, 307.
[27] See Milne and Harvey, 'The Building of Cardinal College', 144–5.
[28] Ibid. 140.
[29] For Wright, see Gee, 'Oxford Carpenters', 157.

Wyllyams, Sir Unspecified, but frequently visited suppliers.
Yorden, Thomas Labourer

CARRIERS AND SUPPLIERS OF MATERIAL

Alam, John Carrier of timber
Archar, Thomas Carrier of stone
Banyst[er], Lawrence Carrier of stone from Headington
Barnes/Barons, Thomas Carrier of wainscot
Boseby, Harry Supplier of dry board
Bowdon, Thomas Carrier of stone
Branne, John Carrier of stone
Bray, John Supplier of stone
Broke, Henry Carrier of stone
Broke, Roger Carrier of stone
Broke/Croke, Wylliam Carrier of Taynton stone
Byshchopp, John Supplier of hurdles
Chare, John Carrier
Chare, Richard Supplier of timber and carrier of lime
Chedwell, Thomas Carrier of stone
Cholsey Carrier
Clare, Wyllyam Carrier of timber and lime (within Oxford)
Cocks/Cooke, John Carrier of wainscot and stone
Colyar, Robert Supplier of timber
Coterell, John Supplier of wainscot
Damaske, Thomas Carrier
Devyn, Robert Supplier of wainscot
Ffrancleyn, John Quarryman, supplier of stone, sand and loam
Ffrancleyn, Wylliam Carrier of timber
Forest, Thomas Supplier of nails
Gely, Robert Supplier of elm board
Grene, Richard Carrier of wainscot
Grene Supplier of lime
Harme, John Supplier of shells (shingles?); probably related to the supplier of sand and loam, Herne/Harne/Horne, listed below.
Harper, John Carrier of timber
Harper, Thomas Carrier
Hart, John Supplier of ragstone
Haryson, Roger Carrier of stone, supplier of timber

Herne/Harne/Horne, Richard   Supplier of sand and loam; also named as supplier and carrier of lime and ragstone. Probably the 'Harme' who was paid for five days carting sand and stone for the building of Wolsey's Cardinal College.[30]
Hyxis, Wylliam   Supplier of hurdles[31]
Jonys, John   Carrier of stone
Knott, John   Supplier of timber; probably the sawyer called John Noytt who was occupied at Lincoln College 1511–12.[32]
Knott, Richard   Carrier of rag and timber; probably related to John Knott listed above.
Larden, Elys   Supplier of lime
Lemesley, Thomas   Supplier of wainscot
Locke, John   Carrier and supplier of stone
March, John   Supplier of loam
Marman, John   Supplier of timber
Marvyng, Thomas   Carrier of timber
Matheow, John   Carrier of wainscot (from London)
Matteson, John   Supplier of ash planks
Medam/Meden, John   Supplier of timber; probably related to Richard and Thomas Medam listed below.
Medam, Richard   Carrier
Medam, Thomas   Carrier of stone, timber
Mede, Thomas   Carrier of various materials including planks; possibly the Thomas Medam noted above.
Nichols, Robert   Carrier of wainscot
Peerson, John   Carrier of wainscot
Phelypps, Roger   Supplier of stone
Phyllypps, John   Carrier of stone
Popley, Wylliam   Supplier of stone
Pownd, Richard   Supplier of wainscot; probably related to Walter and Wylliam Pownd listed below.
Pownd, Walter   Carrier of wainscot
Pownd, Wylliam   Supplier and carrier of wainscot
Pye the carpenter   Supplier of plank board; possibly William Poys

---

[30] See Milne and Harvey, 'The Building of Cardinal College', 141.
[31] Carpenter, John Hykks trimmed timber and helped to make the great gate for Magdalen College in 1471; see Gee, 'Oxford Carpenters', 152.
[32] Ibid. 151.

Pytfeld/Pytford/Pytfyld, Richard   A supplier of timber and carpentry work who worked from time to time as a sawyer for Lincoln College, Oxford.[33]
Raynald, John   Supplier of barrels.
Rede, Kelham   Supplier of ragstone
Robynson   Supplier of penny nayles
Samson/Sampson Gamson, Wylliam   Carrier of stone
Sawndys/Sawnders, Wylliam   Supplier of stone and labouring work
Sharpe, John   Carrier of lime
Slatter, John   Supplier of stone
Swetestarr, John   Carrier of timber
Thycart, Henry   Supplier of elm board
Townesend, Thomas   Supplier of timber
Veer, Richard   Carrier of wainscot
Walker 'the carrier'   Carrier of ironmongery
Waltar, Thomas   Supplier of plank boards
Walton, Robert   Supplier of timber, carriage
Wase, Jasper   Carrier of stone and of timber
Wase, John   Supplier of timber and of stone
Welman, John   Supplier of timber
Wotton   Supplier of dry planks; possibly the carpenter named Wotton who worked in the chapel of Magdalen College 1526–7.[34]
Wylschere, John   Supplier of joists and lime and probably related to Thomas Wylteschere listed below.[35]
Wylteschere, Thomas   Supplier of timber and carriage of various goods and probably related to John Wylschere noted above.

---

[33]   For Pytfeld, see Gee, 'Oxford Carpenters', 150.
[34]   For Wotton, see Gee, 'Oxford Carpenters', 159. A carpenter by name of Thomas Wotton worked in Lincoln College between 1523 and 1525; see Gee , 'Oxford Carpenters', 151.
[35]   They may have been descendants of carpenter, John Wyltsher who had been employed at New College between 1427 and 1455; see Gee, 'Oxford Carpenters', 118, 123–4 and Harvey, 335–6.

BIBLIOGRAPHY

MANUSCRIPTS

BL Additional MS 39959
BL Harleian MS 4795
BL Lansdowne MS 818
BL Stowe MS 146
Bodleian MS Wood D2
CCCO A/1/1/7
CCCO A/2/1
CCCO A/4/1/6
CCCO C/1/1/1
CCCO A1 Cap.1 Fasc.1 Ev.1
CCCO C1 Cap.1 Ev.109
CCCO C1 Cap.1 Ev.145
CCCO C5 Cap.11 Ev.109
CCCO F1 Cap.1 Fasc.1 Ev.25
CCCO Rej. Glos 2
CCCO H/1/4/1
CCCO H/1/4/3
CCCO 280
CCCO 303
HLRO HL/PO/PU/1/1514/6H8n3
HRO, 21 M 65/A1/17–21, 5 vols.
WAM MS 63509
WCL Ledger Book II

PRINTED PRIMARY SOURCES

Allen, P. S., and H. W. Garrod, eds., *Merton Muniments*, OHS 86 (Oxford, 1928)
Allen, P. S. and H. M., eds., *Letters of Richard Fox, 1486–1527* (Oxford, 1929)
Baildon, W. P., ed., *Calendar of the Manuscripts of the Dean and Chapter of Wells*, Historical Manuscripts Commission, vol. 2 (London, 1914)

Bond, M. F., ed., *Inventories of St. George's Chapel, 1384–1667* (Windsor, 1947)
Briquet, C.-M., *Les filigranes: dictionnaire historique des marques du papier dès leur apparition vers 1282 jusqu'en 1600* (New York, 1966)
Brodrick, G. C., *Memorials of Merton College: with Biographical Notes of the Warden and Fellows*, OHS 4 (Oxford, 1885)
Calendar of Patent Rolls 1485–1509, 2 (London, 1916)
Chisholm-Batten, E., *Register of Richard Fox while Bishop of Bath and Wells* (London, 1889)
Erasmus, Desiderius, *Opus Epistolarum*, ed. P. S. Allen, III (Oxford, 1913)
Fox, Richard, *Here begynneth the rule of Seynt Benet* (London, 1517)
Fulman, William, 'De Vita Richardi Foxe, Episcopi Wintoniensis et Collegii Fundatoris', in *Collectanea*, ix, in CCCO MS 303
Gairdner, J., ed., *Memorials of King Henry the Seventh, Historia Regis Henrici Septimi*, vol. II (London, 1858)
Holinshed, R., *The firste volume of the chronicles of England, Scotlande, and Irelande* (London, 1577; repr. 1807–8)
Howden, M., ed., *The Register of Richard Fox, Lord Bishop of Durham, 1494–1501*, Surtees Soc. 147 (Durham, 1932)
Keilway, Robert, *Relationes quorundam Casuum selectorum ex libris Roberti Keilway, Armiger* (London, 1602)
Letters and Papers, Foreign and Domestic, Henry VIII, II.ii, ed. J. S. Brewer (London, 1864)
Rymer, Thomas, *Foedera, conventions, literae et cujuscunque generis acta publica, inter reges Angliae*, vol. 13 (London, 1727)
Second Report of the Royal Commission on Historical Manuscripts (London, 1874)
Valor Ecclesiasticus, vol. 2 (London, 1814)

SECONDARY SOURCES

Allfrey, E. W., 'The Architectural History of the Buildings', in *Brasenose College Quatercentenary Monographs*, I, OHS 52 (Oxford, 1909)
Ayers, T., *Corpus Vitrearum Medii Aevi, Great Britain*, 6, Merton College, part 2 (Oxford, 2013)
Bacon, Francis, *The History of the Reigne of King Henry the Seventh* (London, 1628)
Blair, J., 'Frewin Hall, Oxford: A Norman Mansion and a Monastic College', *Oxoniensia*, 43 (1978), 48–99
Carless, R. H. K., 'Selected Aspects of the Life of Richard Fox, 1446–1528' (M. Litt. thesis, University of Bristol, 1987)

BIBLIOGRAPHY

Chalmers, A., *History of the University of Oxford* (Oxford, 1810)
Clark, J. G., *Benedictines in the Middle Ages* (Woodbridge, 2011, 2014)
Cobban, A. B., *English University Life in the Middle Ages* (London 1999)
Collett, B., 'British Students at the University of Ferrara, 1480–1540', *Filosofia, scienze e cultura alla corte degli Estensi: lo Studio de Ferrara nei secoli XV e XVI. Proceedings of the Commemoration of the 600th Anniversary of the University of Ferrara in March, 1992*, ed. M. Bertozzi (Ferrara, 1994), 125–46
Collett, B., *Female Monastic Life in Early Tudor England with an Edition of Richard Fox's Translation of the Benedictine Rule for Women, 1517* (Aldershot, 2002)
Colvin, H. M., ed., *The History of the King's Works*, 1485–1660, 3 (London, 1975)
Cooper, L. H., and A. Denny-Brown, eds., *The Arma Christi in Medieval and Early Modern Culture* (Ashgate, 2014)
Crook, John, 'Witness from on High', *History Today*, October 2015, 3–5
Crossley, Alan, ed., *VCH Oxon.* iv (City of Oxford) (Oxford, 1979)
Drees, C. J., *Bishop Richard Fox of Winchester: Architect of the Tudor Age* (Jefferson, 2014)
Duff, E. G., *Fifteenth-Century English Books* (Oxford, 1917)
Edwards, H. L. R., 'Robert Gaguin and the English Poets, 1489–90', *Modern Language Review*, 32 (1937), 430–4
Ellory, J. C., Clifford, Helen, and Foster, Rogers, eds., *Corpus Silver: Patronage and Plate at Corpus Christi College, Oxford* (Barton-under-Needwood, 1997)
Emden, A. B., *Biographical Register of the University of Oxford to 1500* (3 vols. Oxford, 1959)
Fideler, P. A., 'Poverty, Policy and Providence: The Tudors and the Poor', in P. A. Fideler and T. Mayer, eds., *Political Thought and the Tudor Commonwealth* (London, 2014), 199–228
Foster, J., *Alumni Oxonienses, 1500–1714* (Oxford, 1891; republished London, 2012)
Fowler, T., *History of Corpus Christi College with Lists of its Members*, OHS 25 (Oxford, 1893)
Gee, E. A., 'Oxford Carpenters, 1370–1530', *Oxoniensia*, 17/18 (1952/3), 112–84
Gee, E. A., 'Oxford Masons, 1370–1530', *Archaeological Journal*, 109 (1952), 54–131
Gwyn, P., *The King's Cardinal: The Rise and Fall of Thomas Wolsey* (Pimlico, 1992)
Harvey, J. H., 'The Building Works and Architects of Cardinal Wolsey', *Journal of the British Archaeological Association*, 3rd ser., 8 (1943), 48–59

Harvey, J. H., *Report of the Society of Friends of St. George*, iv (1962), 3
Harvey, J. H., *English Medieval Architects: A Biographical Dictionary down to 1550* (2nd edn., Gloucester, 1984)
Hearne, Thomas, *The History and Antiquities of Glastonbury* (Oxford, 1722)
Jacob, E. F., 'The Building of All Souls College', in *Historical Essays in Honour of James Tait*, ed. J. G. Edwards, V. H. Galbraith, and E. F. Jacob (Manchester, 1933)
Kendell, Angela J., 'Thomas More, Richard Fox and the Manor of Temple Guyting in 1515', *Moreana*, 23, no. 91/2 (1986), 5–10
Knoop, D., and G. P. Jones, *The Mediaeval Mason* (Manchester, 1933)
Law, E., *History of Hampton Court Palace*, I (London, 1885)
Leach, A. F., *The Schools of Medieval England* (London, 1915)
Liddell, J. R., 'The Library of Corpus Christi College, Oxford in the Sixteenth Century', *The Library*, 4th ser., 18 (1937–8), 385–416
Lincolnshire Notes and Queries, 12 (1912–13), 221
Lobel, M. D., ed., *VCH Oxon.* v (Oxford, 1957)
Luxford, J. M. *Art and Architecture of English Benedictine Monasteries, 1300–1540: A Patronage History* (Woodbridge, reprint, 2012)
McConica, J. K., ed., *History of the University of Oxford, III: The Collegiate University* (Oxford, 1986)
Milne, J. G., 'The Muniments of Corpus Christi College, Oxford', *Bulletin of the Institute of Historical Research*, 10, no.29 (1932), 105–8
Milne, J. G. 'The Muniments of Corpus Christi College, Oxford' *Oxoniensia*, 2 (1937), 129–33
Milne, J. G., 'The Berkshire Muniments of Corpus Christi College, Oxford', *Berkshire Archaeological Journal*, 46 (1942), 32–44, 78–87
Milne, J. G., and J. H. Harvey, 'The Building of Cardinal College, Oxford', *Oxoniensia*, 8/9 (1943–4), 137–53
Milne, J. G., *Early History of Corpus Christi College, Oxford* (Oxford, 1946)
Ollard, S. L., and M. F. Bond, *Fasti Wyndesorienses: The Deans and Canons of Windsor* (Windsor, 1950)
Page, W., ed., *VCH Lincolnshire*, ii (London, 1906); *VCH Durham*, ii (London, 1907)
Pevsner, N., J. Harris and N. Antrim, *Buildings of England: Lincolnshire* (new edn. London, 2002)
Pevsner, N., and J. Sherwood, *Buildings of England: Oxfordshire* (new edn., London, 2002)
Pollard, A. J. *North-eastern England during the Wars of the Roses: Lay Society, War and Politics, 1450–1500* (Oxford, 1990)

Pormann, P. E. *Descriptive Catalogue of the Hebrew Manuscripts of Corpus Christi College, Oxford* (Cambridge, 2015)
Reid, J., 'The Founder's Textile', *The Pelican Record*, 48 (2012), 18–25
Reid, J., 'The Bosses of Corpus Christi Chapel', *The Pelican Record*, 49 (2013), 15–24
Royal Commission on Historical Monuments, *Inventory of the Historical Monuments in the City of Oxford* (London, 1939)
Riall, N., *Renaissance Stalls at the Hospital of St. Cross* (Winchester, 2014)
Richardson, W. C., *Tudor Chamber Administration, 1485–1547* (Baton Rouge, Louisiana, 1952)
Salter, H. E., *Chapters of the Augustinian Canons, Oxford*, OHS 74 (Oxford, 1922)
Salzman, L. F., *Building in England down to 1540* (reprint, Oxford, 1967)
Smith, Angela, 'The Life and Building Activity of Richard Fox, c.1446–1528' (Ph.D. thesis, Warburg Institute, University of London, 1988)
Smith, Angela, *Roof Bosses of Winchester Cathedral* (Friends of Winchester Cathedral, 1996)
Smith, Angela, 'The Chantry Chapel of Bishop Fox', *Winchester Cathedral Record*, 57 (1988), 27–32
Smith, Angela, and N. Riall, 'Early Tudor Canopywork at the Hospital of St. Cross, Winchester', *Antiquaries Journal*, 82 (2002), 125–56
Smith, Angela, 'Bishop Fox and Stained Glass in Early Tudor England', *Journal of Stained Glass*, 31 (2007), 35–52
Somerville, R., *The Savoy: Manor, Hospital, Chapel* (London, 1960)
Streeter, B. H., *The Chained Library. The Evolution of the Library in England* (London, 1931)
Thomson, R. M., *Descriptive Catalogue of the Medieval Manuscripts of Corpus Christi College, Oxford* (Cambridge, 2011)
Walker, S., ed., *Building Accounts of All Souls College, Oxford, 1438–1443*, OHS new series 42 (Oxford, 2010)
Ward, G. R. M., *The Foundation Statutes of Bishop Fox for Corpus Christi College, All Souls College and Magdalen College, Oxford* (London, 1843)
Warton, T., *History of English Poetry* (London, 1775)
Willis, R., *Architectural History of the University of Cambridge and of the Colleges of Cambridge and Eton* (Cambridge, 1886)
Wilson, N. G., *Descriptive Catalogue of the Greek Manuscripts of Corpus Christi College Oxford* (Cambridge, 2011)
Wood, Anthony, *Colleges and Halls in the University of Oxford*, ed. J. Gutch (Oxford, 1786)

Wood, Anthony, *Athenae Oxonienses*, I, ed. P. Bliss (Oxford, 1848)
Wood, Anthony, *Survey of the Antiquities of the City of Oxford*, I, ed. A. Clark, OHS 15 (Oxford, 1889)
Wood, Margaret, *The English Mediaeval House* (London, 1965)
Woolfson, J., 'Bishop Fox's Bees and the Early English Renaissance', *Reformation and Renaissance Review*, 5.1 (2003) 7–26
Woodward, D., *Men at Work: Labourers and Building Craftsmen in the Towns of Northern England, 1450–1750* (Cambridge, 1995)

INDEX

NOTE. Places are assigned to counties as defined before 1974. The following abbreviations are used: Abp., Archbishop; Alex., Alexander; Ant., Anthony; Berks., Berkshire; Bp., Bishop; Coll., College; Edm., Edmund; Edw., Edward; Geo., George; Glos., Gloucestershire; Hants., Hampshire; Hen., Henry; Humph., Humphrey; Lawr., Lawrence; Leics., Leicestershire; Lincs., Lincolnshire; n., note; Nic., Nicholas; Northumb., Northumberland; Notts., Nottinghamshire; Oxon., Oxfordshire; Ric., Richard; Rob., Robert; Rog., Roger; Som., Somerset; Thos., Thomas; Wal., Walter; Warw., Warwickshire; Wm., William; Wilts., Wiltshire.

Abankes, *see* Banks
Abingdon, earls of, 144
Alam, Jn., 68, 158
Alcalá (Spain), university of, x
ale, 57
Allen, P. S., President of Corpus Christi Coll., 99
All Souls College, Oxford, xlix n.
 building accounts, xliii n.
 building of, xliv n.
 Fellows, xxviii, 128–9
 organ, 129
 panelling, xlvi n.
 Warden, 128–9
Almoner, Lord, 22 and n.
Alye (Aley), Geo., 36, 39, 40, 42, 48, 50, 52–3, 55, 57–8, 60–1, 63, 153
Ammonio, Andrea, xxiv
Ancaster, dukes of, 144
André, Bernard, xx
Antony, 43–6, 153
apprentices, l, lxii, 14n.
Aragon, Katherine of, **pl. 16d**
Arborfield (Berks.), xxxiv, 139
Archar, Thos., 66, 75–6, 82, 158; (as Wm.), 78, 84

Arma Christi, xvi, 134
 crown of thorns, 137
armorials, *see* heraldry
arras, *see* tapestry
Arthur, British king, xli
Arthur, prince of Wales, xxii–xxiii
Artificers Act, 1514, xxv, xxxv, 145–51
ash *see* timber
Ashdown, Jn., prior of Lewes, xxvi, 108, 113–15, 122, 124–5
astrolabe *see* Corpus Christi Coll.
Athelstan, king, 134
Atwater, Wm., Bp. of Lincoln, lvi
 chancellor of, 19, 81
 seal of, 19
aumbry, *see* Corpus Christi Coll., chapel
Avenell (Avell, Awell), Jn., 27–8, 30–1, 33–4, 36–7, 39–41, 43–4, 50, 52–3, 55–6, 58–60, 153
axe, 59, 73

Bachelors' Garden, *see* Merton Coll.
Bacon, Francis, xviii–xix
badges, *see* bear and ragged staff; fleur de lys; Tudor badges

bakehouse, 118
baker's peel, 57
baldric, 47
Balliol College, Oxford, xxxvii–xxxviii, xlv, 9
Baltic, xlvi
Banks (Abankes), Jn., xxxix, lvi–lvii, 16, 18, 21–3, 48, 56, 67, 73–4, 76–8, 80–1, 85, 153
Banyster, Lawr., 25, 45, 47, 54, 61–2, 158
barber, 116–17
Barclay, Alex., xxiii
barge, xxxv, xxxvii, liv, 5, 7n., 96
Barker (Barkar):
　Ant., xxxiv, 141, 144
　Jn., 65, 67, 69, 153
　Thos., xxxiv, 139–42
Barnes (Barons):
　Thos., 7, 72–3, 75–6, 158
　Wm., 93
barrels, xxxvii, 6n., 46, 57, 74, 159; and see pipes
Barrington, Little (Glos.), quarry, xlv, 18, 68–9, 72, 75, 78–9, 82, 84, 157
Bartew, see Bertie
Basel (Switzerland), lviii
Basyng (later Kingsmill), Wm., xl n.
Bath and Wells:
　Bp. of, see Fox, Ric.
　diocese of, xxxviii
battles, see Blackheath; Bosworth; Spurs; Stoke
battle-axe, 134
bawdikyn, see fabrics
Bayly, Rob., liv, 96
Baynard's Castle (London), xxx–xxxii, xxxv, xxxvii, xliii, 94
beadle, 24
beams [roof], see Corpus Christi Coll., roofs

bear and ragged staff [badge], 134–5, 137
Beauchamp, fam., 134
Beaufort:
　Lady Margaret, xxii, xxxiv, xxxvii, xl
　fam., 133
　and see Tudor badges, portcullis
beds, x, 15, 46, 109–10
　trussing beds, 110
　and see Corpus Christi Coll, beds; Fox, Ric., personal belongings and napery; tester
Bedfordshire, xxxviii
beer, 147
Beke's Inn, see Oxford
Belgium, see Louvain
Benedictine colleges, see Canterbury Coll.; Gloucester Coll.
Benedictine Rule, xxxvii, xli, 120
　and see Fox, Ric., translation
Benett, Jn., 60, 153
Bere, Ric., abbot of Glastonbury, xxvi, 108, 113–15, 119–20, 122, 124–5
Berkshire, xxxviii, 139–42, 144n.; and see Arborfield; Blewbury; Burghfield; Hinksey; Reading; Sunningwell
Bertie (Bartew):
　Ric., 143–4
　Thos., 143
bills, 20, 33, 38, 43, 48–9, 53, 60, 72–4, 90, 111
Black Death, xiv, xvi
Blackheath (Kent), battle of, xxi
Blackfriars (London), 129
　Conference, xxix–xxx, 94
blacksmiths, lvii, 20, 22–3, 25, 46, 48–52, 55–6, 59, 62, 64, 66, 73–4, 77, 79, 81, 85, 90
Blewbury (Berks.), 61
board, see timber board

Bodkyn, Gerrard (Garrate), 26–8, 30–1, 33–4, 36, 38–9, 42, 153
Bodleian Library, see Oxford University
Bodwyn (Bedewyn), Ric., 153
Boldre (Hants.), xlvii n.
bolster, see cushion
Bond, Jn., 11, 28, 30, 72, 153
book binding, lvii, lviii, 23, 25, 56
book presses, see Corpus Christi Coll., library
books:
  books of 'divers sciences and faculties', 110
  books of Greek, lvi, 79n.
  paper book, lvi
  and see Corpus Christi Coll., library; Fox, Ric., personal belongings, books
Boseby, Harry, 3, 158
bosses (knottes) [roof], see Corpus Christi Coll., chapel; Winchester Cathedral
Boston (Lincs.), xv n.
Bosworth (Leics.), battle of, ix, xvii, xix, xxii
Bowdon, Thos., 24–5, 46, 74–5, 77, 80, 158
Brainton, Isabella, abbess of Godstow, xxxiv, 95, 111, 121–3
Brandt, Sebastian, xxiii
Branne, Jn., 66, 158
Brasenose College, Oxford., xxv, xxvii, xxxiii, xxxviii, xlviii, ln., 92–3, 154
  Principal, xxv, xxvii, 93
Bray, Jn., 84, 158
bread, 58n., 118, 120, 148
breviary, see Fox, Ric., personal belongings
brewing house, 118
Brittany (France), duchy of, xvii, xix

Broke (Brooke):
  Hen., 75–6, 78, 81–2, 84, 158
  Rog., 19–20, 81, 158
  Wm., 18–19, 75–6, 78–9, 81, 158
Brown (Browne), Jn., 25–6, 28–9, 31, 33–4, 36–7, 39–41, 43–6, 48, 50, 52–3, 153
Brussel cloth, see fabrics
Brytton (Brytter, Brytten, Brittayne, Britten), Wm., l, lii, 27, 29–30 (?Jn.), 32–3, 35, 39, 42–5, 47, 50, 52–3, 55, 57–8, 60–1, 63–5, 67, 69, 71–2, 74, 76, 78–80, 82–3, 85, 153, 155
Buckingham, duke of, see Stafford, Hen.
Bull, Jn., 27, 153
Bullock, Thos., 139, 141
Burcot (Oxon.), 70
Burford (Oxon.), 76–8, 141, 154
Burghfield (Berks.), 141
Burton, Jn., prior of St. Frideswide's, Oxford, 110n.
Bustard (Bustared), Garratt, 25–6, 153
butler, 117
Byschopp, Jn., 71, 158

Calais, xv, xx
Cambridge, xvi, xxxiv, xxxviii, xl, xlvi
Cambridge University, xl
  colleges, see Christ's; Pembroke; Queen's; St. John's
Cambye, Mr (Jn. ?), 19
candlesticks, 55, 64, 109, 111–13, 118, 120–1, 125
Canterbury (Kent):
  Abp. of, see Warham
  Christ Church Priory, 4 n.
Canterbury College, Oxford, 4
Cardinal College (Christ Church), Oxford, 4n., 101, 131

Cardinal College *cont.*
  building accounts, xliii, 101, 157
  building of, xlix–l, lvii, 153, 155–9
  design, 154
  master mason of, 104
  Tom Quad, 104
Care, Wm., messenger, 17
carpet, 110, 120
carfs (carves) [timber cuts], 26–7, 29, 31, 37, 39, 41–5, 47, 52
carriers, li, lvi, 3–90, 149; *and see* Appendix 10
Carmeliano, Pietro, xx
Carow, Rob., xxv–xxvi, xxxiv, xlix, lv, lvii, 12, 15, 17, 20, 46, 51, 60, 71, 79, 90, 92, 131, 153, 155
carpenters, xliv, xlvi n., xlix–lii, lvii, lxii, 3n., 6n., 8n., 10, 12, 15, 25–6, 28–9, 31–4, 36–7, 39–41, 43–6, 50–3, 55–6, 58–60, 65, 83, 90–1, 103n., 112, 131, 146, 148n., 153–7, 159–60
  master, xxv–xxvi, xxxi, xxxvii, xlvii–xlix, 103–5, 146, 154
Carter, Wm., 71–2, 77–8, 80, 153
Carthusian Order, xxiv
Carvar, Rob., 83, 85, 153
carvers [specialist], lii, lv, 50, 53, 57, 135, 149, 155–6; *and see* Russell, Jn.; More, Edm.
casements, *see* Corpus Christi Coll., windows
Castell:
  Thos., prior of Durham, xxiv
  Wm., 78, 153
caulk, 145
censers, *see* Corpus Christi Coll., chapel
Chancery, 94, 127–9, 140
Chare:
  Jn., 16, 65, 68, 72–3, 78, 82, 84, 158

  Ric., 10–11, 13, 15–16, 61, 63, 65, 68, 69n., 71, 84, 158
Charles V, Holy Roman Emperor, xli
Chayney, *see* Cheyney
Chedwell, Thos., 19, 158
Chest, Jn., 66, 154
chest [for valuables], 99, 121, 129
Cheyney, Jn., 56, 66, 154
Chilcombe (Hants.), xlvii n.
chimney, 104n.
Cholsey, — ,carrier, 65, 158
Christ Church, Oxford, 101; *and see* Canterbury Coll.
Christopher Inn, *see* Oxford
Christ's College, Cambridge, xl
Church, the English, x, xix, xxi–xxii, xxiv, xxviii–xxxiii, xxxvi, xlii–xliii, li, 94, 144
Cisnero, Ximines de, cardinal, x
Clare, Wm., 6, 158
Clarke, *see* Clerk
Claxton, Mr., 81
Claymond, Jn.:
  President of Corpus Christi Coll., xx, xxvi, xxxv–ix, xliii, liv–lv, lvii, 90, 96
  President of Magdalen Coll., 92, 113–14, 118, 120
clerestory, *see* Corpus Christi Coll., chapel
Clerk (Clarke, Clerke):
  Cornell, l, li n., 8, 11, 25–6, 31, 35, 37–9, 41, 49, 51, 154
  Rob., 31, 154
closets, 59, 62, 82, 87–8, 118
cloth of gold, *see* fabrics
clothing, 109–11, 117, 149; *and see* gloves
coal [for cooking], 118
Coke:
  Christine, lii
  Humph., xxv, xxvi n., xxvii,

INDEX

xxxi–xxxii, xlvii–xlix,
lii–liii, lv, lvii, 6, 12, 17, 50,
54, 67, 90–3, 95–7, 112, 131,
133, 154
  apprentice to, l, 14n.
  assault on, xxv, xxvii, xlviii
    n.;
  designs Fox's chantry chapel,
    xxvii
Colbrond [giant], 134
Colet, Jn., dean of St. Paul's Cathedral, xxiv
Cologne (Germany), xx
Colyar, Rob., 84, 158
Collyns (Collyn, Colyn):
  Ric., 55, 154
  Wm., l, lvii, 14, 31, 33–4, 36–7,
    39, 40–6, 48, 50, 52–3, 55–6,
    58–61, 90, 154
Contarini, Gasparo, xxxvi n.
contracts, x, xxiv, xxvi n., xxviii,
  xxxviii, xliv, xlix, l–li, lv–lvii,
  4n., 6–7, 18, 1–2, 18, 23, 27–32,
  34, 37–9, 41–5, 50–4, 56, 60,
  83–5, 90, 93, 95, 103–5, 107–25,
  128, 154, 156–7, **pl. 11**
  sub-contracts, xxxv, lii, 131
cook, 117
Cooke, Jn., 16, 67, 69, 71, 83–5, 158
cooper, 47
cope, 109
corbel–table, 83–5, 89
Corner Hall, *see* Oxford
corporals, 120
Corpus Christi College, Oxford
  [general]:
  accommodation, xxxi, xxxvi,
    95
  apple-house, 50
  archive, lv, lxi, 99, 102–3, 108,
    127–9
  astrolabe, liv
  bakehouse, 118

barberhouse, 21
bell, 47, 59
benefactor to, xxxviii, lvi
Bible clerk, 117
brewhouse, 118
building of, *see next head entry*
buttery, liv, 6, 13, 22, 24, 55, 58
candelabra, liv
chapel, ix, xxviii, xxxi–xxxii, ,
  xxxvi, xxxix, xliii, li–lii, liv,
  lvi–lvii, 87, 89–90, 95–7, 101,
  112–13, 118, 133
  altar, xxviii, lvi, 57, 74, 87, 93,
    128–9
  aumbry, 21
  bell, 47
  bosses (knottes), lii, 50n., 53,
    68, 87, 97, 136, 154, 156
  candlesticks for, 109
  censers, 66
  choir, 13
  clerestory, 90
  desks, 120
  doors, 13, 21, 46, 59, 86
  panelling, 34, 45, 85, 87
  roof, 87, 90
  vestry, 21, 59, 66
chest, 99, 101
chimney, liii, 71–2, 104n.
cloister, xliii, xlv, lvii, 33, 35,
  51–2, 59, 66, 96
chambers, xlix, liii, lvii, 51, 72
  walls, 32, 53, 65, 79, 89–90
  windows, liii, 18, 42, 49, 73,
    77–8
closet, 59, 62, 82, 87
coal house, 55
courtyard, *see below*, quad
doors, xlvi,–xlvii, li, lvi, 6–7,
  12–14, 21–2, 27, 52–3, 55, 59,
  62, 66, 72–3, 75, 80–1, 88–90
door frames (portals), 7, 14, 146
wicket, 13, 55, 59

Corpus Christi College *cont.*
  endowment, xiv, xxiv, xxxiv, xlvii, 91, 103–5, 112, 130, 135, 139–42, 144
  estates of, 78, 82
  feeder schools, xv
  Fellows, xl, ix, xxxi–xxxii, xxxvi, xxxviii–xl, xliii, li, liii n., liv n., 15n., 95–7, 140
  floors, xlv–xlvi, xlviii, xlix, 7, 90
  foundation of, ix–x, xxxv, xliii, liii, 96; *and see* Fox, Ric., plans
  furniture, xlv, xlviii, li
    beds, x, xlix, 15, 46, 88
    bench, li, 6
    cupboard, li, 7, 14
    dresser, 46
    tables, x, 5, 117, 148
  garden, 4, 6, 89, 117, 123
  gargoyles, 85
  gate, 89
  gatehouse/tower, ix, xxviii, xxxvi, xliii, xlviii, liv, 4, 85, 99n., 101, 132
    fan vault, xlviii, liv, **pl. 5**
    oriel window, xliii, 132, **pl. 4**
  hall, ix, xxvi, xxxiv–xxxvi, xliii, 95, 101, 129, 131–8, 147–8, **pls. 2, 12–17**
    carved detail, xxxiv, xlviii, 131–8
    corbels, xxxiv, xlviii, lv
    glazed window, lv, **pl. 15**
    hammerbeam roof, xxxiv, xlviii–xlix, **pl. 2**
  hen house, 22, 25, 38, 89
  inventories, lvi, 23, 96
  jewels, lvi n.
  jurisdiction over, xxxix, xliii
  kitchen, xxv, xxxii, xxxv–xxxvi, xliii, xlvi, lii, liv, 4, 6, 22, 24, 118, 147
    coal for, 118
    implements, xlvi, liv, 5, 7, 24, 49, 57–9, 96, 118, 147–8
    kitchen yard, 25, 54
    larder, 22
    oven, 24
  lecturers, xxxi, 95, 115–17; *and see below*, readers
  library, xxviii, xxxii, xxxv–xxxvii, xlix, l, lvii, 17, 31, 37, 59, 79, 64, 87, 92n., 100
    book presses, xxxvi
    books, xxxvii, lvi, 37, 79;
      chains for, lvi, 57
    desks, x, l–li, 8, 11, 49, 51, 61, 154
    librarian, lxi, 99, 100–1
    windows, xxxvi, liv
    woodwork and panelling, xxxv, li, lvii, 34, 45, **pl. 6**
  Libri Magni [account books], liv, lvi–lvii
  manuscripts, ix–xi, xiv, xxxix, lvii–lix, lxi–lxiii, 99–102
  maps, liv
  name [Corpus Christi/Winchester Coll.], xxviii–xxix, 94, 128, 130
  occupancy, xxxii, xxxvi, xxxviii–xxxix, 95
  officers, 108, 116–17
  pastry house, 21
  plate, xiv n., liv
  Presidents, xx, xl, xliii, liii, lv, 87–9, 95–6
    lodgings, li, lv, lvii, 6–7, 14, 28–30, 32, 35, 41, 86, 88
    study, 41, 86, 88
    woodhouse, 38, 50
    and see Allen; Claymond
  purpose of, xiv, xxix, xlii
    as chantry, xl

INDEX

Corpus Christi College *cont.*
   quad, xxxii, xxxvi, xliii, liv, 4,
     34, 93, 95
   readers [in Logic, Philosophy,
     Sophistry], 115–17
   refectory, xxviii
   register, 92
   repairs to:
     college fabric, lvii, 13, 22, 38,
       59, 117
     equipment, 25, 47, 64, 73, 82,
       86
     roofs, xlvi, xlix, 87–8, 90
     beams (bemys), 90
     hammerbeam, 129, 131–2
     rooms, ix, xxvi n., xxxi–xxxii,
       xxxvi, xlv–xlvi, xlviii, liii,
       lv, 7, 77, 81, 95, 97, 116
   sacristan, 117
   servants, xxxi, 95, 116–17
   site, ix, xxiv, xlviii, 91, 93, 95,
     97, 101
   stair/staircase, xxxi, 7, 90, 95
   statutes, xiii, xvii, xxxiv,
     xxxvi–xl, lii n., lv n., lvii, 96,
     111n., 117, 123–4, 130
   students, ix, xxvii, xxxi, xxx-
     iii–xxxiv, xxxvii, xxxix– xl,
     xliii, l–li, liii n., liv n., lvii,
     95, 97, 147–8
   treasure house, 52
   treasurer's lodgings, lvi, 13, 21
   Vice-president, *see* Morwent,
     Rob.
   Visitor, xl–xli
   walls, x, xxxv, xlv–xlvi, xlix,
     lvii, 6–7, 32–3, 41, 45, 47, 49,
     53, 56, 88–90, 117
   boundary, xxxv, xliii, liii, 4,
     33, 36
   warden [proposed], 108, 112, 115,
     117
   well, 24, 46, 62, 73, 117

   windows, xlv, liii, lv, lvii, 7, 42, 53,
     46–7, 49, 52n., 59, 68–9, 71–3,
     77–8, 81, 85, 88, 90, 133, 146
     casements, 57, 79, 86
     glass, xxxvi, liii–lv, lvii n.,
       52n., 55, 133, **pl. 15**
     label stops, 77, 80
     lancet (launcelate, lawnslott),
       81, 85
     saddlebars (soudlets), 86
     and see above, cloister, gate-
       house, library
   wine-cellar, 13, 62
   wood house, 53, 73
   wood yard, lii, 4
Corpus Christi College, Oxford
   [building of], ix–x, xiv, xxvi,
     xxxv, xxxviii, xl, 3–90, 93,
     129–31
   accounts, xxxv, xliii, xlv–xlvi,
     xlviii–lii, 3–90, 99–101, 147,
     153–4, 157, **pls. 7–10**
   missing accounts, x, xiv,
     xxvii, lv, App. 2, 129
   building equipment and tools:
     bowl, 66
     brooms, 10, 23
     bucket, 10, 46–7, 66, 85
     candles, li, 51, 54, 56, 59
     cord, 68, 79
     cowl [tub], 5, 15
     frame [structural support],
       xlvi, 52, 68, 79
     mattock, 6
     pail, 5, 68
     packthread [twine], 13
     rake, 62, 64
     saw, 25
     scaffolding, xxxv, 14n.
     scaffolding cord, 56–7, 60, 70
     sieve, 5, 66
     stone-saw, 73, 85
     and see nails

Corpus Christi College [building of] *cont.*
building materials, x, xxxix, xlv, lvii, 3–90, 101
  cement, 70n.
  fern, 49
  glue, 7, 12
  gravel, 11, 20–1, 23, 25, 46–7, 49, 52, 54, 56, 61–3, 66, 68, 80, 83, 157
  iron, 24–5, 52, 55, 59, 85
  lead, 90
  lime, xxxv, xlv–xlvi, 5–6, 8, 10–11, 12, 14, 16–17, 19, 21–3, 47, 49, 60, 63, 66–7, 69, 72, 79, 81–2, 84, 155, 158–60
  loam (clay), 5, 9–10, 13, 17, 157–9
  mortar, xlv, 70n.
  moss, 68
  plaster, xxxv, xlvi, li
  procurement of, xxxv, xliv–xlvi, li, 3–90, 153–60
  resin, 70
  rushes, 17
  sand, xlv, 4–6, 9–10, 16–17, 54, 62, 157–8
  shingles (shellys), 65, 158
  tin, 21
  transport of, xxxv, xliv–xlv, li, liii–liv, 3–90, 157–60
  and see stone; timber
building plans, xxxi–xxxii, 95, 129–30
clerk of works, xxvii, xliii–xliv, lvi, 101
expenditure on, xxxix, xl, xliv, lvii
foundations, digging of, xxxv, liii, 6, 32–3, 35–6, 38, 41–2, 93, 96
master craftsmen, xxv, xliv, lxii; *and see* Carow; Coke,

Humph.; Vertue
paving, x, xliii, xlv, lii, 4, 10, 30, 25, 54
workers' conditions, xxxii, xxxv, lvii, 146–7
Corpus Christi Guild (in Boston), xv n.
Coterell, Jn., xlvi, 16, 158
couriers, *see* messengers
Courtenay, Peter, Bp. of Winchester, xx
craftsmen, *see* Appendix 10
cresse-table (grasse, gresys-table) [? stone slabs], xlix, 18, 54, 63, 81
Creswell, Thos., 142
Crondall (Hants.), 103–4
cults, *see* Virgin; Wounds
Cumberland, *see* Millom
Curteys:
  Hen., xv n.
  Ric., xv
  family chantry, 110n.
cushion, 110, 120

Dalston, Jn., 127–8
Dalton, Thos., xix
Damaske, Thos., 68, 158
Darcy, Lord Thos., xxxi
Davyson, Jn., dean of Salisbury, xvi
Desford, Thos., 66, 154
Devyn, Rob., xlvi, 16, 158
Dogmersfield (Hants.), 103–4
Dorset, *see* Sherborne
Dorsett, Thos., 139–42
Dowman, Jn., 114, 118, 120
Dudley, Sir Edm., xxii–xxiii, xlii
Durham, xviii, xx–xxi, xlvii n., 129
  Bp. of, *see* Fox, Ric.
  bishopric, xiii n.
  castle, xxv, xxxii, xlvii n.
  diocese, xxxviii
  priory, *see* Castell, Thos.

INDEX

East, Wm., xxv, xxviii, xxxiv, xlviii–xlix, lvii, 18, 54, 62–3, 68, 81–2, 91–3, 154
Edward IV, king, xvi–xvii, xx
Edward V, king, xvii
Eger, David, 27–8, 30, 37, 154
Elizabeth of York, queen, xviii, xxii
Elizabeth Woodville, queen consort, xvi–xvii
elm board, *see* timber
Empson, Ric., xxii–xxiii, xlii
England:
  currency of, 105, 124–5
  English church, *see* Church
Erasmus, Desiderius, ix, xiv, xxiv, xl, xliii, 97
Eresby, de, *see* Willoughby
Esher (Surrey), 96, 108, 110
Essex, *see* West Ham
Eton College, Windsor, xlix n., 141
Exeter:
  Bps. of, *see* Fox, Ric.; Oldham
  cathedral, 118n.
  diocese, xxxviii
Exeter College, Oxford, xxxviii

fabrics:
  bawdikyn, 119
  Brussel cloth, 120
  cloth of gold, 110–11, 119–20
  fustian, 110
  linen, 110, 118
  satin, 119
  table cloths, 119
  velvet, 119
  wool, 110
  and see tapestry
Ferrara (Italy), university of, xx
Fest, Thos., 142
Ffrancleyne, *see* Franklin
Fineux, Sir Jn., Lord Chief Justice, xxx

fire (feyer) pike, 58
Fisher, Jn., Bp. of Rochester, President of Queen's Coll., Cambridge, xxii, xxxiv, xl
Fitzhugh, Joan, 135
Flanders, xvi
Fletcher, Wm., 122
fleur de lys, li; *and see* Tudor badges
foreman, 146–7
Forest, Thos., 7, 158
Formby, Jn., xxvii, 93
Forster, Jn., 35, 154
Fox:
  Helena, xiv
  Jn., xv
  Ric., *see next head entry*
  Thos., xiv
Fox, Ric., Bp. of Winchester, ix–xliii, xlvii–l, lii–lvi, 7n., 19n., 83, 91–7, 103–36, 139–44, 147–8
  as Bp. of Bath and Wells, xviii, 110n., 128n.
  as Bp. of Durham, xviii, xxi, xxxii, 110n., 129
  as Bp. of Exeter, xviii, 110n., 118n.
  building activities, x, xv, xix, xxi, xli, xlvii, liv n., 104, 134–5
  burial place, 115
  chantry chapel, *see* Winchester Cathedral
  character, ix–x, xii–xiv, xvi, xviii–xix, xxxiii
  childhood, xiv–xvi
  correspondence, xiii, xvii, liii–liv, 81
  death, ix, xv, xliii
  diplomatic activity, ix, xvi, xviii–xx, xxiii, xxxii
  education, ix, xiv–xvii, li n.
  endowment of Corpus, 112, 135, 139–42, 144

Fox, Ric. *cont.*
  executor, xxxvii, xlvii, 104
  exile, xlii
  family, xiv–xvi, xix
  foreign policy, ix
  heraldry, xxxix n., lii–lv, 133–4, 137–8, **pls. 4, 15, 16**
  his chancellor, *see* Dowman
  his steward, *see* Frost, Wm.
  his treasurer, *see* Gardiner
  his vicar-general, *see* Sylke
  hostility to Richard III, xvii
  land purchases, 7n., xxix, xxxiv, xlvii, 91, 93, 94, 103–5, 127–30
  meritocracy, attitude to, xxxiv, xxxvii
  motto, xxxiv, liv–v, 131, **pl. 13**
  pelican device, xxxix n., lii–lv, 133–4, 137–8, **pls. 15, 16**
  personal belongings:
    beds and napery, 109–10, 119, 125
    books, 110
    breviary (portuose), 118, 120
    choirbooks, 108–13
    furred robes, 110
    images, religious, 109, 111
    jewels, 109–11, 121–3
    liturgical items [altar, plate etc.], 108–13, 118–23, 125
    Massbook, 118, 120
    tapestry, 108–10
    vestments, 109, 111–13, 119–20, 125
    wool mantles, 110
  plans for a college, x, xiii, xxvii–xviii, xxx–xxxvii, xlii, xlvii–liii, 91–7, 104, 108, 129–32, 134
  portraits, **Frontispiece**, xi, xli n., liv n.
  Privy Seal, Keepership of, ix, xviii, xxiv, xxxii, liii, 95
  sermons, xiii
  Secretary [King's], ix, xvii–xviii
  translator of the Benedictine Rule, xiii, xliii–iv, 95
  Visitor of Magdalen Coll., xxxvii
France, ix, xxiii–xxiv, xxvi–xxvii, xxxii, lviii, 93, 107, 109
  king of, *see* Louis XII
  war against, xxix, xlii, xix, 107
  and see Brittany; Calais; Paris; Thérouanne; Tournai
Franklin (Ffrancleyn):
  Jn., quarryman, xliv–xlv n., 5, 9–12, 14, 16–17, 19–21, 23–5, 47, 49, 51, 54–8, 61–2, 64, 66–7, 69, 71, 74–5, 77–8, 80–1, 83–5, 158
  Wm., 70, 158
Fredoli, Berengar, lvii
freemasons, *see* masons
Friars Observant, xxiv
Frost:
  Juliana, lvi
  Wm., Fox's steward, xlii, lv n., lvi, 83
Frulovisi, Tito Livio, xx
fustian, *see* fabrics

Gardiner, Ric., Treasurer of Wolvesey Palace, 107–8, 114–15, 118–20, 126
Garter, Order of, 135
Gely, Rob., xlvi, 19, 158
Germany, xliii; *and see* Cologne; Ingolstadt
Gigli, Giovanni, xx–xxi
gilding, lii, 67–8, 97, 133, 154
Glastonbury (Som.), abbot of, *see* Bere
Glasyer, Rob., liii, 55, 154
glaziers, 55, 146, 149, 154

INDEX

Gloucester, duke of, *see* Richard III
Gloucester College, Oxford, 83
Gloucestershire, xxxviii, 93; *and see* Barrington; Guiting; Hailes; Sudeley; Winchcombe
gloves, lvi, 19
Godstow Abbey (Oxon.), ix, xxvi, 108, 111, 121–3; *and see* Brainton, Isabella
Goldwell, Jas., Bp. of Norwich, xvi
Gossop, Jn., 37, 71, 154
grammar, xv, 108, 115, 117
grammar schools, xv–xvi, xix–xx, xxii, xxxiii
Grantham (Lincs.), xiv–xvi, 110 n.
Greek studies, ix, xiv, xx–xxi, xxv, xxvii, xxxvii, xl, 93, 97, 143; *and see* books
Grene:
   Ric., 16, 158
   —, 8, 10, 158
Grove:
   Ric., 30, 154
   Rob., 29, 32, 154
Gryffith, Rog., li, 34, 53, 154
Grymshave, Jn., 40, 154
Gryth:
   Alice, *see* Polleyn
   Jn., 103
Guildford (Surrey), 114n.
Guiting, Temple (Glos.), xxvii, 82, 83n., 93–4, 127–30, 135, 140
Gunthorpe, Jn., Keeper of Privy Seal, xiii n., xx
Guy of Warwick, *see* Warwick
Gyttens, Thos., 39, 40–1, 155

Hailes Abbey (Glos.), 127n.
Hamond:
   Jn., 53, 155
   Wm., 28, 30, 33–4, 37, 39–40, 42, 67, 77, 79–80, 155

Hampshire, xxiv, xlvii n., 103, 143; *and see,* Boldre; Chilcombe; Crondall; Dogmersfield; Itchenstoke; Mapledurwell; Odiham; Overton; Winchester
Hampton Court Palace (Surrey), 87n., 110n., 104n., 156
Harme, Jn., 65, 68, 70, 158
Harne, *see* Herne
Harper:
   Jn., 68, 70, 158
   Thos., 73, 158
Harrison, Rog., 5, 8–10, 12–13, 16–17, 19–25, 45, 47, 49, 51–2, 54–5, 57–8, 61–4, 66–7, 69, 74–5, 77–8, 81, 83–5, 158
Hart, Jn., 16–17, 20, 64, 158
Harvey, Jn., 99, 101
Hastings, —, scholar, xxv
Headington (Oxon.), quarries, xxxv–xxxvi, xliv–xlv, 5, 8, 10, 12–13, 16, 19–21, 23–5, 45, 49, 52, 54–5, 57, 61, 63–4, 75, 85, 158
Hearne, Thos., antiquary, xliv
Hebrew studies, ix, xiv, xxi, xxxvii, 97, 143
Helyar, Jn., 143
Henley-on-Thames (Oxon.,), xxxv, xlvi, liv, 7, 9, 15–17, 33, 75
Henry VII, ix, xviii, xxiii
   as Henry Tudor, ix, xvii, xxviii
   chantry chapel, 104
   council of, xviii–xix, xxii–xxiii
   founder of Savoy Hospital, xlvii
   monogram, 136
   tomb, 104
Henry VIII, xxiii–xxiv, xxvii–xxxii, xl–liii
   almoner to, 22n.
   as prince, xxiii, 136
   council, xxiv, xxx

Henry VIII *cont.*
dispute with clergy, xxviii
foreign policy, xxxiii
military campaign, xxvi, 93, 107
visits Bp. Fox, 123
heraldry, liii–lv, 45, 130–2, 134–5, 137, 155, **pls. 12, 14**
Herne (Harne, Horne):
  Nic., liii, 20, 26–7, 29–30, 32–3, 35–6, 38–9, 42–5, 47–8, 50, 52–3, 55, 57–8, 60–1, 63–5, 67, 69, 71, 74, 76, 78–80, 82–3, 85, 155
  Ric., 5–6, 10–11, 159
  Wm., 72
hewer [of wood], xlvi
Heys, Ric., 28, 67, 69, 156
Hinksey (Berks.), quarry, xliv n.
Hobbys (Hoogys):
  Jn., 26–7, 155
  Wm., l, 27, 29–30, 32, 71, 153, 155
Holgill, Wm., Master of the Savoy Hospital, xlvii, 75, 144n.
holidays, xv, li, lxi–lxii, 29n.
Holinshed, Ralph, xxxiii
Holman, Simon, 26, 28, 30, 32, 34–6, 38–40, 42–5, 47–8, 50–3, 55, 57–8, 60–1, 63–5, 67, 69–72, 74, 76, 78–80, 82–3, 85, 155
Holy Roman Empire, xxiii, xxxii, 107
  emperors, *see* Charles V; Maximilian
Holywell, *see* Oxford
Homer, xxxvii
Hoogys, *see* Hobbys
Horne, *see* Herne
Horneclyff, Harry, 26, 155
horse hire, 50, 68, 77
Hospital of St. Cross, Winchester, xxxix, lv, 96, 108
  custodian, *see* Launde

Master, xx
Huddleston:
  Jane, xxviii, 93, 127–30, 135
  Sir Jn., xxvii–xxviii, 93, 127–30, 135
  Jn., 94, 127–30, 135, 140
  Ric., 135n.
  Wm., 135n.
  family, 135
  heraldic arms, 137, **pl. 17a**
Humanism, xx–xxi, xxiv, xxxvii, xxxix n., xl, 97
hurdles, 14, 67, 71, 158–9
Hynton, Jn., 58, 155
Hyxis, Wm., 14, 159

Ingolstadt (Germany), lviii
Iordan, *see* Yorden
ironwork, lvii, 46, 73, 76–7, 81–2, 160
  bolts, 21–2, 25, 46–7, 50, 86, 87
  candlesticks, 55, 64
  catches [doors and windows], 47, 50
  chains, 46–7, 57, 66
  crampettes, 14
  curtain rings, 57
  door handle, 14, 59
  grate, 22
  gutter, 4n.
  hinges (garnetts, gymmys), lvi, 6, 13–14, 21–2, 25, 46–7, 50, 58, 61–2, 86
  hooks, 13, 21, 46–7, 51, 57, 62, 66, 86
  hoops, 5, 10, 46, 85
  keys, 13–14, 21–2, 52, 55, 59, 64, 86
  latches, 22, 47, 50
  locks, lvi, 13–14, 16, 21–2, 52–3, 57–9, 61–2, 77–8, 81, 86, 121
  staples [side-pieces for doors], 22, 46–7, 50–1, 59, 66, 86–7, 154

INDEX

window bars, lvi, 52, 56, 58–9, 64, 73
Italy, *see* Ferrara; Padua; Rome
Itchenstoke (Hants), 122

jewels, *see* Corpus Christi Coll., Fox, Ric., personal belongings
Johan [no surname], lii, 62, 155
joiners, l–li, lxii, 6, 8n., 29–32, 38–9, 42–3, 45, 50–3, 83, 85, 146, 149, 154, 157
joists, 65, 72, 81, 90
joll piece [cornice?], 90
Jonson:
  Rob., 58, 155
  Wm., 155n.
Jonys, Jn., 63–4, 66, 79, 159
journeyman, lxii
Joyner, Jn., 36, 155
Justice, Lord Chief, *see* Fineux

Katherine of Aragon, xxii–xxiii, 123, 133, 136–7
Kechynrooffe (Kechynman), Wm., 74, 76, 155
Kelly (Keft), Wm., 27, 84, 155
Kent, xxxviii; *and see* Blackheath; Canterbury; Rochester
keys, lvi, 121, 132, 134
Kidderminster, Ric., abbot of Winchcombe, xxvi, 124
Kingsmill, *see* Basyng
Kingston upon Thames (Surrey), lv, 156
kitchen, xiv, 92; *and see* Corpus Christi Coll., kitchen
kneading trough, xlvi, 5, 148
Knott:
  Jn., 8, 13, 15–17, 19, 24, 159
  Ric., 5, 8, 10, 12, 159
knottes [carved bosses], *see* bosses

labourers, xxv, l–lii, lxii, 26–8, 30, 32–5, 39–40, 42–5, 47–8, 50, 52–3, 55, 57–8, 61, 63–4, 66, 83, 145–51, 153–7
Lancashire, 38
Larden, Elys, xxxv, li, 8, 10–12, 14, 16–17, 20–3, 47, 49, 60, 63, 66–7, 69, 72, 79, 81–2, 84, 159
laths, *see* timber
Lathell, Nic., 118
Latin, ix, xiv–xv, xx–xxi, xxiv, xxxvii, lxiii, 8n., 97, 143
Laund, Thos., custodian of St. Cross Hospital, 108, 110–11
launderer, 108, 116–17
layers [setters of stone], *see* masons
lead board, *see* timber
Lebons (Levibons, Lybyn):
  Alice, *see* Polleyn
  Jn., xxiv, 103–5, 144, **pl. 11**
  Jn., s. of above, 144
Leigh, Jn., xxvii, 93
Lemesley, Thos., 16, 159
Lenche, Jas., 25, 27, 155
Lepton, Ralph, 113–15, 118–20, 128–9
Levibons, *see* Lebons
Lewes Priory (Sussex), *see* Ashdown
Lewis, Ric., xxxv, li, liii, 6, 8, 12, 27–33, 35–6, 38, 40–5, 47, 50–3, 56–63, 65, 67, 69, 71–2, 75–6, 78–80, 82–3, 85, 155
limestone, *see* stone
Lincoln, xx
  Bps. of, *see* Atwater; Russell, Jn.; Smyth, Wm.
  diocese, xxxix, 96
  prebendary of, 141
Lincoln College, Oxford, xxxviii, l, 3n., 104n., 155, 159–60
Lincolnshire, ix, xv–xvi, xxxviii
  quarries in, xv

and see Boston; Grantham; Lincoln; Ropsley
Lindsey, earls of, 144
linen, *see* fabrics
Linstead, Bart., prior of St. Mary Overy, 110n.
Lobel, Mary, 100–1
Locke, Jn., 3, 18, 159
Loggan, David, xxxvi, **pl. 3**
London, xv, xviii, xx, xlvi, lvi, 5, 14, 17, 24, 50, 52, 64, 79, 94, 97, 148, 154, 159
   city of, xviii
   St. Paul's Cathedral, *see* Colet
   Tower of London, xvii, xxiii
   Westminster, lii, liv, 87, 96, 133, 156
      Abbey, 104
      hall, xxiii
   and see Baynard's Castle; Blackfriars; Savoy Hospital; Southwark
Looder, Wm., 42, 155
Louis XII, king of France, 107
Louvain (Belgium), university, xvi
Luther, Martin, xxxvii n.
Lybyn, *see* Lebons
Lytyll, Thos., 26–7, 29–31, 33, 35, 37–9, 41, 155

Machiavelli, Niccolò, xxiii, xxxvii n.
Magdalen College, Oxford, xvi, xx, xxxvii–xxxviii, xliii n., xlvi n., xlix n., l, li n., lv, 3n., 6, 8, 46, 88n.
   carpenter at, 153–4, 157
   great gate, 159n
   President, *see* Claymond
   pytt [quarry], 60
   statutes, xxxvii
Makegood, Ric., 27–9, 31, 33–4, 36–7, 39–41, 43–4, 71–2, 76–7, 79–80, 83, 155
Makyns, Jn., 26–8, 30, 32, 34–6, 38–40, 42, 155
Malowse, Jn., 26–8, 30–1, 33–4, 36–7, 39–40, 42–5, 47–8, 67, 69, 71, 74, 76, 155
Manchester Grammar School, xxxiii
Mapledurwell (Hants.), lvi
March, Jn., 9–11, 13, 17, 159
Marman, Jn., 82, 84, 159
Marvyng, Thos., 75, 159
Mary, queen, 144
Maryn, Jn., 34–5, 155
masons, xxiv–xxv, xxxi, xxxv, xliv–xlv, xlvii–xlix, li, lxii, 5, 27, 53, 93, 143–4, 146, 149, 153–5, 157
   freemasons, xliv, 28, 30, 49, 50, 54, 58–61, 85, 103–5, 112, 146, 149, 154–7
   master masons, xxv, xxxi, xlviii, 18n., 91, 103–5, 143n., 144, 146, 157
   roughmasons [stone layers], xliv, lxii, 26, 31, 33–4, 36–7, 39–40, 42, 51, 53, 56–8, 61, 146, 149, 153–7
Matheow, Jn., 17, 159
Matteson, Jn., 5, 159
Mawe, Jn., 155
Maximilian, Holy Roman Emperor, 107
meat, 118, 146–7, 149
Medam (Meden):
   Jn., 8, 16–17, 68, 77, 159
   Ric., 12, 159
   Thos., 5, 8–11, 13, 19, 159
Mede, Thos., 5, 68, 70, 72–3, 75, 159
Meden, *see* Medam
Mekyns, Jn., 155
merchants, xv n., lvi, 79

INDEX

Merton College, Oxford, xxiv–xxvi, xxix–xxx, xxxiii, xxxvii–xxxix, 4, 6, 7n., 22n., 51, 89, 91–2, 108, 111, 122
  Bachelors' Garden, xxvi, xxix, 92, 94
  Fellows, xxiv, xxvi, 94
  library, liii n., lv
  statutes, xxxvii
  Warden, see Rawlins
Merton Priory (Surrey), see Salyng
messengers, xiii, liii–liv, 57, 59, 61, 64, 68, 74, 81–2, 139; and see Care; Roper
Millom (Cumb.), 135n.
mitre, 133, 137
monks, xxxi–xxxiv, xxxvii, xxxix, xl–lii, 91, 94–6, 107–8, 111–12, 115, 117–18, 120, 131, 134
More:
  Edm., lv, 45, 156
  Nic., l, lvii, 25–6, 28–9, 33, 52, 55, 57, 60–1, 65, 71, 79, 81, 90, 156
  Ric., 39, 43, 48–9, 51, 68, 76, 156
  Rob., li, 34, 53, 156
  Sir Thos., xix, xxv, xxxii, xxxvii, xl, 94, 127n.
Morwent;
  Rob., Vice-president of Corpus Christi Coll., xxxvi n, 6n., 78, 88
  Rog., li, 6–7, 28–30, 32, 34, 41, 53, 156
  Wal., xxvi, 6n., 92
Morys, Wm., 70, 156
Myller (Myles), Jn., 10, 58, 156
Myllet, Wm., 57, 156
Myllwell, Wm., 72, 156
Mylton, Thos., 25, 27–9, 31, 33–4, 36–7, 39–41, 43–4, 156

nails, 5, 7, 8, 13, 17, 48, 81
  broddes, 13, 22, 24–5, 47, 49, 51, 55, 73, 78
  cord (chord) nails, 86
  lath-nail, 15, 17, 21, 54, 66, 83
  penny nails, 5, 15, 17, 21, 23–4, 54, 63, 69, 71, 74, 80, 160
  seallyng [panelling] nails, 51
  sprig nails, 5, 12, 14, 17
Navarre (Spain), papers from, lviii
Nettlebed (Oxon.), xxxv, xlvi, 42, 56, 66, 72, 80
  carpenter at, 33
  timber from, 3, 8, 10–13, 15–16, 22–4, 46, 61–2, 65, 68, 70, 73, 75, 82, 84
  sawyers at, 39, 42–6, 49, 55, 57, 61
Neville family, 135
Neville's Inn, see Oxford
New College, Oxford, xx, xxxviii, xxxix n., xliv n., xlvi n., 21, 134n., 143n.
New Learning, xxvi, xxxvii, 124n.; and see studia humanitatis
Newland, Ric., 140–2
Nichols, Rob., 75, 159
Nix (Nykke);
  Ric., Bp. of Norwich, 108, 110n.
  Thos., 110n
Norham Castle (Northumb.) xv, xxi
Norwich, Bps. of, see Goldwell; Nix, Ric.
Nottinghamshire, see Stoke
Noytt, Jn., 159
Nun Hall, see Oxford
Nykke, see Nix

oak, see timber
Odiham (Hants.), 103–4
Oldham, Hugh, Bp. of Exeter, xxxiii, xxxviii, lv, 45, 156

Oriel College, Oxford, xxxviii, xlix n., 154
Osney Abbey (Oxon.), 85
overseers, 146
Overton (Hants.), 91
Owen, Matt., 28–30, 32, 34–6, 38–40, 156
Oxford, xiv–xvi, xx, xxiv–xxv, xxvii, xxxiv, xxxvii–xl, xliv–xlvi, xlviii–l, lii–liv, lvi, lxii, 8–9, 15, 82–3, 91–3, 95–7, 102–4, 108, 131, 139–40, 153, 156
  archdeacon of, see Urswick
  Beke's Inn, 95
  Christopher Inn, 104n.
  Corner Hall, xxvi, xxix, 92, 94
  Holywell, 6
  Neville's Inn, xxix, 92, 94
  Nun Hall, 95
  St. Frideswide's Priory, xxvi, xxxiii, 4, 88, 95, 108, 110n., 111, 123, 157
  sweating sickness, xxxix, 97, 140
  university, see next head entry
  Urban Hall, xiv–xv, 95, 147
Oxford University, ix, xv, xxiv, xxvii, xxxvii–xxxviii, xl, 81n., 83n., 91, 100
  Bodleian Library, 102
  chancellor's court, xxv
  classical studies, ix; and see studia humanitatis
  colleges, xxxiv, xxxvi; and see All Souls; Balliol; Brasenose; Canterbury; Cardinal; Corpus Christi; Exeter; Gloucester; Lincoln; Magdalen; Merton; New; Oriel; Queen's; St. Hugh's; University
Oxfordshire, xxxviii, xlvi; and see Burcot; Burford; Godstow Abbey; Headington; Henley-on-Thames; Osney; Taynton

Padua (Italy), xx
panelling, xlv, xlviii, li, 7, 28–30, 32, 34, 41, 45, 85, 87–8, 90
pans [kitchen], liv, 118
Pantry(e), Thos., 24
Papacy, xxx, xxxviii
paper, lvii–lviii, 23, 49, 56
parchment, lvi–lviii, 23, 25, 83, 118
Paris (France), xvii, 140
Parker, Ric., liii, 58, 60–1, 65, 67–9, 71–2, 75, 77–8, 80–1, 83–5, 156
Parliament, xviii, xxix, 114n., 140, 145, 149
Passion of Christ, xvi, 136
  see Arma Christi
pastry boards, xlvi, 5, 148
patens, 118, 120–1
paviers, lxii, 4n., 25, 30, 34, 157
paving, see Corpus Christi Coll. [building of]
Peerson, Jn., 9, 159
pelican vulning, see Fox, Ric., pelican device
Pembroke College, Cambridge, xxxvii
Perpoynt, Harry, 28, 156
pewter, 24
Phylypps (Phelyppys):
  Jn., 21, 63, 84, 159
  Rog., 18–19, 21, 159
  Thos., 76
piecework, lxii, 50, 87
Pigot, Wal., xv
pillows, 110
plasterers, xxxv, li, 5, 26–8, 30, 33, 36, 39, 153, 155, 157
plate, see Corpus Christi Coll.; Fox, Ric., chantry chapel; Fox, Ric., personal belongings, liturgical

INDEX

Plato, xxxvii
platt [design], 90, 95, 112–13
plumber, 13, 72, 146, 149, 157
Polleyn (*alias* Waterygge):
    Alice, m. 1 Jn. Gryth, 2 Jn. Lebons, 103–5
    Jn., 103–4
pomegranate, *see* Tudor badges
Popley, Wm., 18, 159
portcullis, *see* Tudor badges
porter, 108, 117
portraits, *see* Fox, Ric.
pots [kitchen], liv, 24; *and see* pans
Pownd:
    Ric., 15, 159
    Wal., 9, 159
    Wm., 9, 16, 159
Poys, Wm., 38, 156
Privy Seal, *see* Fox, Ric.; Gunthorpe
Pye, —, carpenter, 12, 159
Pynson, Ric., xxxv
pipes (*pypys*) [containers for books], lvi, 79n.
Pytfield (Pytfed), Ric., l, 9, 20, 26, 39–40, 44–5, 47–8, 51–3, 160

quarries, *see* Barrington; Headington; Hinksey; Lincolnshire; Magdalen Coll.; Sherborne; Sunningwell; Taynton
quarrymen, xliv, lv n.; *and see* Franklin, Jn.
Queen's College, Cambridge, President of, xxii
Queen's College, Oxford, xxxviii, xlvi, xlix n., 9, 154
quilts, 110

ragstone, *see* stone
rates of pay, *see* wages
Rawlins, Ric., Warden of Merton Coll., xxix, xxxiii, 22n., 94, 111

Raynold, Jn., 74, 160
Reading (Berks.), xxxiv, 139
    Abbey, *see* Thorne
Rede, Kelham, 16, 19, 20–3, 64–5, 160
Redmayn, Hen., 104
relics, xli–xlii, 134–5
Renaissance, ix–x, xiv, xxiv, xxvii, xxxvi, xxxix n., xl, xlii; *and see* Humanism
Richard III, ix, xix, xl, xlii, 135n.
    as duke of Gloucester, xvii
Robynson, —, supplier, 5, 160
Rochester, Kent, Bp. of, *see* Fisher
rochit [vestment], 110
Rockingham, barons of, 144
Rome, xx, xxviii, xxx–xxxi, xxxviii
roofs, *see* Corpus Christi Coll.
Roossell, *see* Russell
rope, 14, 51, 83
Roper, Geo., messenger, liv, 19, 57, 61
Ropsley (Lincs.), xiv–xv, xix
Roses, Wars of the, *see* Wars
roughmasons, *see* masons
Rous family, xv
Rudbourne, Thos., 134
rush matting, xxxv
Russell (Roossell):
    Jn., Bp. of Lincoln, xx
    Jn., carpenter, lii
    Thos., lii, 53, 87, 97, 133, 156
Ryckes, Thos., 129
Ryley, 27, 156

St. Cuthbert, xxviii, 93, 128–9
St. Frideswide's Priory, *see* Oxford
St. George's Chapel, Windsor, xxxi n., 141
St. Hugh's College, Oxford, 100
St. John's College, Cambridge, xxii, xxxvii, xxxix

St. John the Evangelist, symbol, 134, 137
St. Mary Overy, see Southwark
St. Paul, sword of, 132, 134
St. Peter, keys of, 132, 134
St. Swithun's Priory, Winchester:
   arms, **pl. 4**
   monks of, xxvi, xxxix–xl, 131, 134
   prior and convent of, xxix, xlvii, lv, 92–4, 107–26, 128–9, 131–2, 134, 141, 143; and see Silkstede
   visitation of, xli
Salisbury (Wilts.):
   Bp. of, see Woodville, Lionel
   Cathedral, xvi
   dean of, see Davyson
   diocese, xvi
   and see Sarum
Salter, Revd. H. E., 100–2
Salyng, Wm., prior of Merton, xxxiii
Samson (Sampson), Wm., 64, 66, 68, 72–3, 79, 160
Sarum [Salisbury], use of, 118
satin, see fabrics
Savoy Hospital, London, xlvii, lii, liv
   bailiff of, liv, 96
   master carpenter of, see Coke, Humph.
   Master of, see Holgill
   statutes of, xlvii
Sawnders, Wm., 18, 27, 69, 160
saw pit (pytt), 39, 60
sawyers, l, lxii, 26–7, 29–31, 33, 35, 37–40, 42–5, 47–9, 51, 53, 55, 57, 60–1, 67–8, 70–2, 74–5, 78, 80, 84, 159
Saxon kings, xli–xlii, 134–5; and see Athelstan
Schelman, Jn., 36, 156

Schiner, Matthäus, cardinal, xxxii, 94–5
Scotland, xviii, xix, xxi, xxiii
   Scottish friars, see Friars Observant
scribe, payment to, 23
seal [wax], 19, 112, 122, 124, 126
secretary hand, xliii, lxi
Secretary [King's], ix, xvii–xviii, xxix n.
Sexton, Chris., 26–7, 29–30, 32, 34–6, 38–40, 42, 50, 67, 69, 71–2, 74, 76, 156
Sharpe, Jn., 11, 13, 15, 160
Sheen Priory (Surrey), xxiv
sheets, 110
Sherborne (Dorset), quarry, xliv n.
shovel, liv, 24, 57, 66
Silkstede, Thos., prior of St. Swithun's, Winchester, xxvi, xxxiii–xxxiv, xxxix–xli, xliii, xlvii, 92–4, 107–26, 128–9, 132, 134, 136, **pl. 14**
Slater, Lancelot the, 3, 10, 15, 17, 24, 38, 41–2, 156
slaters (slatters), 10, 17, 27, 38, 41–2, 155–7
Slatter, Jn., 18–19, 160
slytting-work [timber], 26–7, 29–31, 33, 35, 37–45, 47–8, 52–3, 60, 72, 74
smiths, see blacksmiths
Smyth:
   Garatt, 6, 13, 79, 156
   Jn., carpenter, 15, 25, 27–30, 32, 34–5, 38–40, 42, 146, 156
   Jn., plasterer, 36, 156
   Wm., Bp. of Lincoln, xxxiii
social mobility, xiv–xvi, xxxiv, 140–1, 143–4
Somerset, see Glastonbury; Taunton
Southwark (London), St. Mary Overy in, 108, 110n., 129

INDEX

Southwell, Rob., 127–8
Spain, xix
  alliance with, 107
  ambassador of, xiii
  Anglo-Spanish marriage, xix, xxii–xxiii
  and see Alcalá; Navarre
Spyllisby(e):
  Jn., 28, 30–1, 33, 58, 71, 156
  Wm., 57, 60–1, 156
Spurs, battle of the, 107
squinches (squynchys), 77, 80–1
Stafford:
  Hen., duke of Buckingham, xvii
  Hen., earl of Wiltshire, 140
Standish, Hen., friar, xxviii–xxx, xxxii
Stanley:
  Jn., 28, 62, 156
  Thos., 127–8
  Wm., 62, 156
steps [stone], xlv, xlix, 18n., 89
Stevyns, Ric., 31, 157
Steyle, Jn., 31, 157
Stoke (Notts.), battle of, xviii
Stone, Thos., 65, 67, 77–8, 81, 83, 85, 157
stone, xv, xxxv, xliv–xlv, 4–5, 56, 75, 82, 84, 122, 131, 158–60
  freestone, xliv–v, liii, 9–11, 17, 21, 24, 47, 49, 51–2, 54–5, 57–9, 61–2, 64, 66–7, 69, 71–2, 74–8, 80–1, 83–4
  limestone, xlv
  paving stone, 54
  polled (*pold*) stone, 20, 23, 25, 46–7, 49, 51, 85
  slate, 22, 24
  square stone, 18
  ragstone (ragg), xxxv, xliv–xlv, 5, 8, 10, 12–13, 16–17, 19–21, 23–5, 45–7, 49, 51–2, 54–5, 57–9, 61–4, 66–7, 69, 71,
74–8, 80–1, 83–5, 158–60
  and see quarries
studia humanitatis, ix–x, xiv, xx–xxii, xxiv–xxv, xxvii, xxxvii
Sudeley Castle (Glos.), xi, xli n., 127n.; *and see* **Frontispiece**
Suffolk, duke of, 144
Sunningwell (Berks.), quarry, xliv n.
suppliers [of building materials], *see* Appendix 10
Surrey, *see* Esher; Guildford; Hampton Court Palace; Kingston upon Thames; Merton Priory; Sheen Priory; Sutton; Wandsworth
Sussex, *see* Lewes
Sutton (Surrey), 103–4
sweating sickness, *see* Oxford
Swetestarr, Jn., 12, 60, 160
Switzerland, xxxii, 107; *and see* Basel
Sylke, Wm., vicar general to Fox, 118
Symons, Jn., 27, 157

table cloths, *see* fabrics
tapestry (tapetts), 108–10: *and see* verdures
Taunton (Som.), xvi
Tayler, Thos., 30–1, 33–4, 157
Taynton (Oxon.), quarry, xlv, xlviii, 18–19, 21, 50, 53, 57, 59–60, 64, 154
tester [for a bed], 109–10
Thérouanne (France), 109
Thomas, Wm., 72, 157
Thorne, Jn., abbot of Reading, 108, 113–15, 122, 124–5
Threder:
  Ric., 25–6, 29, 31, 33–4, 36–7, 39, 40–1, 43–6, 48, 50, 52–3, 157
  Thos., 26, 28, 157

Thycart, Hen., xlvi, 14, 160
tilers, 143, 146, 149
timber, xxxv, xliv–xlvi, 22n., 131, 156–60
  ash, xlvi, 5, 159
  board, 60, 75–6, 81–2, 84, 90, 158
  elm board, xlvi, 14, 19, 158, 160
  dry board, 3
  laths, xlvi, lxii, 3, 9–10, 15, 22, 24
  lead board, 65, 90
  oak, xlvi, 132
  plank (board), xlvi, 3, 9, 12, 15, 17, 20–4, 61–2, 68, 78, 84, 159–60
  transport of, xxxv, xliv, xlvi, 3–90
  and see carfs; panelling; *slytting*; wainscot
tippet, 110
Tournai (France), 109
Townesend:
  Jn., 3–4, 6, 8–11, 16–17, 19–25, 34, 46–7, 49, 51–2, 54–6, 61–3, 66, 68–9, 76, 80, 83, 157
  Thos., 11, 160
tradesmen, xliv, lxii; *and see* Appendix 10
'Trojans', xxv, xxvii
Tudor badges, lii, 133, 135–8, **pl.16**
  fleur de lys, 133, 137–8
  pomegranate, 133, 137
  portcullis, 133, 138
  Tudor rose, 133, 136–8
Twyne, Brian, 92n., 101n.

universities, *see* Alcalá; Cambridge; Ferrara; Louvain; Oxford
University College, Oxford, xxxviii
Urban Hall, *see* Oxford
Urswick, Chris., archdeacon of Oxford, xxviii, 93, 127–30, 135

Vanderbye, Peter, 31, 62, 157
Veer, Ric., 15, 160
velvet, *see* fabrics
verdures, 110n.
Verona, Guarino da, xx
Vertue, Wm., xxv, xxvii, xxxi–xxxii, xxxiv, xlvii–xlix, liii, liv n., 17, 50, 91–3, 95, 97, 112, 157, **pl. 5**
Virgin Mary:
  cults, 136
  monogram, 136–8, **pl. 17**
Vitelli, Cornelio, xx

wages, x, xxxv, xliii–xliv, xlviii, li, lxi–lxii, 3–90, 145–50, **pl. 8**; *and see* Corpus Christi Coll. [general], officers
wainscot, xlvi, li–lii, 7, 9, 15–17, 26, 29, 31, 33, 37–9, 42, 44–5, 47–8, 50–1, 75, 87, 155, 158–60
Wales, xvii
Walker (Walkar), —, carrier, 14, 160
Waltar, Thos., 20, 160
Walton, Rob., 5, 9–10, 12–13, 16, 19–25, 45, 47, 49, 51–2, 54–5, 57, 59, 61–4, 71, 75, 77–8, 81, 83–5, 160
Walton (Warw.), 74, 78, 82
Wandsworth (Surrey), 103–4
War, Ric., 27, 157
Ward, Jn., xlv, liii, 18–19, 21, 42, 49–50, 52–3, 59, 64, 68, 71, 76, 79, 81, 84, 157
Warham, Wm., Abp. of Canterbury, xxviii, xxx–xxxii, 91, 94–5, 129
Wars of the Roses, xvi, xxiii
Warwick the Kingmaker, 135
Warwick, Guy of, 134
Warwickshire, *see* Walton

Wase:
   Jasper, 5, 8–12, 16–17, 19–25,
      45, 47, 49, 51–2, 54–5, 57–8,
      61–4, 66–7, 69, 71, 74–5,
      77–8, 80–1, 83–5, 160
   Jn., 11, 45, 47, 49, 51–2, 54–5,
      57–8, 61, 64, 66–7, 69, 71,
      74–5, 77–8, 80–1, 83–5, 160
Waterygge, see Polleyn
watermarks, lviii
wax, 70, 120
Wayneflete, Wm., Bp. of Winchester, xxxviii
Welman, Jn., 15, 160
West Ham (Essex), 141
whitewash, xlv
Whorlton:
   Jn., 30–1, 33–4, 157
   Wm., 26–8, 157
Whyght:
   Jn., 30, 33, 35, 37, 42–5, 157
   Rog., 26–7, 36, 157
   Wm., 31, 36, 38–40, 42, 157
Whytakars, Thos., 33, 37, 67, 69,
   71–2, 74, 157
Willoughby, Katherine., Baroness
   Willoughby de Eresby, 144
Willoughby de Eresby, barons, 144
Wiltshire (Wylschere)
   (Wylteschere):
   Jn., 10–11, 65–6, 84, 160
   Thos., 11, 13, 15–16, 65–6, 68,
      82, 84, 160
Wiltshire, earl of, see Stafford, Hen.
Wiltshire, xxxviii; and see Salisbury; Wroughton
Winchester, xviii, xx, xxv, xxxii–
   xxxiii, xxxix, xl–li, liii–lv, 19,
   82–3n., 93, 96, 108
   Bps. of, xl, 96, 143; and see
      Courtenay; Fox, Ric.;
      Wayneflete; Wykeham
   Cathedral, see next head entry

   diocese, xxxiv, xxxviii, xlvii n.,
      95, 131–2, 134, 137, 139, 141
   Winchester College, 103n.
   and see Hospital of St. Cross; St.
      Swithun's Priory; Wolvesey
      Palace
Winchester Cathedral, ix, xvi,
   xxvi–xxvii, xxxiv, xli, xlvii,
   93, 97, 107–9, 116, 122, 131
   arms, pl. 14
   bosses (knottes), xvi, xli, lv, 133,
      135n., 136
   east end, xli, xlvii n., 135
   Fox's chantry chapel, ix, xvi,
      xxvi–xxvii, xl–xli, xlvii, lv,
      93, 97, 107–8, 115–16, 119–21,
      pl. 1
      dedication, 118
      ornaments, 109, 111–13,
         117–18, 120–1, 125
      plate (liturgical), 118, 120–1, 125
      priests, xxvii, 107–8, 110n.,
         115–16, 118, 120–1
   mortuary chests, xliii, 135n.
   presbytery screens, xlii, 135n.
   St. Swithun's shrine, 108
   Silkstede's chantry chapel, 136
   wooden chests, xli–xlii
Winchcombe Abbey (Glos.), 124;
   and see Kidderminster, Ric.
Windsor, see Eton; St. George's
   Chapel
Wolsey, Thos., cardinal, ix, xiii,
   xxiv, xxvii, xxx–xxxii, xl, lv,
   lvii, 4n., 22n., 103–4, 107n.,
   109–10n., 143, 153, 156
Wolvesey Palace, xxxvi n., xliii n.,
   liii, 114, 118n., 126
   Treasurer, see Gardiner
Wood, Ant., 143
Woodville:
   Elizabeth, see Elizabeth
      Woodville

Woodville cont.
  Lionel, Bp. of Salisbury, xvi
  family, xvii, 140
wool, see fabrics
Wotton, —, supplier, 3, 160
Wounds, cult of the, 134
Wright, Hen., 93
writing materials, see paper; parchment
Wroughton (Wilts.), 141
Wryght, Rog., l, 27, 157
Wrykysham, Jn., 29–30, 32, 34–6, 38–40, 157
Wykeham, Wm. of, Bp. of Winchester, xxxiii, xxxix n., 143n.
Wyld, Rob., 48, 50, 157
Wylliams, Sir, 56, 66, 76–8, 80, 157
Wyllyngton, Geo., 36, 38–9, 158
Wylschere (Wylteschere), see Wiltshire, Jn.
Wynford:
  Jn., 143n.
  Wm., 143n.
Wynsemore, Ric., 7

Yorden (Iordan) Thos., 27, 29–30, 32, 34, 36, 157
Yorkists, xvii–viii, xl, 127n., 135